Thomas Rainborowe – Dangerous Radical

Stanley Slaughter

Copyright © 2015 Stanley Slaughter

All rights reserved.

ISBN: 1512091316
ISBN-13: 978-1512091311

Contents

Foreword 1

Acknowledgements 3

Chapter One: 'Horrid Murder' 5

Chapter Two: Origins 21

Chapter Three: The Men from New England 40

Chapter Four: Parliament's Great Warrior 59

Chapter Five: The Army's Great Radical 89

Chapter Six: The Attempted Army Coup 136

Chapter Seven: Revolt at Sea 167

Chapter Eight: Aftermath 211

Bibliography 245

Foreword

"For really I think that the poorest he that is in England has a life to live as the greatest he."

"I do think...that every man born in England cannot, ought not, to be exempted, neither by the law of God nor the law of nature, from the choice of those who are to make laws, for him to live under."

"That which is dear unto me is my freedom."
Thomas Rainborowe at the Putney Debaters in October, 1647.

Thomas Rainborowe is one of the forgotten heroes of the English Civil Wars. The son of a wealthy merchant and national naval hero, he rose to prominence in Parliament's New Model Army as a brilliant siegemaster and man of astonishing courage. By the end of the first civil war in 1646, only Oliver Cromwell, a cavalry leader of genius, stood above him in terms of military prowess.

But Rainborowe also became the admired leader of the radicals in the Army. As a major spokesman for these men at the Putney Debates, Rainborowe presented a revolutionary vision. This was of an England where all men had the vote, where the people were sovereign and where no tyrannical king could again reap the havoc on the nation as Charles I had done.

He put himself on a collision path with the innately conservative Cromwell by supporting An Agreement of the People, written by the nascent republican John Wildman. This called for the people to have inalienable rights and made no mention of any role for a king.

Rainborowe subsequently helped lead a revolt where the radicals tried to have the Agreement acclaimed as the Army's policy. Cromwell, in a desperate act of bravado, put the revolt down.

Within a year, Rainborowe was dead, killed by a troop of royalists in Doncaster with the help of disenchanted Parliamentarians. It happened just as the Army was moving towards backing his demand that the king be put on trial. With Cromwell undecided on the issue, the leadership was in Rainborowe's grasp.

His funeral was among the largest London had ever seen, with thousands accompanying the corpse to its burial in Rainborowe's birthplace of Wapping. His battle colours of green and black subsequently became the colours of the Leveller movement which continued his fight for a radical solution to England's problems.

But Rainborowe's early death - he was about 38 when he died - was not the only lethal blow to his reputation. The great, visionary words he spoke in the radical cause at Putney were lost to posterity for more than 200 years. Even when they were discovered in the archives of Worcester College, Oxford, Great Britain still did not have one man, one vote.

Britain seems reluctant to honour its radicals who fought for change. It says much that in the grounds of the "Mother of Parliaments" at Westminster, there is a statue of Cromwell, the man who opposed one man one vote but no acknowledgement of Thomas Rainborowe, the man who first proposed what is now seen as a bedrock of democracy.

This book is an attempt to raise his reputation.

Author's note: In the 17th century, Thomas Rainborowe's name was spelt many different ways, including Rainsborough, the version commonly used by most of his contemporaries. I have used Rainborowe because that is the way he and his family always spelt it.

Acknowledgements

Many people have helped me with this book and I am most grateful to them all. However I would like to thank some people in particular whose help has been exemplary. First Professor Henry Woudhuysen, Rector of Lincoln College, Oxford University who secured access for me to Oxford colleges and libraries and kept me going with his constant encouragement.

I must in particular thank Dr Joanna Parker, Librarian of Worcester College, Oxford who gave me access to the Clarke Papers and the ever tolerant staff of the Bodleian Library.

In London, I must also profoundly thank Ms Sally Brooks, librarian at the Museum of London who gave me access to the Tangye collection of Cromwelliana and Adrian James, assistant librarian at the library of the Society of Antiquaries of London.

I also received much valued help from staff at Birkbeck Library, University of London, the Institute of Historical Research, the National Archives and from Chris Gravett, curator of Woburn Abbey.

Further afield, I would like to thank Ashley Cataldo of the American Antiquarian Society and Daniel Hinchen of the Massachusetts Historical Society for their guidance on the early settlers to New England.

I would also like to thank my wife Linda who must have been heartily fed up with the name Rainborowe by the time this book was finished but assured me she wasn't.

Finally, I would like to acknowledge two men who made a vital though indirect contribution to this book. Sloane Grammar in Chelsea was blessed with many, many excellent teachers while I was there in the 1960s. But two inspirational teachers stood out for me. Mr G. A. Eversfield left me with a lifelong love of history while Peter Carlen introduced me to novels, plays, the theatre, poetry and the beauties of the English language. Without these two outstanding men, this book would never have been written.

Chapter One: 'Horrid Murder'

Just before sunrise on Sunday, October 29, 1648, a troop of 22 Royalists, headed by Captain William Paulden, rode into the small Yorkshire town of Doncaster. They had slipped out of Pontefract Castle, 12 miles away to the north, at midnight the day before. Riding through the night, they had reached Mexborough by the early morning where they rested. From there they sent an outrider to spy out the land at Doncaster. At noon, the party moved onto Conisbrough where it waited until its spy returned to assure them that Doncaster was quiet. After a further overnight wait, the men rode the last mile into Doncaster, approaching the town from the south west.

At the town's St Sepulchre Gate at about 7.30am, they received the signal they wanted. As arranged by their outrider, a man walked down the street carrying a Bible. It denoted all was clear. From there the men moved along the street to the main guard house where they said they were from Colonel William White's regiment, stationed in nearby Rotherham, and that they had a letter from Oliver Cromwell, the Lieutenant General. Luck was on their side. The man supposed to be in charge of the guard house, Lieutenant-Captain John Smith was not there, allegedly in the local whorehouse, quite possibly lured there the previous night. With Smith absent and three other guards asleep, the sole sentry accepted their story, apparently not wondering why it took 22 men to a deliver one letter, and let them through. Paulden then divided his troops into four parties.

According to Paulden's brother, Captain Thomas Paulden,[1] who was part of the troop, six were ordered to stay at the main guard; six were to guard Friar's Bridge to the north – their escape route out of town back to Pontefract; another six, led by William, were to patrol the streets; the last four were directed to Alderman Taylor's lodgings house on the north side of the market square. At Friar's Bridge the guards were put to flight and their arms thrown in the river. At the same time, the four men ordered to the lodgings began their short ride. Armed with swords and pistols, they eastwards through Baxter Gate and past the great St George's Church which dominated the town towards their quarry.

This was Colonel Thomas Rainborowe, a highly accomplished soldier and brilliant siegemaster in Parliament's New Model Army. A tall, formidable though short tempered Londoner in his late thirties, he had been ordered up to Yorkshire by General Lord Fairfax,[2] commander-in-chief of all the Parliamentary forces, to take Pontefract Castle. This was the last stronghold of Charles I in the north. It was a crucial task – if Rainborowe took that castle it would effectively end both Royalist resistance and the second civil war that had raged unwantedly throughout England for much of the year.

The Royalists were fearful that Rainborowe would bring the siege to a quick and successful end, just as he had previously done in the far larger cities of Worcester, Oxford and Colchester. But it was not just his ruthless skills as a siegemaster that motivated Paulden and his men; neither was it his raw and often reckless courage that had on at least one occasion turned a battle for Parliament; nor was it his dangerous radical politics that had caused him to fall out with Cromwell, call for one man, one vote and demand the King be put on trial for his crimes against the people. Paulden and his men had a baser motive: revenge. Rainborowe had been a major player at the recent siege of Colchester. When this bitter and nasty confrontation had ended two months earlier in August in Parliament's favour, Fairfax and Rainborowe were among the council of war that had condemned two leading Royalist officers, Sir George Lisle and Sir Charles Lucas, for their part in the siege. As punishment, they were summarily shot beneath the castle wall. Executed according to the rules of war, said the Parliamentarians, murdered said the Royalists – with the extremist Rainborowe the driving force.

The executions made him a hate figure among Royalists and within a month, the first attempt was made on his life. As Rainborowe and a captain rode from London to Army headquarters at St Albans in late September, they were attacked by three men.

"The Cavaliers seeing their Gallantry and Resolution, put Spurs to their Horses and rode for it, and being extraordinary well mounted over rid them."[3] It was a minor incident, which probably did little to disturb a man of Rainborowe's mettle, but it was a straw on the wind. He needed to be on his guard.

But if Colchester had ended the war in the south, that in the north was going less well. Fairfax and Colonel John Lambert, commander of the Northern Alliance and another outstanding soldier thrown up by the war between King and Parliament, were becoming increasingly agitated by the lack of progress of their forces at Pontefract. The castle had been under Parliamentary control until June 3 when its occupants was surprised by a dozen men led by a Colonel John Morrice.

The castle's military governor, Sir John Cotterill, alerted by the prospect of an invasion by the Royalist Duke of Hamilton, had begun moving his men, then scattered around Pontefract, into the castle along with provisions and beds. Morrice, William Paulden and ten others, the first two dressed like country gentlemen with swords, the rest "dressed like plain Countrymen and Constables" but armed with pistols and daggers, accompanied the men carrying the beds into the Castle. Morrice gave some of the soldiers inside a crown to go and buy drinks for their fellows and as soon as they left, lowered the drawbridge. He then forced the remaining soldiers down to the dungeon and fetched Cotterill to join them. Expecting a siege, the Royalists acted quickly. More men were called to join them, pushing their number up to 500, while corn and cattle were brought in from the country.[4]

The Parliamentary Committee of Yorkshire appointed two local commanders, Sir Edward Rhodes and Sir Henry Cholmley, at the head of 5,000 troops, to besiege Pontefract Castle. But the efforts of these two were never more than half-hearted. Paulden said there was always a gate open on the south side of the castle for people to come and go.[5] Cholmley and Morrice, who knew each other, seem to have been in touch from the start and were happy to grant passes for people to come and go from the castle and to exchange prisoners. Rows, quarrels and petty jealousies between various Parliamentary factions also blunted hopes of a successful siege. Even Cromwell, at that time engaged in the more serious matter of fighting off a Scots invasion, was dragged into the squabbling, being asked to arbitrate between two junior officers over the theft of two horses.[6]

On another occasion, Cromwell asked Rhodes, Cholmley and two other colonels to raise some men to pursue Hamilton who, after defeat at the battle of Preston,[7] was heading east towards Yorkshire.[8] Cromwell repeated his request three days later and Charles Fairfax, uncle of the commander in chief and commander of the forces in Yorkshire, passed on this urgent message to Cholmley.[9] There is no evidence he ever acted upon it. By early September, Lambert was getting fed up and pointedly asked Charles Fairfax what progress had been made on the surrender of the Castle.[10] By the end of the month Lord Fairfax had had enough. On September 23, he ordered Rainborowe and his regiment to march to the North.[11] The general gave him a considerable force, two regiment of horse and two of foot, indicating the importance he attached to ensuring a swift resolution to the siege. In a letter four days later from "your very affectionate nephew", he told Charles of his action: "Finding it needful that you be assisted with more forces for the speedy reducing of Pontefract Castle, I have ordered Col Rainborowes regiment to march to your assistance who I hope will be very industrious in that charge committed to him and have ordered him to command the forces there which will be an ease of that trouble which otherwise would necessarily continue upon you. I have acquainted Sir Henry Cholmley herewith that there may be fair correspondence in this matter."[12]

Fairfax was well within his rights. It had been nearly four months since Morrice and his men had taken the castle. In that time, Cholmley and Rhodes, perhaps understandably as it was well defended, had made no attempt to storm it but, far more incompetently, had not even managed a secure blockade. Not only was the inept siege delaying a successful end to the war but the county was sinking into lawlessness. The Commons was told on October 16, 1648 "that notwithstanding the besieging of the castle, the enemy sallies out, went a good way in the country, fetched away Sir Arthur Ingram from his house and carried him into the Castle. But when Col. Rainsborough's Regiment is come up to us, they will keep them up closer."[12] Sir Arthur was released and allowed home in return for £1,500, an enormous sum in the 17th century.

An anonymous letter from a visitor to Pontefract sent to Parliament later the same month painted an even more disturbing picture: "They have, since I came from London, taken at least two hundred head of cattle, above one hundred oxen, from graziers; they sound a parly for a cessation and make a fair of their horses near the castle, sell them to Sir Henry Cholmley's troopers and in the cessation, they drink to one another 'Here is to thee, brother Roundhead' and 'I thank thee, brother Cavalier'"[14]. After Cromwell arrived in Pontefract, he found the Castle had enough food for a year, including "two hundred and twenty or forty fat cattle within these last three weeks."[15] Nonetheless the proud Cholmley was beside himself with fury at being usurped by someone he saw as a junior colonel on a patch he regarded as his own.

Fairfax must have known the effect his letter would have. The Fairfaxes of Denton were, after all, one of the oldest and most dominant families in a county run by its landed gentry. So were their friends the Cholmleys, the Hothams and their long-time enemies the Wentworths. Sir Henry Cholmley's elder brother, Sir Hugh, had 25,000 acres and an income of £1,000 in the Whitby area.[16] But the split between king and Parliament in the 1640s had turned Yorkshire into a political snakepit. Thomas Wentworth, a scion of the Wentworths, had switched from fierce critic of the king to being one of his senior ministers. For his allegedly treasonous conduct in Ireland, Wentworth, later the Earl of Strafford, had been condemned by the Long Parliament[17] and executed on Tower Hill in 1641. The Hothams, Sir John and his son John, after famously refusing Charles entry to Hull and its sizeable arsenal and holding out against a Royal siege in 1642, also changed sides. After Parliament discovered they were in talks with the king, both were put to death in 1645. Sir Hugh Cholmley, held Scarborough for Parliament until 1643 and then defected to the Royalists. He later exiled himself to the continent, from where he stayed in touch with his brother who saw nothing to condemn in his actions. Morrice, a page to Strafford while a boy, changed sides twice during the wars. He rose to the rank of lieutenant-colonel with the Royalists before deserting them for Parliament after the fall of York in 1644.

Four years later, he switched back to the king.[18] The latest defection was that of Colonel Matthew Boynton, governor of Scarborough, who on July 27 declared for Charles.

Sir Henry Cholmley had committed himself to the Parliamentary cause in 1642 but by 1648 he longed, like many others, both in Yorkshire and throughout the country, for an end to the fighting and a return to his home. Before the war, the county had suffered the expense and disruption of billeting English troops during the Bishops' War, while the peace was negotiated.[19] The county, which had an ambivalent attitude to both Charles and Parliament, was also the most heavily taxed during the conflict.[20]

Cholmley, again like many others, could not quite see men he had known for much of his life as enemies – men with whom he would have to live after the fighting stopped. This played a part in his lax attitude to the siege. But rivalling Sir Henry's desire for peace was his fear of social disorder, the rise of the people. In his eyes the man sent to take his command at Pontefract embodied exactly that threat, the anarchy that Cromwell and Henry Ireton,[21] the Army's commissary general, had predicted at the Putney Debates a year ago in 1647 if Rainborowe, the political extremist, got his way. Cholmley, aware of his immense standing in Yorkshire and of his men's general distrust of outsiders, determined to see off upstart colonel.

Rainborowe seems to have arrived in Yorkshire by about October 15, 1648. He must have been immediately aware of

Cholmley's hostility as he wrote to Fairfax that day about the cordiality of Thomas Fairfax and John Mauleverer, a former governor of Hull but now part of the force besieging Pontefract, compared to the animosity of Cholmley.[22] Cholmley was not slow to act. On October 16, the day before he was due to meet Rainborowe in York, he had written to Cromwell asking him to take charge of the siege. Cholmley later claimed he received a favourable reply to this letter but Cromwell would have been in no position to offer immediate help. After victory at Preston, the lieutenant general had moved northwards.

On October 20-21, he was in Durham when he received the request from the York committee for help in reducing Pontefract. Cromwell replied that two regiment of foot and two of horse - presumably Rainborowe's - were on their way. As an extra measure, Cromwell also ordered three troops of Derbyshire dragoons to join them in Yorkshire. There is no indication that he ever received Cholmley's letter or, if he did, that he specifically acted upon it. He then moved further south to the seat of Sir Henry's Vane[23] at Barnard Castle, west of Middlesbrough. By October 28 he was in Boroughbridge, still 41 miles north of Doncaster.

The York meeting between Rainborowe and the Yorkshire officers on October 17 almost produced a solution. Three days after it, Rhodes and four others wrote to the House of Commons Speaker, William Lenthall,[24] saying a compromise had been suggested "to prevent the mischief." In this, the two colonels, Cholmley and Rainborowe, "should command their own forces at their distinct posts until the pleasure of the Parliament were further known." This had apparently been agreed, but the next morning Rhodes said Rainborowe "acquainted us that upon second thoughts he cannot conform to his last nights resolution" nor was he prepared to be anything other than commander in chief of the siege. However the letter admitted they were short of foot soldiers and that Rainborowe's men were "very welcome to us."

Cholmley was far from appeased by what happened at the meeting and poured out his hurt feelings in a letter to Lenthall, probably written that day. Parliament received it on October 20. In the letter, Cholmley says it would be a "wrong" to Rhodes and Mauleverer if he obeyed Rainborowe's orders as he, Rainborowe, was a younger colonel than either of these two men and that he would not do so until "I shall first hear that it is your pleasure to have it so."

This sounds disingenuous, as Fairfax said he had already informed Cholmley of his decision to put Rainborowe in charge. Cholmley said such a move would be "hard recompense of our services". Then the real reason for his anger spilled out: jealousy. Cholmley bewailed that he had engaged against the enemy night and day for five months. "We should now have one put over us, that is but a bare colonel of foot in the Army, and a younger colonel than any of us. Sir, the kingdom being now in this posture there may perhaps be little use of us, yet we are unwilling that another should reap the reward of our labours and with double the force that we have had, come now and gain the prize for which we ventured our dearest blood."[25]

This was not how Rhodes and the others felt. Nor did the Commons have any time for Cholmley's complaints, ordering a letter to be written "to require him, and all others, to obey the Commands they shall receive from the General in this Business, touching the Siege, and reducing the Castles of Pontfract and Scarborough."[26] The rebuke did little to allay Cholmley's festering anger.

By October 20, Rainborowe had installed himself at Alderman Walker's lodgings house in Doncaster - said to be the "best inn of the town"[27] - and began to quarter his troops in the surrounding countryside. Three companies were sent to Hatfield and Woodhouse to combat a local brigand called Robin Partington. He and his band of men had won such a terrible reputation that he was known as "Robin the Devel." A story went about that "a poore mad women came crying into the Town that Robin was coming out of ye levels with a great army and was resolved to kill everybody; upon that the above three troupes, being almost frightened out of their wits, mustered upon the Lings in the greatest confusion imaginable, and immediately fled, as fast as their horses could carry them, to Doncaster."[28]

This sounds like propaganda - these men were veterans of fighting in Kent and the recent siege of Colchester. But it is likely to have been lapped up by the locals. It also indicates the hostility of the county to the soldiers, who were mainly Londoners. But despite this and the recent attempt on his life, Rainborowe was dispersing his men when he might have needed them to protect him. His guard in Doncaster probably amounted to no more than 60 men, spread around the town.

It was amidst this stalemate and Cholmley's stern rebuff from Parliament, Rainborowe and possibly Cromwell, that William Paulden hatched his plot. Ostensibly it was to kidnap Rainborowe and exchange him for Sir Marmaduke Langdale, a doughty Royalist fighter who had been captured at Preston and now languished in the jail of Nottingham Castle. He was expected to be executed. Paulden and his men left Pontefract Castle through the gate which was always left open, and then rode "over the Meadows, between two of the Enemy's Horse-Guards, whom, by the favour of the Night, we passed undiscovered."[29] It sounds highly suspicious that none of the guard noticed this. The party also had good intelligence. They knew Rainborowe, whom they said was "esteemed a Person of great Courage and Conduct, exceeding zealous and fierce in their Cause", had 1,200 foot and had deployed one of his regiments of horse three or four miles east of Doncaster and the other the same distance to the west.[30]

When the four Royalists arrived at Rainborowe's lodgings in Doncaster on October 29, they "pretended to bring letters to him from Cromwell, who had then beaten the Scots; they were met at the door by the General's lieutenant, who conducted them up to his Chamber."[31] This was a clever ruse as Rainborowe was most likely was expecting some communication from the lieutenant general over his stand off with Cholmley.

He was still in bed when the men handed him the alleged packet from Cromwell "wherein was nothing but blank paper." As Rainborowe opened the packet, "they told him he was their Prisoner, but not a hair of his Head should be touched, if he would go quietly with them." The lieutenant was disarmed and Rainbrowe led down the stairs to where a horse was waiting for him. He was ordered to mount it. "He seemed at first willing to do it, and put his Foot in the Stirrup; but looking about him, and seeing none but four of his Enemies, and his lieutenant and Centinel (whom they had not disarmed) standing by him: he pulled his Foot out of the Stirrup, and cried *Arms, Arms*.

"Upon this, one of our Men, letting his Pistol and Sword fall, because he would not kill him, catch hold of him, and they grappling together, both fell in the Street. Then General Rainsborough's lieutenant catching our Man's Pistol that was fallen, Captain Paulden's Lieutenant, who was on horseback, dismounts and runs him through the Body, as he was cocking the Pistol. Another of our Men run General Rainsborough into the Neck, as he was struggling with him that had caught hold of him; yet the General got upon his legs with our Man's Sword in his hand; but Captain Paulden's lieutenant ran him through the Body, upon which he fell down dead."[32] It is a bitter irony that Langdale had escaped from Nottingham Castle the night before Rainborowe's death. Paulden's men then returned to Pontefract Castle, again somehow escaping the notice of Cholmley's guards.

Thomas Paulden's account is one of several that exists. A more graphic account, written in a letter by a J. Bernard a day after the killing, describes a far bloodier affair. An immediate difference is that he said Paulden's party numbered 47 of which 22 went to the lodgings house. This figure does not tally with what Bernard himself described. But the main difference is that Bernard described Rainborowe as resisting from the start. He wrote: "Being brought out, they bid horse, but he answered 'he would die in the place rather than go with them' it's thought being confident of rescue from his main guard. They attempted per force to have horsed him, but, he striving, they ran him through the body." Rainborowe then called for a sword so he could die like a man but he was run through again. Paulden's men then tried to shoot him but the pistol failed to go off. It was then thrown at his head, the bruising blow caused him to stagger.

"Being again run through the body, he fell, having before flung one of them upon the ground. They rode away from him; he got up and followed them some twelve yards which they seeing, swore 'the dog was following them' and returned again upon him, but with faintness he was fallen before they came back. Yet they ran him some eight times through the body. The last words the maid of the house heard him say before he fell was that 'he was betrayed, oh, he was betrayed.'"

Bernard recounted how the men returned to Pontefract and "presently the Governor sent out a sealed letter... to Sir Henry Cholmley that 'he had now decided the controversy about the command for his men had left Rainsborough dead in a Doncaster street, at the reading of which the base, treacherous perfidious Cholmley very much laughed and rejoiced for a long time together as was observed by some honest men that were by at the reading of the letter from his brother in evil, so that it is more than probable that Sir Henry was an absolute complotter in the murder." He ended with a clarion call: "And can the soldiery of this kingdom be silent, and not revenge this barbarous murder of this incomparable commander, the like for sea and land service never came out of the bowels of this nation. The Lord stir up your hearts to be avenged of these bloody enemies".[33]

A more reliable source of Cholmley's pleasure comes from Cromwell's secretary, Robert Spavin. He wrote on November 2: "Cholmley, a very knave, hates us to the death; leapt at the news of Col. Rainborowe being killed."[34] In the House of Commons, the death of Rainborowe, the MP for Droitwich, was solemnly reported on Friday, November 3. It immediately ordered "That it be especially recommended to Lieutenant General Crumwell, forthwith to make a strict and exact Scrutiny of the Manner of the horrid Murder of Colonel Rainborow; and to certify the same to the House".[35]

It is highly questionable that William Paulden and his men wished only to kidnap Rainborowe and exchange him for their general, Langdale. Thomas Paulden, in his 1702 account, makes the claim twice as well as saying they told Rainborowe he would not be hurt if he went with them. This has the ring of someone protesting too much. Paulden clearly knew the nature of the man they were trying to kidnap and would have realised he was not one to come quietly. Was the use of only four men at the lodgings a deliberate ploy to encourage Rainborowe to struggle and so give them a reason to kill him? The idea that they would later hand back the country's best siegemaster so he could wrought their own destruction also seems unlikely.

But if Paulden's real aim all along was to kill Rainborowe, did he get help or encouragement from the other side? Certainly Sir Henry Cholmley seems to have played a role for petty, personal reasons. It is unlikely that he was part of the conspiracy but he allowed Paulden and his men in and out of the castle without hindrance, completely careless as to what their mission was.

But what of Lord Fairfax and Cromwell? Were they involved? Rainborowe's extreme politics must have tired and tested the goodwill of the non-political Fairfax to the limit. Rainborowe had stayed out of politics since the Putney Debates the previous October and the subsequent Army Revolt, in which he played a leading party, at Corkbush Field in November, 1647. But this was largely because, for much of the time, he had been at sea as vice admiral. He returned to the mainland only when he was put ashore by his men after they revolted against him in May, 1648. For part of this time, he worked with Fairfax at the siege of Colchester and shortly after that he was sent north to Pontefract. But there were weeks when Rainborowe was in London and quite likely to have been in touch with radical colleagues.

During the wet autumn of 1648, radicals such as Rainborowe had much to concern them. Much of the country still favoured a quick deal with the king which would restore him to his throne. In the capital, Royalists were becoming more and more forceful in their demands for a settlement with Charles. But this was not the view of the radical minority. Levellers - the name for the largest group of radicals - were again becoming increasingly vocal against any deal with the "man of blood". But they were now joined not just by the Army rank and file but also by some of its grandees.

At the Putney Debates, Henry Ireton, Cromwell's dry as dust son-in-law, had argued strongly against the radicalism of Rainborowe and for a deal with the king. A year on, he had changed his mind and opposed any agreement with Charles. In September, the Levellers published their "large petition", which called for the payment of arrears for soldiers and indemnity for any acts committed during the wars – the same grievances for which the Army had been demanding redress since the spring of 1647. But the petition also denounced the fresh talks, due to start that month, between the king and Parliament. The negotiators included the Army's old foe, Denzil Holles, who had once called the soldiers the enemy of the people and who favoured a lenient settlement with Charles.

Thomas Rainborowe had been one of the most outspoken opponents of a settlement with the king, a man he both disliked and distrusted. Did Fairfax conclude that, with the new talks starting, Rainborowe would again become a prominent radical spokesman against the king. Better then to get him out of the way, up north? But Fairfax was a soldier, not a politician, and certainly not a radical. Like many others, he was sick of the fighting and wanted a quick and successful siege of Pontefract. In military terms alone, Rainborowe was by far the best man to achieve this. The decision to send him to Yorkshire may have had the bonus of removing him from the politics of London though also plunging him into the bitter squabbles and jealousies of Civil War Yorkshire. But it was, first and foremost, the correct military decision.

But what of Cromwell? It was Cromwell who gained most from Rainborowe's death. The two had clashed dramatically over Rainborowe's wish to be vice admiral, over Rainborowe's unbending opposition to his attempts to settle with Charles and over his call for one man one vote at Putney, which Cromwell believed would lead to anarchy. But the ensuing year had changed much and by autumn, the opposition to Charles was no longer confined to a handful of radical officers. A majority of all officers now were against the king. Crucially, it was Cromwell, who at this stage had kept quiet on what should be done with Charles, who was out of step. If the Army did move against Charles, it would be Rainborowe, not Cromwell, who would be seen as the driving force. This would have renewed the rivalry between the two men which had seen Cromwell bested over the vice admiral's job and out manoeuvred at Putney. It is likely that Cromwell, as astute and sometimes devious a politician as he was a brilliant cavalryman, reasoned this.

With Rainborowe out of the way, Cromwell's life would be less fraught and less complicated as he considered the magnitude of executing a king and of his beloved Army ruling the country. If that happened, there would be no serious opposition to him as leader.

So just who was this man Thomas Rainborowe? What had he done and what did he stand for that the two starkly opposing causes of King Charles I and Oliver Cromwell both benefited from his untimely death?

Notes for Chapter One

1. Thomas Paulden, *An Account of the Taking and Surrendering of Pontefract Castle*, (Oxford, 1747). This is one of several accounts of the killing of Colonel Thomas Rainborowe though the only one by someone who was there. It was written as a letter to an unnamed friend in 1702, 54 years after the event, when Paulden was 77. There is a ring of truth about some of it but it is also consistently and predominantly self-serving. Tantalisingly, Paulden does not say if he was one of the four men who went to Rainborowe's lodgings.
2. Lord Fairfax was Sir Thomas Fairfax until March 1648 when he succeeded his father Ferdinando as the 3rd Lord Fairfax. He is referred to subsequently as Fairfax.
3. John Rushworth, *Historical Collections*, (London, 1721-2), vii, p. 1280
4. Paulden, *An Account*, pp. 9-11.
5. Ibid., p. 12.
6. Museum of London, *The Tangye Collection of Cromwelliana*, Item 706, The Fairfax Correspondence relating to the Siege of Pontefract Castle 1645-1648. The collection contains 160 letters.
7. The Battle of Preston, fought on August 17-19, resulted in a decisive victory for Cromwell over the Royalist and Scots forces led by the Duke of Hamilton.
8. Tangye Collection, letter number 44, dated August 20 from Warrington.
9. Ibid., letters number 50, dated August 23, and number 51, dated August 25.
10. Ibid., letter 67, dated September 4.
11. Rushworth, *Historical Collections*, vii, p. 1280. Rainborowe's regiment was known as the "Tower" Regiment having been originally raised in 1647 to defend the Tower of London. It later saw service in Kent and at Colchester before going north with Rainborowe. See Charles Harding Firth and Godfrey Davies, *The Regimental History of Cromwell's Army*, (Oxford, 1940), i, pp. 571-4.
12. *Tangye Collection*, letter number 80, dated September 27, written from Army HQ at St. Albans.
13. Rushworth, *Historical Collections*, vii, pp. 1281-1314.
14. Ibid., iv, ii, p. 1294 and p. 1314. Quoted in Edward Peacock, *Archaeologia*, (London, 1881), 46, p. 40.
15. Edward Peacock, 'Life of Thomas Rainborowe,' *Archaeologia*, XLVI (London, 1881), p. 44; *The Moderate*, 31 October- November 7 1648 (E470/12), pp. 4-5.
16. Jack Binns, *Yorkshire in the Civil Wars*, (Pickering, 2004), p. 14.
17. What was subsequently named The Long Parliament was called by Charles in November, 1640 and initiated a series of severe measures which curbed the power of the king and executed two of his main counsellors, Strafford and Archbishop William Laud. It lasted, in varying forms, until 1660.
18. Binns, *Yorkshire in the Civil Wars*, p. 139.
19. The Bishops' War was fought with the Scots in 1639-40 over Charles's misguided attempts to impose the English prayer book on the Scottish kirk. No major battles were fought but a Scots army occupied Newcastle while Charles's troops were quartered in Yorkshire, causing such resentment that the local gentry petitioned the king to move them.

20. Binns, *Yorkshire in the Civil Wars*, p. 2. Before the war started, the Fairfaxes had actually signed a treaty of neutrality with Royalist neighbours. See Binns, p. 37.
21. Henry Ireton (1611-51) was an Oxford-educated lawyer who fought in many major battles and sieges for Parliament, including Edgehill, Newbury, Naseby, Bristol, Oxford and Colchester. He was the main opponent of Rainborowe in the debate on the franchise at the Putney Debates. He later became one of the first of the Army Grandees to demand Charles be tried. He was married to Cromwell's daughter, Bridget. He died of a fever while campaigning in Ireland.
22. Thomas Carlyle, *The Letters and Speeches of Oliver Cromwell*, ed. S. C. Lomas, (London, 1904), pp. 382 and 385N. The letter, part of Clarke MSS, is now in Worcester College, Oxford.
23. Sir Henry Vane the younger (1613-1662), a zealous believer in religious freedom, he was a friend of Cromwell's until the pair fell out over England's governance in 1653. Vane played no part in the execution of Charles I and refused to endorse it but Charles II had him beheaded for treason in 1662.
24. William Lenthall (1591-1662) was MP for Woodstock in the Long Parliament and, having been chosen by Charles to be Speaker of the House, he remained in that position until 1653. He was regarded as timid and pliable but made the famous remark, when Charles, having entered the Commons to arrest the Five Members, asked for support, Lenthall replied: "May it please your Majesty, I have neither eyes to see nor tongue to speak in this place but as the House is pleased to direct me, whose servant I am here."
25. *The Moderate*: impartially communicating Martial Affairs to the Kingdom of England, No 17, October 31-November 7, 1648. The letter is quoted in full in Peacock, *Archaeologia*, 46, p. 42. The full part of the paraphrased quote reads: "That we engaged in the kingdom and our countries greatest need, as it then was, and having now been five months upon the imployment, and upon every other nights duty with our foot and 50 horses together with our horse whereby we have driven the enemy, who was master of the countrey into his last strength and begun our Lines about him."
26. *Commons Journal*, vi, pp. 60-1.
27. Earl of Clarendon (formerly Edward Hyde), *The History of the Great Rebellion and Civil Wars in England*, ed. W. Dunn MacRay, (Oxford, 1888), iv, p. 402.
28. From *Warburton's Collections for Yorkshire*, Lansdown MS 897, fol. 207. Quoted in Peacock, *Archaeologia*, 46, pp. 40-1N
29. Thomas Paulden, *An Account*, p. 14.
30. Ibid., p. 13.
31. Ibid., p. 15. Paulden wrongly calls Rainborowe a general. According to Clarendon, Rainborowe's men addressed him in that way. His lieutenant was William Raisine of Pontefract.
32. Ibid., pp. 16-7.
33. The letter appeared in *The Moderate*, October 31-November 7, 1648. British Library E472 (15). It is reprinted in Hugo Ross Williamson, *Four Stuart Portraits*, (London, 1949), pp. 138-141 and Firth and Davies, *Regimental History*, pp. 574-6.
34. Thomas Carlyle, *The Letters and Speeches of Oliver Cromwell*, ed. S.C. Lomas, (London, 1904), p. 385N. He names his source as Historical MSS Commissioners' Report on Mr Leyborne Popham's MSS, pp. 7-8.
35. *Commons Journal*, vi, pp. 68-9.

Chapter Two: Origins

Thomas Rainborowe, born about 1610 in the Thames-side hamlet of Wapping, was "bred to the sea."[1] His paternal grandfather, also Thomas, was a wealthy mariner and merchant; his father, William, a national naval hero; his maternal grandfather Roland Coytmore sailed with Sir Francis Drake and was secretary to the Admiralty. These men lived through the heroic Elizabethan seafaring age, great days of exploration, expanding trade, national pride and rampant piracy. The daring exploits of Drake, "the most spectacular freebooter of his time"[2], the circumnavigation of the world, the raid on Cadiz, the thwarting of the Spanish Armada, the swashbuckling theft of Spanish gold, were still fresh and vibrant in English minds. This was the stuff of schoolboy dreams and young Thomas is likely to have heard the great stories from a grandfather who knew them first hand. Coytmore sailed on Drake's last voyage in 1595-6 as master of a merchant ship which accompanied six galleons sailing to Central America to capture Spanish gold. He would no doubt have enthralled young Thomas with his account of Drake's reckless storming Puerto Rico, his attack on Panama and, most poignant of all, the great sea captain's death on his way home.[3]

The mariners of Wapping were a tightly-knit community whose families shared the dangers of their calling. They regularly intermarried but, perhaps most crucially, they were bound together by a staunch Protestantism. Besides the Rainborowes and Coytmores, there were the Grays, the Graveses, the Bournes, the Hoxtons, the Woods and the Harrises. These were substantial families. They were wealthy from their sea trading; they built ships, owned ships and had shares in ships; they owned property in London, land in Essex, Surrey, Suffolk and New England. They were among the outstanding men of their profession who provided commanders for the Royal Navy and MPs for Parliament.

Thomas's father, William Rainborowe was offered - but turned down - a knighthood by King Charles I. Both he and Thomas were

MPs in the Long Parliament, William as a firm supporter of Parliament, his son as an independently minded radical. Of their neighbours, Thomas Graves, born in Wapping's neighbouring hamlet of Ratcliffe in 1605, rose to become a rear admiral; Coytmore also served as a secretary to Richard Rich, 2nd Earl of Warwick, one of the grandest men in the kingdom and Lord High Admiral of the Parliamentary navy for much of the Civil War; Nehemiah Bourne, who emigrated to New England, built the first major ship in the colony, returned to fight in Rainborowe's first regiment and, under the Commonwealth, became a commissioner of the navy.

But if seafaring provided their livelihood, religion was their guiding light. Many members of these families, including Thomas's brothers and sisters, were among the thousands who emigrated to New England in the 1630s. Some left for economic reasons – the economy, particularly the cloth industry, was in the doldrums in the 1630s. But most wanted to escape what they saw as the persecution of their deep Puritan beliefs during Charles's personal rule (1629-1640) by his Archbishop of Canterbury, the constantly meddling William Laud. When the first English Civil War broke out in 1642, many hundreds returned, including Thomas's brothers William and Edward, to fight for the Parliamentary side. Thomas's first regiment was officered by several New England returnees, one of whom, John Leverett, later rose to be governor of the Massachusetts Bay Colony. It is likely that the political views of these men, with their emphasis on personal freedom and liberty, strongly influenced Thomas.

The origins of the Rainborowes – also variously spelt Rainsborowe, Rainborough and Rainsborough - are obscure. Two earlier biographers[4] suggested the family could have come from Regensburg in Bavaria. This seems to be based on the thinnest of evidence, that the English version of Regensberg is Raynesbourg and that there was no one with the surname Rainborowe in England before the late 16th century.[5]

But, practically, it seems fat-fetched. Regensburg, a city built at the confluence of the Danube and Regens rivers in south east

Germany, adopted the Protestant religion in 1542 and was ruled by a council of Lutherans until the early 19th century. It seems improbable therefore that the Rainborowes had religious grounds to flee. Thanks to its position on the Danube, Regensburg also seems to have been a prosperous trading town which may rule out economic reasons. It is also landlocked which again is an unlikely location for a family which within a generation were master mariners.

It is more probable the family came from England and began its rise to prominence in the mid-16th century. Their name could have originated in the part of England from which they came. There are rainbarrows, ancient burial sites, in various parts of the country and a Rainsborough Camp in Northamptonshire. There is an interesting but possibly diverting story from Peacock that the coat of arms of a Captain Ransbrowe, consisting of "checquy or and azure, a Moor's head proper, wreathed argent, bearded sable", bore a strong resemblance to that of Guy of Warwick, a popular figure in romantic legend dating back to the 13th century.

His coat of arms consisted of "chequy or and azure, a man's head affronte, filleted argent." Guy's son was variously referred to as Rainburn, Raiburn or Sir Raynbrown. The Moor's head could be a reference to the successful expedition of Thomas's father to Sallee on the North African coast where he rescued hundreds of hostages held by Barbary pirates. Thomas Rainborowe, when an MP, apparently sealed his letters with a ring bearing this coat of arms.[6]

Peacock's description of the Rainborowe family as "gentle, but...probably of little note" rings true. Thomas's paternal grandfather, also Thomas, was the man who began their rise to prominence. He lived in East Greenwich, a settlement on the south shore of the Thames several miles east of the City, but also had a "not inconsiderable leasehold estate"[7] at Claverhambury, near Cheshunt on the Essex-Hertfordshire border. He married Martha Moole, from the nearby parish of St Bride's in Fleet Street, at St Mary's church, Whitechapel. The marriage was recorded in the parish register on November 11, 1582. The couple had seven children of whom six survived into adulthood. This Thomas Rainborowe was a merchant and mariner who made his fortune from currants.

To exploit the great potential for trade in the eastern Mediterranean and Turkey, a group of mainly London merchants set up the Turkey Company in 1581.[8] In 1588, it changed its name to the Levant company and spread its trading as far north as Venice. The company prospered mightily over the next 40 years – the years in which Thomas Rainborowe the elder was most active. Trade in the Levant was "probably the most profitable branch of the country's overseas trade" from 1580-1620[9] and within that trade, "the most lucrative branch" of the business were currants bought from the islands of Zante and Cephalonia.[10] In return Rainborowe offered cloth, lead and tin. By 1626, the trade to Turkey was worth £250,000 a year and "many of the merchants amassed considerable fortunes."[11]

By the time he died in 1622, Thomas Rainborowe was a rich man. He owned property and land in East Greenwich, leased land in Essex and had shares in four ships. His will[12] revealed that he had paid Edward Lord Dennie, Baron of Waltham Holy Cross in Essex £2,300 for a 22 year lease on the estate at Claverhambury in 1619. In the will he left his household goods, his one sixteenth share in the ship the *Barbara Constance* and a annuity of £100 from the rents of the Essex estate to his wife Martha.

To his elder son, William, Thomas's father, Rainborowe left shares in three ships, the *Rainbow*, the *Lilley* and the *Royal Exchange*, £200 and an annuity of £20 from the Essex estate. To his other son, Thomas, who became an armourer in the City of London, and his surviving daughters Barbara, Martha and Sarah he left £200 each and a £20 annuity.[13] The rest of his estate, including the house and land in East Greenwich was divided equally between his widow and William. There also a gift of £10 to the poor children of Greenwich.

William Rainborowe – Thomas's father - was born and baptised in the parish of St Mary's, Whitechapel in 1587. He followed his father into seafaring and traded in currants from the two Greek islands. But he also built a growing reputation as a respected mariner.

Trading in the eastern Mediterranean meant ships had to pass the Barbary coast of North Africa which was infested with pirates ever ready to attack and take hostages. It forced the English seamen to travel in convoy with heavily armed merchantmen.

For this purpose, Rainborowe and his business associates had the 500-ton *Sampson* built at Limehouse, just east of Wapping. It probably the biggest ship of the day and the Lord High Admiral, the Duke of Buckingham, gave permission for her to carry whatever guns she needed to combat the pirates. This not only helped enhance English sea power but it also made William Rainborowe, *Sampson's* master, highly adept at warfare at sea.

It also brought the *Sampson* regular work. The Levant Company[14] picked the ship in 1625 to deliver goods, including cloth and pepper and to bring home "fine goods" valued at £7 a ton. The next year, William was asked by Lord Edward Conway, the secretary of state, to carry the trunks and possessions of Sir Thomas Phillips to his newly appointed post as ambassador to Constantinople. In 1627, Letters of Marque, formal authority to attack and capture marauding enemy vessels and bring them before the admiralty courts, were issued to Rainborowe as commander of the *Sampson*.[15]

By now Rainborowe was also an elder of Trinity House, a charitable guild granted a charter by Henry VIII in 1514, to "regulate pilotage of ships in the king's streams." In 1604, as William began his rise to eminence, James I had given the charity the exclusive and extremely lucrative rights on compulsory pilotage and of licensing pilots in the Thames. In 1633-4, Rainborowe held the exalted position of Master of Trinity House.

By the 1630s he was among a small group of senior mariners whom Charles I consulted on maritime matters and was one of only two professional seamen on the Lord Treasurer's, Sir Richard Weston, (created the Earl of Portland in 1633) list of officers suitable to serve in Charles's new ship money navy. In 1632 he was part of a commission which included Admiral Sir Robert Mansell which looked at how best to man the king's ships.

In 1635 when England assembled a fleet under Admiral the Earl of Lindsay to frighten off the Dutch and French and restore English sovereignty in the Channel, two of the ships were the *Sampson* and the *Royal Exchange*. Rainborowe himself was made captain of the fleet's flagship, the *Merhonour*.[16]

William graduated from highly respected mariner to national hero after the successful raid on Sallee in 1637. The Barbary coast of North Africa was the stronghold of pirates who were disrupting shipping, including trade with the Levant, as well as seizing ships and imprisoning sailors. Despite exhaustive talks of retaliation, nothing was actually ever done until the pirates staged a daring raid in the Bristol Channel in 1636. Towns were plundered and women and children carried off as hostages.

The king consulted Rainborowe who suggested a siege of the most active of the North African ports, Sallee. The plan was backed by the Earl of Northumberland, who later became Lord High Admiral of England, and Rainborowe was appointed commander of the expedition and admiral of the *Leopard*. He was to be accompanied by three other ships and two pinnaces. Five of the skippers were Wapping men handpicked by Rainborowe.[17] The English ships arrived off the coast of Sallee in March 1637 and in the first exchange of fire, 28 of the pirates' corsairs were destroyed. The port finally surrendered on July 28 and 300 hostages were released. Rainborowe then sailed down to the port of Saffee and secured the release of a further 1000 hostages.

The expedition returned to England in triumph, accompanied by the Emperor of Morocco's ambassador. Amid much pomp, a great procession of the freed prisoners, some of whom had been held for decades, was held in London while ministers across the land delivered sermons to mark the great event. The Ambassador was presented to a delighted Charles to whom he offered hawks and four steeds "the choicest and best in all Barbary. These, "led by four black Moors in red liveries, were caparisioned with rich saddles embroidered with gold and the stirrups of two were of massive gold, and the bosses of their bridles of the same metal."[18] Charles played his part in the national celebrations by offering Rainborowe a knighthood. This he refused but he did accept a gold chain and medal, valued at that time at £300, and the captaincy of Charles' new flagship the *Sovereign of the Seas*.

The Sallee expedition was a little more than a "side show"[19] when compared with the epic feats of Drake. But it was a rare victory for the Caroline navy which had become a shadow of the dashing Elizabethan fleet. Its nadir was the shameful retreat from Cadiz under the hopeless Duke of Buckingham in 1625.

Rainborowe's success was largely forgotten within a few months as England faced more immediate problems like continually poor harvests and increasing religious dissent. But it did Rainborowe no harm at all. He wanted to launch further attacks in the Mediterranean and planned a much larger expedition in 1638 – but the scheme never came off and he settled down into a more sedentary role as an expert on naval matters.

Northumberland also made him the more interesting offer of the Parliamentary seat of Aldborough in Suffolk which he accepted. He was an MP from 1640, in what became the Long Parliament, until his death in February, 1642. He was buried in the new St John's church in Wapping which had been paid for by gifts from many of the local mariners.

William Rainborowe married twice. His first wife, whose name is not known, was a daughter of Roland Coytmore[20] who was born in Wapping in 1565 of Welsh parents. By the time of his death in 1626, Cotymore, an associate of the earl of Warwick, had property in Prittlewell, Essex and Surrey. Rainborowe's first marriage produced three children: Thomas, William and Martha. There appears to be no record of when this wife died. His second marriage was to Judith Hoxton, daughter of Reynold Hoxton, a master shipwright of Wapping. There were three surviving children: Judith, Joan and Edward. Four others died in infancy.

Wapping, the chosen home of the Rainborowes, was a riverside hamlet which dated back to the 5th Century AD when Roman rule in Britain was coming to an end.[21] It was first known as the home of Waeppa's People, a small tribe which settled there before becoming Wapping on the Wose (in the mud) and finally just Wapping. Its first wharf was built in 1395 and by 1516, "royal ships were being fitted and victualled at Wapping."[22]

During that century, more wharfs, warehouses and docks were built along this stretch of the Thames as Wapping expanded as a maritime centre. As Elizabethan merchants took a greater share in world trade, the old City harbours of Greenhithe, Dowgate, Puddledock and Billingsgate could no longer cope. Docks and harbours to the east, beyond the City Wall, like Wapping, Ratcliffe, Deptford and Greenwich became far more suitable and important.

In the early 16th century, Wapping was a still a small settlement hedged in to the south by the Thames, to the west by the London Wall and to the north by marshland. But the draining of the marshlands by a Dutchman, Cornelius Vanderdelft, provided more space for development. The population increased as did the number of inns and brothels to entertain the seafarers. "By the end of the Tudor period, having been a sparsely populated marsh on the fringe of a great farming estate, the riverside hamlet had become the most densely populated part of Stepney, the busiest and the most lawless."[23]

John Stow, the great 16th century antiquarian, also cast his eyes over the thriving village. He did not much like what he saw. His first opinion was that St Katharine's Hospital, first established in 1148 (now the site of St Katharine's Marina) was "pestered with small tenements, homely cottages, having inhabitants, English and strangers, more in number than in some cities in England."[24] He also noted its darker side. "This precinct of St Katheren to Wapping in the Woze and Wapping itselfe, is the usall place of execution for hanging of Pirats & sea rovers at the low water marke there to remaine, till three tides had overflowed them, was never a house standing with these 40 yeares; but since the gallows being after removed further off, a continuall streete, or filthy strait passage with alleys of small tenements or cottages builded, inhabited by saylors' victuallers along by the river of Thames, almost to Radcliff, a good mile from the Thames."[25] The "filthy strait road" was a new highway built in 1570.

It is now Wapping High Street. Stow was describing Execution Dock, London's "most famous" gallows.[26] The men to be hanged, pirates, smugglers and mutineers, were kept in either Newgate Prison in the City or Marshalsea Prison across the river in Southwark and on the day of their death marched to the infamous Dock where, before taunting crowds, they suffered their fate, "danced the hempen jig" as the locals put it. Thomas as a boy would have been familiar with the regular executions.

By the end of the 16th century, Wapping was a rough, lawless hamlet teeming with life, packed with sailors of many nationalities, warehousemen, lightermen, wherrymen, ships' builders and repairers, smugglers, thieves and every sort the river attracted. Ships were moored mid-steam and dozens of lighters and wherries plied their trade around Wapping's pontoon.

Its dark, muddy lanes were packed with lodgings, tenements, workshops, warehouses and numerous inns and brothels. It was this area into which the seafaring Rainborowe family moved sometime in the early 17th century and where Thomas, the first child of his parents, was born about 1610.[27]

Little is known of his childhood. There are just three hints of the type of upbringing he may have had. At the Putney Debates, Rainborowe referred to the books he had read, which suggests an education of sorts. As the son of wealthy and strongly Protestant parents, he would almost certainly have gone to a grammar school. There were at least five in London as Thomas was growing up. Middle class Protestants like the Rainborowes valued education as the best way to enable their children to learn to read the Bible, the guiding light of their life. The late 16th and early 17th centuries saw a massive expansion both in the number of grammar schools in England and the levels of literacy.

The curriculum, heavily influenced by religion, consisted, first and foremost, of Latin, followed by Greek and Hebrew – all languages helpful in reading the Bible. Rainborowe's remarks at Putney suggested he also read some history.[28] Grammar school lasted until a boy was 13 or 14. After that it is likely that Thomas joined his father at sea. An anonymous author wrote, in the 1660s, a lament at the apparently declining standards of the Royal Navy. He cited a list of admirals who had previously been cabin boys which included Sir Francis Drake, Sir John Hawkins, General Deane, Col Rainsborough, Sir John Narborough and Sir William Penn. "All these came to deserved honour from having been cabben boyes."[29]

That Thomas grew up with the sea is also acknowledged by the Earl of Clarendon, a royal devotee who had little time for the radical Rainborowe, when he wrote "he had been bred to the sea and was the son of an eminent commander lately dead."[30] It is likely that Thomas became a currant trader like his father and grandfather and may also have joined his father on the Sallee expedition when he would have been about 27.

When William Rainborowe died in 1642, aged 55, he left significant property and money. Thomas received his houses in Southwark, south west of Wapping and across the Thames. His second son, William was left the houses in Gun Alley, Wapping[31] as well as £1,000. It would have taken an unskilled labourer in those days 100 years to earn that amount. His third son Edward received £1,200, his eldest daughter Martha £700 and his younger ones, Judith and Joan £1000 each. There were also bequests to nephews and nieces, other family members and to the poor children and mariners of Wapping.

Within a few months of his father's death, Rainborowe married. His bride was Margaret Jenny who came from a prominent family in Suffolk. The ceremony took place in Woodbridge, Suffolk on June 9. Some records suggest there were Rainborowes in Suffolk in the 16th century. These included a Robert Rainborowe who died in Ipswich, not far from Woodbridge, in 1544. It is possible the two families knew or more likely knew of one another. However nothing is known of Margaret, her parents, or when and where she was born. The couple had two children, Mary and William.

At the age of 32, Thomas was a tall and powerfully built man, full of self confidence, but known to be short tempered and fiery. He also now a wealthy man, with property in Southwark and a share in a profitable shipping business. The one portrait which exists of him seems to come from his later years. It shows a well built man, his hair thinning on top but at the sides falling down onto his shoulders. The face, black eyebrows, soft eyes, a prominent nose, a light coloured moustache over pursed lips, is one of contentment, perhaps with a trace of smugness, certainly one of a man who knew his own worth.

But the world in which he was making his way was in the throes of rapid and fundamental change. These were political, economic, social but, most of all, religious, sparked to a large extent by the policies of Henry VIII the previous century. It was Henry Tudor, who reigned from 1509-47, who set England on its Protestant path. In his need to produce a son and heir, he defied Pope Clement VII, divorced his wife, Catherine of Aragon, and married his wilful and pregnant mistress, Ann Boleyn, in January 1533.

Amid fury from the Catholic Church, Henry broke from Rome with a series of new laws which made him the supreme head of the church in England.[32] He completed his reform of the church by dissolving the monasteries and other religious houses between 1536-41. These were often immensely powerful and rich institutions – religious houses owned about a quarter of England's land. But they were also seen by many as corrupt houses whose occupants peddled fake relics to gullible believers and lived as idle hedonists too well off the fat of their extensive lands. In the Dissolution, many of the buildings were destroyed and most of the land went to the Crown. It was a significant windfall for the cash strapped monarchy.

But Henry's reforms also encouraged a wave of dissent. On the continent, criticism of the corrupt and authoritarian Roman Catholic Church was rife.[33] This was attracting a growing band of sympathisers in England, later known as Puritans. With the aid of the printing press, the unsettling ideas spread with hitherto unknown rapidity. Henry's daughter, Queen Elizabeth, (1558-1603) struggled to control it with her Settlement of 1559. But while this confirmed the break with Rome, it kept the monarch as the supreme head of the church in England and gave considerable power to bishops and clergy.

The Settlement left the Puritans, who wanted a large measure of freedom of worship, profoundly disappointed. But if Elizabeth firmly established Protestantism in England, she never fully soothed Puritan anger. It festered throughout her reign. Then "On a world heaving with expanding energies, and on a Church uncertain of itself, rose, after two generations of mutterings, the tremendous storm of the Puritan movement. The forest bent; the oaks snapped; the dry leaves were driven before a gale…a new world, it was evident, had arisen."[34] It was her successors, James I and Charles I who reaped this bitter harvest.

But while this Puritan storm gathered force, the country also began its rise as a major trading nation. The two in fact went hand in hand. England produced cloth, lead, tin, coal and copper and it needed markets for its products. Most were in Europe but trade to the continent was, by the 1580s, becoming more difficult. This was not just through the actions of the likes of the Barbary pirates but also the restrictions placed on imports by countries on the continent. The need for new markets saw the establishment of the first big trading companies, Muscovy in 1555 and the Levant in 1581.

These were accompanied by repeated attempts to find the north east passage to the fabled Cathay or the north west passage to the far east. It was the need for trade, not exploration, that sparked these expeditions.[35] They may have failed in themselves but they helped open up some new markets. Further south, thanks to the mariners and merchants of the Levant Company, like the Rainborowes, exports to the eastern Mediterranean were steadily increasing.

The buccaneers also played their role. Men like Drake, his cousin Sir John Hawkins and dozens like them, through their plunder of Spanish possessions in the Caribbean and their enthusiastic participation in the slave trade from Africa, increased English knowledge of the world and found areas for possible expansion. The greatest of these was the New World. The idea gathered pace in the late 1570s and in the 1580s and the first attempts at colonisation were made. Sir Walter Raleigh, poet, soldier, courtier and explorer, took his first group of settlers to Roanake Island in Virginia in 1584 but the venture soon failed. The second attempt, three years later on the same island, ended disastrously with the disappearance of the would be colonists. The failures put off further colonisation for two decades but the idea never faded.

By the end of the 16th century, religion was tearing Europe apart. England was at war with Spain, the continent's foremost Catholic power and the ready military arm of the Pope in Rome. France, Europe's other great power, was riven by constant civil war between the Huguenots and the Catholics. As Elizabeth successfully fought off recurring attempts by Rome to re-impose its writ, like the Ridolfi plot which saw the Duke of Norfolk and others executed in 1572, and the Spanish Armada of 1588, Catholics increasingly came to be seen as synonymous with traitors. By the latter years of her reign, it was not altogether safe to be a Papist in Elizabeth's England.

But if Protestantism became the religion of the majority, they were increasing disputes as to the real form these beliefs should take. Some still hankered for at least a measure of the elaborate ceremonies of Rome, the great mystique, the elevated power of the bishops. Others favoured a far simpler form of worship, in chapels stripped of decoration and ostentatious wealth, where the congregation could concentrate on the all important words and message of the sermon rather than be beguiled by the ritual. It was a dispute that grew in intensity in the last years of the 16th century and the first of the 17th century. In the words of Tawney, a new world was arising.

When the old queen died in 1603, her irascible, heavy drinking and pompous successor stepped into this religious maelstrom. But James VI of Scotland, now also James I of England, was nowhere near the man for the job. He was a spendthrift obsessed with hunting and further marred by a damaging predilection for attractive young men. His court was perpetually bankrupt, both financially and morally. It sunk to its nadir with the murder of a courtier, Sir Thomas Overbury, in which one of his former favourites was heavily implicated. James's management skills were little better. A solid believer in the divine right of kings, he had considerable difficulty in coming to terms with an increasingly vocal and self confident parliament eager to discuss its rights and powers.

In religious affairs, James was a Presbyterian with little sympathy for the Puritans. He appointed the strongly anti-Puritan Richard Bancroft as Archbishop of Canterbury in 1604 whose strict new church laws were thrown out by Parliament. When Bancroft died six years later, James was astute enough to replace with the more Puritan-friendly George Abbot. Initially this kept dissent in check.

But James was tested by the outbreak of the Thirty Years War in 1618. This long and devastating religious conflict was ostensibly sparked by the attempt of the Bohemians to place the Protestant Frederick V of the Palatinate on their throne in preference to a Catholic candidate backed by the powerful Habsburgs. What complicated matters was that James's daughter, Elizabeth, was married to Frederick. Englishmen, anti-Catholic and anti-Spanish, expected their monarch to intervene on behalf of both his family and his religion. There were good practical reasons for not intervening but James appeared to the growing anger of his countrymen as a do nothing ditherer. It broke the already fragile religious consensus.

Thomas Rainborowe was born into this world of stark religious division. The Thirty Years War lasted for the rest of his life. In England he grew up witnessing Parliament and the new king Charles

I, who succeeded his father in 1625, increasingly at odds. The disputes were over the rights and role of Parliament, the boundaries of a king's power, the king's finances and, most fundamental of all, the question of religion. Most Englishmen saw popery as the religion of the enemy and feared and utterly opposed a return to the Catholic Church. But that was where the policies of Charles and his insensitive archbishop of Canterbury, William Laud, seemed to be taking the country in the 1630s.

For many people, the answer was one that was close to Rainborowe, his family and his community in Wapping: emigrate to the New World. The idea had been put aside after Raleigh's two failed enterprises, but was soon back on the agenda. One of the leading protagonists was Richard Hakluyt,[36] a writer, chaplain and adventurer, who tirelessly sought to convince Robert Cecil, James's secretary of state, of the benefits of colonising Virginia. The land was finally and successfully settled around the St James River in what was later named Jamestown in 1607.

But there was also interest in other potential settlements. Captain John Smith, a tough, no nonsense "solider of fortune"[37] was the driving force behind the settlement in Virginia, three times threatening to blow up the ship in which discontented settlers planned to flee the colony. After ensuring the colony's survival, Smith returned home and was next employed by the Virginia Company in 1614 to explore land further north, around Maine and Massachusetts Bay, which he named New England. His subsequent book, *A Description of New England*, published in 1616, created enormous interest. It was a land, Smith claimed, that was flowing with something akin to milk and honey. It appealed not only to those in England suffering from the decline the cloth trade but also those who longed for religious freedom.

Thomas Rainborowe, as a boy of about ten, might have seen, looking across the Thames to the settlement of Rotherhithe in 1620, a "staunch, chunky, slow sailing vessel, square rigged, double decked, broad abeam [and] with high upper structure at the stern."[38] This was the *Mayflower*,[39] about to embark for Southampton to pick up its passengers to settle in the New World. The Mayflower unleashed a growing emigration of English people to the New World. After several short-lived settlements, the New England Company for a Plantation in Massachusetts Bay settled 100 people there in 1628 and 300 the following year.

In the same year, the Massachusetts Bay Company was founded and, in 1830, it organised a fleet of 11 ships with up to 700 people, led by John Winthrop, to sail to a new life in New England. Winthrop, "the first great American",[40] was a deeply committed Puritan, of the same generation as Oliver Cromwell, John Hampden and John Pym, all great leaders of the opposition to Charles. Like Cromwell, he came from the Eastern Counties with an estate in Groton, Suffolk; like Cromwell, whose family lived in genteel poverty, Winthrop, like many of his fellow emigrants, had suffered from the decline of the cloth trade. But it was the chance to build a new society based on his Puritan beliefs, his "city upon the hill", that was his main inspiration.

Thousands of Englishmen followed in Winthrop's wake. During the decade of personal rule, "the 11 years' tyranny", up to 20,000 people left England for Massachusetts Bay and the growing number of other settlements in New England. Rainborowe's brother, William, later a staunch support of his radical views, arrived in Charlestown, Massachusetts in 1639. Their sister Martha arrived with her husband Thomas Coytmore in 1638.[41] Coytmore died at sea in 1644 and Martha married John Winthrop, by now governor of the Massachusetts Bay Colony, in 1647. Rainborowe's younger sister Judith was also in New England by 1644, when she married one of Winthrop's sons, Stephen.

Nehemiah Bourne, William Rainborowe's business associate and neighbour in Wapping, left for the colony in the late 1630s and built his first ship, the *Trial* in Boston in 1640. Its master was Thomas Graves, born in Ratcliffe, the next settlement on the Thames to Wapping. He had emigrated in 1638 but may have sailed as mate on the *Arabella*, the ship which carried John Winthrop to America in 1630. Graves, who later served in Cromwell's navy, brought his wife, Katherine and two children to the colony. Katherine was the daughter of Thomas Gray and Katherine Myles. When Gray died, Katherine married Roland Coytmore and when he in turn he died, she emigrated with her son Thomas, his wife Martha and another of her daughters, Elizabeth to Charlestown.

By the 1640s, as England took its fateful steps to Civil War, Thomas Rainborowe had strong bonds with New England. They were to prove invaluable. Many New Englanders, including Bourne, joined Rainborowe's first regiment in 1644. More crucially, it is highly likely that the men who enjoyed a freer and more equal society in the New World played a significant role in developing Rainborowe's radical ideas.

Notes for Chapter Two

1. Earl of Clarendon (formerly Edward Hyde), *The History of the Great Rebellion and Civil Wars in England*, (Oxford, 1888), i, p. 646.
2. George Malcolm Thompson, *Sir Francis Drake*, (London, 1972), p. 318.
3. Ibid., pp. 301-14.
4. Peacock, Rainborowe, *Archaeologia*, pp. 10-11; Williamson, *Four Stuart Portraits*, pp. 109-110.
5. Peacock, Rainborowe, *Archaeologia*, pp. 10-11.
6. Ibid., p. 10.
7. Ibid., p. 9.
8. The Turkey Company, later the Levant Company, was the second major trading company to be founded in Elizabeth's reign. The first was the Muscovy Company which was granted its charter in 1555. They were followed by the biggest of them all, the East India Company, founded by several of the wealthiest members of the Levant Company which received its charter in 1600.
9. Kenneth R. Andrews, *Trade, plunder and settlement Maritime enterprise and the genesis of the British Empire 1480-1630*, (Cambridge, 1984), p. 97.
10. Alfred Wood, *A History of the Levant company*, (London, 1935), p. 24.
11. Ibid., p. 42.
12. Henry Fitz-Gilbert Waters, Henry F Waters and Isaac Greenwood, *The Rainborowe Family* (New York, 1886), pp. 3-4.
13. Thomas Rainborowe became an armourer in the City of London and lived until 1670. Martha married a local mariner Anthony Wood who died in 1625. He left her his house in Surrey, shares in two ships, one the *Exchange*. He left his share in the *Rainbow* to his son Richard. Wood's brother-in-law, the two Rainborowe sons and their mother were also beneficiaries of the will.
14. The Levant Company also used two other of Rainborowe's ships the *Royal Exchange* and the *Rainbow* for commissions to the eastern Mediterranean in the 1620s.
15. W. R. Chaplin, 'William Rainsborough (1587-1642) and his associates of the Trinity House,' *The Mariner's Mirror* 31, 4 (1945), p. 179.
16. Ibid., p. 180.
17. These were Brian Harrison, an elder of Trinity House, a relative of Nehemiah Bourne and master of the *Hercules*, which was used by the Levant Company, George Hatch, elder of Trinity House, a business partner of Rainborowe's and master of the *Mary*, another Levant ship, Thomas Trenchfield, an elder of Trinity house, a shipowner and master of the *Mary Rose*, Thomas White in the pinnace the *Expedition* and Edmund Seaman in the pinnace the *Providence*. A sixth captain was Vice Admiral Sir George Carteret in the *Antelope*, the only one who subsequently fought on the Royalist side in the Civil War. He was a later appointed Comptroller of the Navy and, in the war, Bailiff of Jersey.
18. Waters, Waters and Greenwood, 'Rainborowe Family', pp. 10-11.
19. Kenneth R. Andrews, *Ships, Money and Politics: Seafaring and naval enterprise in the reign of Charles I*, (Cambridge, 1991), p. 131.
20. Captain Roland Coytmore married three times. His first wife was Christian Haynes and it must have been their daughter whom William Rainborowe married. Coytmore's third wife was Katherine Myles who outlived him. In his will Coytmore referred only to the children of this marriage, his son Thomas and his daughter Elizabeth. Thomas married Martha Rainborowe, sister of Thomas. In effect she married her half uncle.

21. Madge Darby, *Waeppa's People: A History of Wapping*, (London, 1988), p. 5.
22. Ibid., pp. 28 and 32.
23. Ibid., p. 38.
24. John Stow, *A Survey of London*, (London. 1598), p. 148.
25. Ibid. p. 383.
26. Peter Ackroyd, *Thames Sacred River*, (London, 2007), p. 160
27. There are birth records for all the Rainborowe children except Thomas. It is not clear where the Rainborowes lived in when they arrived in Wapping.
28. Rainborowe's words at Putney were: "If writings bee true there hath been many scufflinges between the honest men of England and those that have tryranniz'd over them", Clarke Papers, I, p. 246. He also made references to the law of God.
29. British Library, Addl. MS11, 602, fol 38.
30. Clarendon, *Great Rebellion*, i, p. 646.
31. William Rainborowe said in his will he bought these houses from Reynold Hoxton, the father of his second wife. It is possible the family lived there at some stage after the second marriage. Gun Alley no longer exists but seems to have been one of the numerous alleys off Wapping High Street.
32. The main new laws were the Act of Succession which made Anne Boleyn's children with Henry legitimate heirs, the Act of Supremacy which made Henry head of the church and the extended Statute of Treason which tightened the law of treason. All were passed in 1534. The second act did not establish an independent church but one that was entirely under Henry's control.
33. This came from men such as Martin Luther who questioned the sale of relics as a way to redemption, Ulrich Zwingli and John Calvin.
34. Richard Henry Tawney, *Religion and the Rise of Capitalism*, (London, 1926), p. 197.
35. The expedition to find the north east passage was led by Sir Hugh Willoughby and Richard Chancellor in 1552-3 with the aim of finding new markets for English cloth. Sir Martin Frobisher led three expeditions to find the north west passage in 1576, 1577 and 1578. All failed.
36. Richard Hakluyt (c.1552-1616) was a director of the Virginia Company of London from 1589 and the chief promoter of the petition for rights, granted in 1606, to colonise the land. He also wrote several books extolling the virtue of English settlements in the New World. The best known, *The Principall Navigations, Voiages and Discoveries of the English Nation*, was first published in 1589 and aroused considerable interest.
37. Hugh Brogan, *The Penguin History of the United States of America*, (London, 1985), p. 20.
38. Charles M. Andrews, *The Colonial Period of American History*, (Yale, paperback edition 1964), i, p. 269, quoted in Brogan, *Penguin History*, p. 36.
39. After a series of mishaps, the Mayflower finally sailed from Plymouth on September 16, 1620 with 105 passengers, of whom 35 were religious dissenters, later known as the Pilgrim Fathers. She made landfall at Plymouth Rock on November 9.
40. Brogan, *Penguin History*, p. 41.

Some sources say Martha arrived in New England in 1642.

Chapter Three: The Men from New England

As the king travelled through England in the summer of 1642, attempting to rally men and money to his cause, Thomas Rainborowe was headed for Ireland, hoping to pick up some real estate. Irish Catholics had rebelled against English rule on October 23, 1641. Amid ferocious violence, many thousands, Catholic and Protestant, men, women and children, died. Exaggerated reports reaching a fearful London suggested the death toll had reached 30,000. But the English government was slow to react. Charles himself was in Scotland trying to mend fences after his ill advised Bishops' War.[1] The visit was a disaster with Charles actually accused of being involved in a plot to capture – and perhaps kill – the Scots Covenanter leaders. There is no evidence that Charles was personally involved but such was the level of trust the monarch enjoyed, most people thought he was.

In England, the king's relations with the Long Parliament[2] had sunk to a similar low. Led by the implacably anti-Catholic lawyer John Pym,[3] caustically known by his enemies as "King Pym", MPs were reluctant to allow Charles to raise an army as they feared he would use it against them. So despite fears of a Catholic invasion reaching hysterical heights, no agreement was reached over whether Parliament or the king had the authority to send in the troops. In the resulting stalemate, little was done over the winter of 1641-2.

The situation changed dramatically early in 1642. On January 4, Charles made his fateful and foolish attempt to arrest five the MPs he judged to be the biggest thorns in his flesh.[4] In the cold light of failure, Charles, fearing for the safety of his family, retreated to Hampton Court on January 10. It was the last time he saw his capital for seven years. When he returned in 1649, it was as a prisoner of Parliament's victorious army. But his flight left Parliament as the *de facto* government of England. One of its pressing problems was the situation in Ireland.

At first, it looked as though English money and Scots soldiers would combine to create the army needed to subdue the rebels. As early as November, 1641, Pym had tried to raise £50,000 in the City to finance an army. But it was not until February 11, 1642, that King Pym got an offer he could not refuse. A group of London merchants offered to subscribe money for their own expedition to Ireland to crush the rebels. In return they wanted two and a half million acres of Irish land confiscated from the rebels.

The idea of an expedition to Ireland had immense appeal. It offered the opportunity of fighting the hated and feared Papists; it offered the chance of adventure; but most of all to these entrepreneurs, it offered the chance to make money. The men who flocked to support it ranged from colonial traders to MPs, both existing and future, and London merchants and adventurers.

The common thread was their Puritanism and radical political beliefs. Almost to a man they supported Parliament's cause. This was not a surprise. For 15 years, the opposition of merchants to the government of Charles I had been growing. The wars with France and Spain in the late 1620s were disastrous for trade. An increased levy on the import of currants, the livelihood of the Rainborowe family, led to merchants from the Levant Company – some of the richest men in London – to break into a customs house in 1628 to retrieve their precious cargo.

It was again traders from the Levant Company who were foremost in refusing to pay tonnage and poundage in the 1630s.[5] By 1630, opposition in Parliament to the king was "fully merged" with that of the merchants.[6] By 1642, this had had become "something like a party of opposition.[7] Many of these men were among those who, months later, seized control of the Royal Navy for Parliament. By 1647, many, including Thomas Rainborowe, were among the radicals and Independents who wanted to curb the power of the king and force the Army to adopt more extreme policies. A new radical grouping, in which Rainborowe was to play a leading role, was now forming.

Within weeks, Parliament had passed the Adventurers Act. But despite raising £55,000 by mid-April from some 80 subscribers, including Rainborowe and his brother William, the expedition never left port. But nothing daunted, a second, smaller venture, in which Rainborowe played a prominent part, took shape.

This was the Additional Sea Adventure to Ireland. In June, this group, headed by Sir Nicholas Crisp, one of the few Royalists involved, the Thomson family of Maurice, George, Robert and William, Gregory Clement, William Willoughby and Rainborowe petitioned Parliament for permission to raise money. They promised to take 12 ships, pinnaces, soldiers, cavalry and sailors "to reduce the rebels in the said realm of Ireland to their due obedience and (as much as in them shall lie) to prevent and hinder all such supplies as shall be sent unto the said Rebels...and to infest, spoil and waste the said Rebels by Land and Sea."[8] Again subscribers rushed to the cause. Parliament sanctioned the raising of £40,000 but in the event, £43,300 was raised from 180 investors.

Again the deal was that land would be awarded to the subscribers in accordance with the sum they had invested. Parliament also gave the venture permission to hold onto any "ships, goods, monies, plate, pillage and spoil"[9] they laid their hands on. Among the investors were John Hampden, Sir Arthur Hazelrige, Denzil Holles – all the king's bête noirs - Oliver Cromwell, Sir Henry Mildmay, later an ally of Rainborowe's in his pursuit of the vice admiralty of the Parliamentary fleet in 1647, and Philip Skippon, already by 1642 one of Parliament's established soldiers. The Rainborowes contributed £800.[10] This was a substantial investment, higher than most. It would have "bought" them more than a thousand acres of high quality land in Ireland.[11] But politically it was also significant. The Additional Adventure was "an early and spectacular project of London's radical party or alliance."[12]

The expedition gained pace with remarkable speed and on June 17, an Act of Parliament appointed 16 commissioners for the scheme. They included several colonial traders who were close associates of the Thomsons, traders, among them Crisp, who were active in the Guinean trade, Lord Brook, a long time radical opponent of the king, ship owners like Clement and Thomas Vincent and Thomas Rainborowe, described as a seaman. He, Clement and George Thomson later became radical MPs. Thomson and another supporter of the scheme, George Snelling, were the MPs for Southwark when Rainborowe marched his brigade through the borough to occupy London in August, 1647.

Other major supporters included two prominent opponents of the king, the Earl of Warwick,[13] soon to be admiral of the Parliamentary fleet, and Lord Saye and Sele. Warwick was a regular and heavy investor in colonial and privateering adventures in the Caribbean with "an unrivalled network of contacts with fellow shipowners and colonial investors in London's merchant community."[14] Warwick's secretary was Rainborowe's grandfather, Roland Coytmore. But, Warwick, a staunch Presbyterian, was an opponent of Rainborowe by 1647.

Brook was the leader of the expedition although he never travelled to Ireland. The practical leader was Alexander Lord Forbes, the admiral of the Fleet was Benjamin Peters, a London merchant and half brother of Hugh Peter, the radical chaplain who had recently returned to London as the representative of the Massachusetts Bay Colony. Rainborowe was appointed vice admiral while his brother William, also lately returned from New England, sailed with the expedition.[15] William was part of a strong New England element to the expedition. The second in command was John Humfrey, a deputy governor of the colony, while Robert Thomson, appointed rear admiral, was a resident of Boston.

The fleet left Dover on June 29 with 15 vessels, 1,000 soldiers and 500 seamen. Hugh Peter, who kept a daily record of the expedition, *A True Relation of the Passages of Gods Providence in a Voyage for Ireland* [16] claimed it was a great success. But this was obvious propaganda. The expedition was poorly planned and badly executed. In fact it achieved little more than "six months of private war and plunder", before running out of money.[17] It did little, if anything, to strengthen or advance the English position in south and west Ireland.

The fleet arrived off Kinsale on July 11 and three days later, Forbes led 800 men on a march to Rathberry Castle at Bandonbridge to relieve a garrison of 100 Englishmen led by Lord Kynalmachy. In various clashes at Clonakilty and Rathberry, hundreds of rebels were said to have been killed. Peter estimated the number at 500-600. But Forbes also lost a good number of his men. From Kinsale, Forbes sailed north with the intention of relieving Galway. But the city stayed loyal to its Royalist governor, Lord Clanrickard. In revenge, Forbes ordered 500 of his men to despoil Connaught.

Forbes then sailed back southwards to Limerick but again met with little success. The rebels were adept at avoiding a direct battle, leaving Forbes with only the consolation prize of storming a royalist castle at Glyn. Peter left expedition to return to London – by which time civil war had began in England. News of the one tangible success of the expedition, the seizure of five ships along with arms and ammunition to the value of £20,000, followed Peter to London.

Rainborowe's role in all this seems to have been as muted as the expedition itself. Peter reported in his journal that he did not join the fleet until July 29, although he served on its guiding committee. Of his one foray ashore at an un-named port, Peter wrote: "our vice-admiral's boat went ashore, and took some cattle, burnt some houses and killed some rebels."[18] It also left him pursued by creditors. Less than a year later, in May, 1643, "Captain Thomas Rainborow" petitioned Parliament to have them call off several men demanding that their bills for the Additional Sea Adventure be paid.

Rainborowe claimed that he had paid and undertaken to pay "divers great sums, far exceeding the sums received by him." These were for provisions and other unspecified items. He asked that the Committee for the Irish Expeditions pay the bills. The Commons, now locked in the war with the king, had more pressing matters to worry about and ordered that the creditors, named as Thomas Clare, John Hales, Leonard Dewden and others stay their suits "until the said Captain Rainborow shall return from the public service of the kingdom."[19] Rainborowe also received no land for his investments and efforts. When the Cromwellian Settlement was finalised in the 1650s, he had been dead for several years. There is no record of his land entitlement being passed onto his surviving widow and children who had, in any case, emigrated to New England.

Rainborowe had sailed to Ireland in the *Zante Merchant*, a ship whose name suggests she was engaged in the import of currants from the eponymous Greek island. When Forbes' expedition returned to England in the autumn, Rainborowe and the *Zante*, a ship of 117 tons but no guns, stayed on as part of the nine-strong winter guard for Ireland.

By the summer guard of 1643, he had been promoted to skipper of the much larger *Swallow*, a vessel of 380 tons and 42 guns. Within a few months, certainly by June, Rainborowe was again promoted, this time with the rank of vice-admiral, to the *Lion* under the Earl of Warwick, his former business associate. Warwick had seized the vessel on July 9 after she had returned from taking Charles's wife, Henrietta Maria to the Netherlands,[20] ostensibly for her safety, practically to raise munitions and support for her husband's cause.

It was aboard the *Lion*, a great ship of 620 tons and 40 guns, that Rainborowe saw his one piece of action as a sailor. He captured a vessel sailing from Leith in Scotland to Newcastle packed with 200 men intent on joining the Royalist army of the Earl of Newcastle. The Earl, Charles's most effective soldier in the north east, was causing all sorts of problems for the Parliamentarians. An addition of fresh men would only have strengthened his position. Rainborowe delivered his prisoners to Yarmouth and was sufficiently proud of his achievement to go to Westminster and inform Parliament personally. Parliament ordered on June 20 that the matter of the prisoners be referred to the Committee for the Navy.[21]

It was in the autumn that Rainborowe's career changed dramatically. The switch from vice admiral in the Navy to colonel in the Army put him on the path to become one of Parliament's greatest soldiers. But it also brought him into close contact with the men from Massachusetts who helped form and radicalise his political outlook.

Yorkshire became involved in the pending conflict between king and Parliament before most other counties. When Charles left London to rally his supporters, it was to the city of York that he turned first. But on his arrival on March 19, 1642, he got scant response. The county was the most heavily taxed to pay for his Bishops' War; its cloth industry in West Riding had suffered as much as East Anglia's in the economic doldrums of the 1630s; and this area was also strongly Puritan, later providing Sir Thomas Fairfax with the backbone of his Army. The county itself was also split between the Royalist factions of the Wentworth family, formerly headed by the king's widely loathed counsellor, the earl of Strafford and the Cholmleys, Fairfaxes and Hothams who supported Parliament. Despite his warm reception in the city the year before, this was no longer fertile territory for the king.

Yorkshire also had one of the biggest magazines outside the Tower of London with weapons for 16,000 men stored at Hull. Control of this arsenal was vital for either side. Parliament had appointed Sir John Hotham as governor of the city and its deep water harbour in January 1642. Charles had countered by giving the same position to his ally, the earl of Newcastle. The inevitable clash came in April. The king and his entourage arrived at the gates of the city on April 23 but Hotham, acting on Parliament's order, refused him entry. The spurned monarch returned to his base at York but two months later returned to Hull with Newcastle and 3,000 infantrymen and 1,000 cavalry.

But by then Parliament had shrewdly removed most of the weapons to safer keeping in London. At the king's approach, the citizens of the Hull opened the sluices on the River Humber and flooded the surrounding land for two miles. A party of Royalists troops which moved towards the city, burning buildings at it approached, was driven off. It was the first major action of the first English Civil War.

Hull was shortly strengthened by the arrival of Sir John Meldrum, a seasoned Scottish soldier who had left Charles for Parliament. His presence with 1,500 soldiers made the city safe. Charles abandoned his siege and returned to York. But his fortunes changed remarkably in the county in the next 12 months. Sir Hugh Cholmley, elder brother of Sir Henry, later Rainborowe's nemesis at Pontefract, defected to the king, taking the vital port of Scarborough with him. Next, in June, Sir John Hotham and his son John were arrested for treason and taken to London.[22] By the summer of 1643, Parliamentary forces in the county were in disarray and Newcastle was the master of the county. On September 2, he duly began the second siege of Hull.

The siege slipped into stalemate by October until the gallant Meldrum once again rode – or rather sailed – to the rescue. On October 11, he landed with just under 2,000 men, both soldiers and seamen. The same day, with Colonel John Lambert, a Yorkshireman from Malhamdale and another of the great soldiers thrown up by the Civil War, vice admiral Rainborowe and 1,000 of the party stormed the enemy's defences on the north bank of the Humber.

Amid fierce fighting, the Royalist defences were overrun and heavy cannon captured. But in the melee, Rainborowe was taken prisoner. First reports said he had been killed. Meldrum, in his letter to the Speaker, William Lenthall described the "happy success" of the action. But it was not that straightforward. Meldrum described how two bodies of 500 musketeers under Lambert and Rainborowe "carried themselves very bravely marching amongst the enemy's line of approach on every side, the enemy abandoning one work after another, until we made ourselves masters of their ordinance."

But a Royalist counter attack by 100 pikemen threw the van of the Parliamentarian infantry into disarray. They were scattered, lost the just captured cannon and forced into a "shameful" retreat. "In this retreat [Rainborowe] is either taken prisoner or killed and fallen into some ditch but cannot be found, his man's body is found," Meldrum wrote. His forces re-grouped, re-captured some of the ordinance and, after more fierce fighting, forced the enemy to flee by about midnight. But as his finished his account, the veteran soldier received some good news. "Since the beginning of my letter we understand that Colonel Rainsborough is safe."[23]

Rainborowe was later reported as saying that he, "riding up to their horse, which he thought had been ours, was carried away captive, but is since released by Captain Bushell who begged him of the earl of Newcastle as his prisoner, whom he sent back to Hull upon his promise of giving him £500."[24] It was an irony that Rainborowe should be the prisoner of Captain Browne Bushell who was a cousin of the Cholmleys and had defected to the Royalists with Sir Hugh Cholmley. It is unclear for how long Rainborowe was held captive. Parliament only gave permission for a prisoner exchange for him on November 4, 1643, after a petition by his wife Margaret.[25] The prisoner for whom he was exchanged was another defector, Captain Thomas Kettleby whom Rainborowe had succeeded as captain of the *Swallow* earlier that year. When Rainborowe returned to the Parliamentarians, he was a a soldier and no longer a sailor.

The Army which he joined was being assembled by the Earl of Manchester.[26] This was the army of the Eastern Association, a network of six counties in 1642: Norfolk, Suffolk, Essex, Cambridgeshire, Hertfordshire and the Isle of Ely. It was joined by two others, Lincolnshire and Huntingdonshire in 1643. These were the counties said to hold the "sacred fire of liberty which history has justly credited to the old Puritan stock."[27] The army Manchester raised was the "largest and most effective" then in Parliament's cause and later formed the "backbone" of the war winning New Model Army.[28] It was paid for through local levies and saw the defence of the eastern counties as its prime role. This differed slightly in Lincolnshire which paid for both Colonel Huw Rossiter's horse regiment and Rainborowe's foot. The county was never entirely free of Royalist enclaves or incursions so these two regiments as well as a garrison at Grantham were permanently stationed the county in 1644.

Rainborowe's regiment was raised in June 1644 and the senior officers chosen by Manchester. It was Manchester's policy to pick able men as his officers rather than merely rely on the landed gentry to fill the posts; nor did it matter where these new order of men came from. So Rainborowe, a Londoner with strong ties to trade, was put in charge of a foot regiment consisting largely of men from Lincolnshire. But it was a regiment that needed strengthening. John Hotham had previously been in charge of forces in Lincolnshire but when his treachery was revealed and he escaped to Hull, some of his men followed while others simply dispersed.

This led to another major difference in Rainborowe's regiment compared to many others. Three of his senior officers and perhaps dozens of his men were recruited from New England. Israel Stoughton became Rainborowe's lieutenant-general, Nehemiah Bourne became a major and John Leverett a captain of a troop of foot. A Boston innkeeper, William Hudson, became Leverett's ensign. It has been estimated that between 80 and 150 New Englanders served in Rainborowe's regiment.[29] John Winthrop, governor of the Massachusetts Bay Colony, described the whole group as "our best military men."[30]

The officers at least came from the top echelons of Massachusetts society. Stoughton, born in Essex but who later moved to Rotherhithe, across the Thames from Rainborowe's home of Wapping, emigrated in 1632 with his brother William. He became a freeman of Boston a year later and was actively involved in politics. Stoughton became the leader of a campaign which opposed the colony's governor, Winthrop, having both executive and magisterial powers. When the colony established its general court – its chief judicial and legislative body – in 1634, Stoughton was elected as one of its deputies.

In his continuing row with Winthrop, who called him a "worm and underminer of the state", Stoughton was banned from office the following year but re-admitted in 1636. A year later he was a captain in the Dorchester Militia and led the Massachusetts forces in the brief war against the Pequot Indians in 1637. In 1641, Stoughton was promoted to sergeant-major-general of the Massachusetts militia. He was the leader of the men who returned to England in the winter of 1643 and joined Rainborowe in the summer.[31]

Bourne came from the same generation of the tightly knit Puritan and seafaring community in Wapping as Rainborowe. The two, born a year apart, would have known each other for years. He emigrated to New England in 1638 in the *Confidence*, a ship owned by Rainborowe's father,[32] and settled in Charlestown, where Thomas's brothers, William and Edward and his sisters, Martha and Judith lived from 1639. Bourne moved onto to Boston where he built the colony's first ship, the *Tryal*, and became a member of the Boston church. After fighting alongside Rainborowe until 1645, Bourne returned to New England but came back a year later and stayed. During the Commonwealth years, he was a naval commissioner and built a new shipyard at Wapping. His career ended with the Restoration and he moved to the Netherlands.

John Leverett was another rising star of the Massachusetts colony. He was born in Boston, Lincolnshire and emigrated with his family in 1633. He was a member of the Massachusetts Artillery Company from 1639-71, a transatlantic merchant in the 1640s and appointed a commissioner to negotiate with native Indians in 1642. He served with Rainborowe from 1644, seeing action at Crowland in his native Lincolnshire, at the capture of Gaunt House in Oxfordshire, the Battle of Naseby in 1645 and possibly at Bristol and the siege of Sherbourne in 1646. On his return to Massachusetts, he rose to be deputy governor of the colony in 1671-3 and governor from 1674-9.

A fourth New Englander, who served briefly under Rainborowe at the siege of Worcester in 1646 and for a longer spell with William Rainborowe, was Stephen Winthrop. Son of John, he was born in Groton, Suffolk in 1619 and emigrated with his family and hundreds of others in 1633 when he was 11. In 1644, Stephen married Judith Rainborowe and in either late 1645 or early 1646, he returned to England and made contact with his brothers-in-law. He spent much of the rest of his life in England.

These four men had all came from the eastern counties where the "sacred fire of liberty" burned. But they had something else in common which must have fascinated the Rainborowe brothers, two men increasingly exercised by how England was governed through a strict, hierarchical structure. They all had a vote in how their community was run.

Massachusetts was different from other colonies. In Virginia, the hierarchical society still thrived. Many of the immigrants there were single young men who were indentured to masters for up to seven years before gaining their freedom. In Massachusetts no such system ever existed and the immigrants were mainly families, friends who were united by their Puritan beliefs and planned, from the start, to form a new style of community. Nor were they feckless wanderers. These immigrants comprised skilled men with a wide variety of trades: shoemakers, coopers, blacksmiths, millers and yeomen. The Winthrops themselves could be classed as minor gentry. They also had a far higher than average level, of literacy, reflecting again the Puritan belief in the value of education.[33]

The primary cause of their decision to leave England was the feeling that under the personal rule of Charles I, their religious beliefs were under increasing attack. The prime culprit in this was William Laud, bishop of London until his translation to Canterbury in 1633. While Laud's policies seemed to be edging the Church of England closer to that of Rome, the ministers they admired and respected preached a far more democratic style of worship where an individual church and its members were supreme.

Foremost among these ministers was William Ames who came from the next village in Suffolk to John Winthrop. Ames, described as a "gifted theologian" was a congregationalist who believed that power should reside in an individual church and its members. Church elders might play a part but there were no bishops. He "would have been the clerical guiding light of Massachusetts had he not died [in 1633] before he could cross the Atlantic."[34] His contemporary Paul Baynes preached that the greatest authority in England should be the people and that the monarch could be deposed. Robert Parker was another strongly anti-bishop minister whose son and grandson both became prominent Massachusetts clergymen. Several of preachers of these pronounced anti-conformist views fled to the Netherlands and set up a network of English puritans criticising the works of Laud from afar.

Another leading light in this group was John Cotton from Lincolnshire. Thomas Leverett, father of John, was a strong supporter of Cotton's and both had led the county's protests against the forced loan Charles tried to impose in 1627. There were also protests, among other places, by Essex and Suffolk men and by London merchants. It was out of this civic protest – not religious – that the idea of the Massachusetts Bay Colony was born.

The Cottons and the Leveretts emigrated together in 1633. Thomas Leverett became a ruling elder of the church at Boston while the constant theme of Cotton's sermons in the 1630s was the abuse of power by the king. Dudley Thomas, another prominent forced loan protestor from Lincolnshire was one of the four founding members of the Boston and Charlestown congregationalist church.

It was with these radical beliefs and a strong sense of guiding their own destiny that the emigrants to Massachusetts set about creating their "city on a hill." Winthrop pulled a master stroke when he insisted that the Royal Charter permitting the settlement of Massachusetts Bay should physically accompany the emigrants. It made it nigh on impossible for Charles or anyone else in England to change it[35] but easy to do so for those in Massachusetts.

Within months of setting up the colony, Winthrop began to do exactly that.[36] He proposed that all male settlers should become voters and they should elect the members of the Court of Assistants once a year. A year later in 1631, it was agreed that the settlers by their votes could add to or remove Assistants. Another year on and the settlers were given power to vote annually for the governor, his deputy and the Assistants. In 1834, a new Central Court, in addition to the Court of Assistants, was formed. This became the colony's main legislative and judicial body.[37] A form of democracy was beginning to take a hold.

It was not that Massachusetts was wholly out on a limb. There had been increasing calls in England from respected lawyers as well as radicals about limiting the power of the king in England in the reigns of both James I and Charles. There was also a growing trend to grant charters to English towns and cities under which a wide section of the community had a vote. Freemen, burgesses in boroughs, citizens in towns, often through patrimony or purchase, and even those with seven-year apprenticeships under the authority of a freemen were enfranchised.[38] But this was not mainstream; it was on the fringes. In Massachusetts it was central to how the settlers wanted the colony to develop. They were "looking to create not just churches but a state. What they wanted was a godly republic."[39]

This all gave the men of Massachusetts an aura envied or even marvelled at by some Englishmen. Nathaniel Mather, a settler who visited England, wrote home to a friend: "'tis a notion of mighty great and high respect to have been a New-English man, 'tis enough to gain a man very much respect, yea almost any preferment." Their experiment in trying to create a new church and new state "gave them an authority that many Englishmen hoped to learn from."[40]

Thomas Rainborowe could certainly be counted among these Englishman. His family's strong and sympathetic connection with New England, his friendship with Bourne and his need for trained officers for his new regiment made the colony an obvious recruiting ground for him. From their point of view, Rainborowe's regiment, where the colonel was known to be open to their views, was the most attractive one for them to join.

During the long periods of inactivity as Rainborowe's regiment was garrisoned in Lincolnshire in 1644, it seems beyond dispute that political issues were talked of again and again. "No doubt this connexion with the New Englanders influenced Rainborowe's political views."[41] It was here that Rainborowe's views, which he so eloquently expressed at the Putney Debates three years later, began to take shape. It was not just his belief in the sovereignty of the people. Perhaps more important was his growing belief that individual men should have their own measure of freedom. "That which is dear unto me is my freedom", he said at Putney.[42]

Rainborowe's foot was one of two regiments stationed in Lincolnshire – the other was Colonel Edward Rossiter's horse - largely because it was paid for by the locals. It was a much disputed county with the Royalists strong in the north and Parliament holding the south. Parliament's grip had been tightened when it had taken Crowland in April 1643. Crowland, in the deepest Fen country and just north east of Peterborough, was not an obviously important town but both sides seemed to see it as vital. It may have been more of symbolic value.

Either way, the Royalists were determined both to make inroads into the south and take Crowland back. In the absence of Manchester and much of his army fighting in the north and west,[43] they swooped down, taking Grantham and Stamford. In November they seized back Crowland. Rainborowe's regiment was among the 4,000 strong force that Parliament quickly assembled to re-take the town. But despite an overwhelming superiority of numbers – the Royalist force numbered 260 men and 25 horse – the Parliamentary troops were foiled by the incessantly heavy rain in what was already a marshland. As the area turned into a quagmire, Rainborowe's men were kept in place but many of the horse and trained bands were sent back to their bases.

Two Royalist attempts to relieve Crowland were beaten off, the bigger skirmish being at Denton where Parliament took about 1,000 prisoners. The embattled Royalists at Crowland, holed up in the little town's Benedictine abbey on the hill, also managed regular sallies out into the countryside, no doubt to gather food. Manchester put

Rainborowe in charge of taking the town. It was a good choice. The town was surrounded by water and had to be approached in boats. Rainborowe, recently a vice admiral, was best equipped to oversee such an advance.

His first move was to cut off the Royalists with no sorties out of the town and no supplies getting in. Long boats were called in, mounted with guns which both blocked off the town and enabled the attackers to begin a battery of the abbey. The siege lasted a few weeks before the Royalists surrendered. By that time, they had run out of both bread and salt. Rainborowe was hailed as a hero, his victory widely celebrated. One report of the operation by John Vicars noted "that a brave party of the Parliament's forces in those parts [Lincolnshire], led by the valiant and virtuous Colonel Rainsborough, under the command of the Earl of Manchester, having much battered Crowland with the ordnance which they brought by water in long boats against it, the enemy, at last, was forced to parley."

Under the terms of surrender, the Royalists were allowed to march out of the town, the officers with their swords and pistols "but the common soldiers to leave all their arms behind them, as also all the ordnance and ammunition therein to be left for the Parliaments use."

In his account, Vicars suggests that the town was of "so great concernment" because while it took only a few men to hold it, hundreds were necessary to besiege it. Had Rainborowe not recovered it, Crowland "might have proved a kind of Dunkirk to the Parliament, both by land and water too, had the enemy continued in it."[44] It stayed in Parliament's hands for the rest of the war. Rainborowe had begun to establish his reputation as a great solider. He had also been given plenty to think about by the men from New England.

Notes for Chapter Three

1. The Bishops' Wars (1639-40) amounted to minor skirmishes over Charles's rash attempts to impose the English prayer book on the Scots and, in turn, thwart their wishes to abolish episcopacy. It was his desperate need for money, after eleven years of personal rule, that forced Charles to call the short Parliament in April 1640 and the Long Parliament which sat from November 1640 to 1660.
2. Since first sitting in November 1640, the Long Parliament had curtailed the power and prerogatives of the king and increased its own powers. In the process, two of Charles' favoured counsellors, the Earl of Strafford and William Laud, Archbishop of Canterbury, were arrested. Strafford had been beheaded in May, 1641; Laud was executed in January, 1645.
3. John Pym (1584-1643) had a long record of challenging royal power. Like many other radical Puritans, among them the Earl of Warwick, he was involved in the Providence Island Company which tried to establish a Puritan haven on the central American island. Pym was also led Parliament's efforts to raise the loans and taxes which financed the Civil War and ensured eventual victory. He died in 1643, probably of cancer.
4. Charles, accompanied by armed guards, had tried to arrest Pym, John Hampden, Denzil Holles, Sir Arthur Hazelrige and William Strode in the Chamber of the House of Commons on January 4. Tipped off, they had retreated to the safety of the City of London. They returned to Parliament in triumph the day after the king fled.
5. For a full account of the opposition of the merchants to the Crown, see Robert Brenner, *Merchants and Revolution: Commercial Change, Political Conflict, and London's Overseas Traders 1550-1653*, (Cambridge, 1993), pp.199-234.
6. Brenner, *Merchants and Revolution*, p. 233.
7. Ibid., p. 400.
8. Charles Firth and R.S. Rait (eds.), *Acts and Ordinances of the Interregnum 1642-60*, (3 volumes, London, 1911), i, pp. 9-12, quoted in Raymond Stearns, *The Strenuous Puritan Hugh Peter*, (Urbana, 1954), pp. 189-90.
9. Stearns, *Strenuous Puritan*, p. 190.
10. There is a full list of subscribers in both Karl Bottigheimer, *English Money and Irish Land*, (Oxford, 1971) and J. R. MacCormack, 'The Irish Adventurers and the English Civil War', *Irish Historical Studies*, x, no. 37, (March, 1956), pp. 21-58. They do not exactly tally but both say the Rainborowes contributed £1,000. Bottigheimer says it was £200 to the first, aborted Adventure and £800 to the second. MacCormack says they subscribed £1,000 for both expeditions but only actually paid up £500.
11. MaCormack said the breakdown for the first expedition was £600 for 1,000 acres in fertile Leinster, £450 for 1,000 acres in Munster and £200-300 for 1,000 in the less good lands of Connaught and Ulster. The breakdown for the second expedition is likely to have been similar. MacCormack, 'Irish Adventurers', p. 30.
12. Brenner, *Merchants and Revolution*, pp. 403-4.
13. Robert Rich, the second earl of Warwick (1587-1658) was typical of many aristocrats of the mid-17th century, completely owing his place and wealth to Henry VIII's

Reformation and the subsequent dissolution of the monasteries in the 1530s. Rich's great grandfather, Richard Rich who presided over the dissolution of many of the monasteries was granted Lees Priory, a former friary in Essex as part of his reward. Richard was later made Baron Rich by Edward VI and his grandson the 3rd Baron purchased his earldom in 1618. His son, Robert, succeeded him in 1619. See John Adamson, *The Noble Revolt*, (London, 2007) for a fuller look at his life although Adamson exaggerates his influence on events in the early 1640s.

14. John Adamson, *The Noble Revolt*, (London, 2007), p. 27.
15. Stearns, *Strenuous Puritan*, p. 191.
16. It was endorsed by Forbes and published by Parliament in London in 1642.
17. Brenner, *Merchants and Revolution*, p. 404.
18. Hugh Peter, *A True Relation of the Passages of Gods Providence in a Voyage for Ireland*, (London, 1642), pp.10-11, quoted in Whitney Jones, *Thomas Rainborowe, Civil War Seaman, Siegemaster and Radical*, (Woodbridge, 2005), p.15.
19. Commons Journal, iii, pp. 131-4.
20. John Rowland Powell and E. K. Timings (eds.), *Documents Relating to the Civil War 1642-48*, (London, 1963), pp. 3-4.
21. Commons Journal, iii, pp. 136-8. On the same day, Parliament ordered that some Irish pirates taken prisoner and now in Yarmouth be tried under martial law by Warwick. It is not clear if these were the same men.
22. The Hothams became disillusioned and at odds with Parliamentary commanders including Fairfax and Cromwell. Both were in contact with the earl of Newcastle, probably with the intention of turning Hull over to the king. After a long delay they were tried for treason and beheaded in January, 1645.
23. Portland MSS, 13th report of the Historic Manuscript Collection, i, pp. 138-9.
24. Powell and Timings, *Documents Relating to the Civil War*, p. 97, quoting from Thomason E. 59, p. 11.
25. Commons Journal, iii, p. 302.
26. Edward Montagu, 2nd earl of Manchester (1602-71) was a strong opponent of Charles I and the only member of the Lords the king tried to arrest in 1642. He served under the earl of Essex, Warwick's cousin, before being put in command of the army of the Eastern Association. He resigned after leading Parliamentary forces at Marston Moor as he thought the war should then end. His Presbyterian views led him into opposition with Rainborowe in 1647. After the Restoration he was a strong supporter of Charles II. He married Warwick's daughter.
27. Alfred Kingston, *East Anglia and the Great Civil War*, (London, 1897), p. 2. Quoted in Clive Holmes, *The Eastern Association in the Civil War*, (Cambridge, 1974), p. 1.
28. Ibid.
29. Francis J. Bremer, *First Founders*, (Durham, New Hampshire, 2012), p. 214.
30. John Winthrop, *The Journal of John Winthrop 1630-1649*, (Harvard, 1996), eds. Richard S. Dunn and Laetitia Yeandle, pp. 287-8.
31. Roger Thompson, *Oxford Dictionary of National Biography*, vol 52, p. 969.
32. Barnard Capp, *Oxford Dictionary of National Biography*, vol 6, p. 855.
33. See Susan Hardman Moore, *Pilgrims: New World of Settlers and the Call of Home*, (London, 2007).
34. Michael P. Winship, *Godly Republicanism*, (Cambridge, Massachusetts, 2012), p. 93.

35. Charles planned to send ships to the colony in 1634 to recover the Charter but nothing came of the threat.
36. Under the original terms of the Charter only the freemen or stockholders of the colony, i.e. the investors, had a vote. Not all were in Massachusetts. They would meet in theory four times a year to make company laws, elect a governor, his deputy and a Court of Assistants. This court was the law making, executive and magisterial body.
37. See Winship, *Godly Republicanism*, pp. 185-95.
38. Phil Withington, *The Politics of Commonwealth* (Cambridge, 2005), p. 8.
39. Winship, *Godly Republicanism, p. 185*.
40. Bremer, *First Founders*, p. 123. He does not give a source for the Mather remarks.
41. Charles Harding Firth and Godfrey Davies, *The Regimental History of Cromwell's Army*, (Oxford, 1940), two volumes, i, p. 418.
42. Sir William Clarke, *The Clarke Papers*, (London, 1891), Ed. Charles Harding Firth, i, p. 273.
43. Manchester was in command of the Parliamentary forces at the Battle of Marston Moor in Yorkshire on July 2, 1644.
44. John Vicars, *The Burning Bush not Consumed*, (London, 1646), p. 76 in his *Englands Parliamentary Chronicle*, vol iv, p. 76.

Chapter Four: Parliament's Great Warrior

Rainborowe was now a rising star of the Parliamentary Army. Pamphlets and newspapers supporting Parliament gleefully reported the victory at Crowland and raised Rainborowe almost to the status of national hero. He became "a much talked off and popular man."[1] His reward was a new foot regiment which he largely raised himself in London.

However for the months following Crowland, Rainborowe remained stationed in Lincolnshire. During this time, the regiment suffered two major losses. First Israel Stoughton, the leader of the New Englanders and probably the colony's top soldier, died of a sickness either in late 1644 or early 1645. Secondly Nehemiah Bourne, Rainborowe's old friend from Wapping, returned to Massachusetts to resume his career at sea. He rejoined the Parliamentary cause a year later and rose to the rank of rear admiral by 1652.

One of the reasons the victory at Crowland shone so brightly was that it came at a time when the Parliamentary forces were in a state of unrest. There were growing problems egarding arrears of pay among the soldiers, leading to an increasing number of desertions. Equally damaging, there were the first signs of the crippling split between the Presbyterians and the Independents – the first group wanted a peace with Charles while the second wanted a victory. But the major and immediate problem was the Earl of Manchester, the commander of the Eastern Association's army.

Following his decisive victory at Marston Moor, the earl wanted little to do with anymore fighting. He retired to Lincolnshire "where he was impervious alike to the Committee of Both Kingdoms' orders to go to the rescue of Essex [who was faring badly in the West Country] and to his own officers' pleas to move against Newark."[2] He did eventually agree to aid Sir William Waller who was retreating before the king's stronger forces also in the West. But he moved so slowly he only reached in Reading by mid-October.

As the year progressed, Manchester's dilatoriness got worse. He was slow in moving his troops during the second battle of Newbury on October 27 which helped cost his side the expected outright victory. He then refused to let Cromwell and Waller take their cavalry to pursue the king after his tactical retreat until it was too late. Finally in November, at the prospect of the third battle of Newbury, he refused to engage at all. He told Cromwell and Sir Arthur Haselrig, also a cavalry officer, "the king cares not how oft he fights but it concerns us to be wary, for in fighting we venture all to nothing. If we beat the king ninety-nine times, he would be king still, and his posterity, and we subjects still; but if he beats us but once we should be hanged, and our posterity be undone."[3] There may have been truth in what he said but it was hardly the right attitude for an army commander. Manchester had had enough.[4]

It was a time for fundamental reform and out of the disarray of the Parliamentary forces the New Model Army (NMA) emerged in the spring of 1645. Cromwell was the driving force behind it. He laid bare – as did Waller – his quarrel with Manchester before the Commons in the last months of 1644, highlighting the earl's continual tardiness in action. The solution was twofold: an end to MPs and peers having commands in the army – the Self Denying Ordinance – and a national and professional army in place of the current regional forces. The Commons heartily endorsed the proposals; the Lords did their best to derail them.

By December, the Commons had approved both the Self Denying Ordinance and the New Model Ordinance. Next month they approved Sir Thomas Fairfax as the new army's commander-in-chief. It was a risk. They were limited in their options by the Self Denying Ordinance: Fairfax was just 32 and had no so far not distinguished himself in the war. But he came of solid Yorkshire fighting stock, had the toughness and charisma of the born leader and, not least, had no marked interest in politics. It turned out to be an inspired choice. He turned out to be a firm but fair general, much admired by his men. In their turn they called him "Black Tom" because of his dark looks.

The Lords felt otherwise. They delayed accepting the Self Denying Ordinance until it was modified, which, ironically, allowed Cromwell to take up the post of second in command of the NMA and passed Fairfax's appointment by just one vote. They then set about rejecting many of his choices for commissions in the NMA. In all, they wanted 57 changes to Fairfax's original list of 193, 35 because of their Independent or radical views. A good number of these were from Manchester's former army which had become heavily politicised and where Rainborowe had served.[5] It is not clear if Rainborowe was among those to whom the Lords objected. Fairfax, however, was having none of it and simply ignored much of the Lords' objections. It was a style he often adopted when faced with orders he disliked.

But unexpectedly the list worked to Rainborowe's advantage. There was one name to which the Lords objected which Fairfax acknowledged, that of Colonel Thomas Ayloffe. After agreeing to remove this man, Fairfax replaced him with Rainborowe who had not been on the original list. This was not entirely remarkable as Fairfax did not then know him. More surprisingly, Rainborowe was approved by the Commons on March 1.

Under the restructuring, Parliament moved Rainborowe's Lincolnshire regiment across the Pennines to Lancashire in April and transferred the command to a Lieutenant Colonel Grey.[6] Rainborowe's new charges had been raised by Ayloffe, an Essex man, in Huntingdonshire in 1643. They had already been involved in two minor battles. They took part in action under Waller at the defeat at Cropredy Bridge in June 1644 and then against Prince Rupert[7] at Abingdon in January 1645 under Major-General Sir Richard Browne.

By the spring of 1645 it was much depleted. 174 of its men were transferred to Colonel John Pickering's new regiment of foot while most of the remainder, basically no more than a handful, stayed on as part of Rainborowe's new command. He was given three of Ayloffe's captains, Sterne, Dancer and Drury and men and officers from the regiments of Colonel Francis Russell, brother of the earl of Bedford and a former member of the earl of Essex's life guard, and Major-General Lawrence Crawford, commander of the infantry in Manchester's army and an unwavering Presbyterian.[8]

Rainborowe also did his own recruiting in his home town of London. On July 31, he was given £1,000 of public money to recruit 1,457 men to the NMA. With 15 officers in tow, he completed the job for under half the money, returning £675/10/- to the treasury. Fairfax sent out many officers to recruit for the NMA and one of the most fertile grounds were the poor areas of St Giles Cripplegate, Clerkenwell, St Martin-in-the-Fields, Finsbury, St Clement Danes and the Savoy.[9] It is likely that Rainborowe also recruited in other London districts including Southwark where he owned property and was well known.[10]

But by this stage, Rainborowe's new regiment was already in the field. On May 8 it was ordered to join Cromwell who, with Browne, was monitoring the king's activities around Oxford. This was one of the last Royalist strongholds. Fairfax and the main army were themselves planning to march on the other stronghold at Bristol, held by Prince Rupert. Within a month, Rainborowe's men saw action. They were ordered to take Gaunt House, near Oxford on May 31. Within a day it was theirs.

The House was owned by Dr John Fell,[11] a committed Royalist who had lent his home in the village of Standlake, 12 miles west of Oxford, to the king. It served as a base for a garrison to secure New Bridge, a 14th century crossing over the River Thames on the vital road between Witney and Abingdon. Rainborowe and his foot, strengthened by horse from Colonel Thomas Sheffield's regiment, "battered it [the house] for all that day; but by reason of the moat, the access was ill to it." The governor also refused a summons to surrender from Rainborowe.

The next day, Rainborowe drew up "carts and all things necessary" to storm the house. Whereupon "the governor, perceiving the same, sounded a parley waving the consideration he insisted on the day before, and surrendered the house, with all the arms and ammunition therein, upon quarter for himself and his soldiers."[12] A similar account is given by Bulstrode Whitelock, who reported "Col Rainsborough with his regiment of foot and three troops of Colonel Sheffield's horse, took in Gaunt house, ten miles from Oxford and therein the governor, with all his soldiers, arms, ammunition and provisions."[13]

This was a mere skirmish compared to what followed next. Inevitably in war, it emerged from confusion. The king with Rupert moved first north towards Scotland, then east to storm Leicester with immediate success on May 31 and then south to relieve Oxford. After the unforeseen loss of Leicester, Fairfax was ordered by a rather alarmed Committee of Both Kingdoms to abandon his siege of Oxford and engage the king's army. This was located by the NMA's commissary general Henry Ireton near Naseby, in Northamptonshire, 12 miles south west of Market Harborough. The king had the choice of doing battle or retreating. He chose the former.

The two sides lined up against each other on the foggy morning of June 14. The Royalist line spread out over one and a half miles between Clipston Naseby and Sulby Hedges. Rupert with nearly 3,000 cavalry men was on the right, Lord Astley with three infantry brigades and a regiment of horse in the centre and the doughty Sir Marmaduke Langdale commanding 1,500 of his cavalrymen from the north on the left.

Fairfax's army occupied a two mile long ridge north of Naseby. Ireton's five and a half regiments of horse were on the left wing, backed by Colonel John Okey's regiment of dragoons. In the centre, Serjeant-Major General Sir Philip Skippon commanded five regiments of foot with three more in reserve. These included Rainborowe's men. On the right was Cromwell with his six and a half regiments of cavalrymen. In reserve was Fairfax and his own regiments.

Amid the mist both sides advanced their infantrymen until they were engaged in hand to hand fighting. Skippon was badly injured but could not leave the battlefield in case it destroyed morale. Ireton and his men rode to his aid but the commisary general was unhorsed and captured.

Rupert's cavalry broke through and scattered Ireton's men. Some rallied with the help of fire from Okey's dragoons, others fled the battlefield with Rupert's men in hot pursuit. As Astley's foot advanced, Skippon's men retreated. One observer, the king's secretary, Sir Edward Walker reported: "The Foot on either side hardly saw each other until they were within Carabine Shot, and so made only one Volley; our falling in with Sword and butt end of the Musquet did notable Execution, so much as I saw their Colours fall and their Foot in great Disorder."[14]

It was here that Rainborowe, ready in reserve, played his part in the fierce battle. "The reserves advancing, commanded by Col Rainsborough, Col Hammond and Lieutenant-Col Pride repelled the enemy forcing them to a disorderly retreat."[15] But the decisive action came from Cromwell. In short order, he stopped Langdale's advance and, counter-attacking, routed his cavalry. He sent two of his regiments in pursuit of Langdale and turned the rest on the Royalist centre and right wing. Fairfax moved his regiments of horse and foot to attack on all fronts while Okey with his now mounted dragoons joined with the remainder of Ireton's men in a renewed attack on the enemy's left flank.

It was over. Fairfax is said personally to have taken the standard of the last resisting regiment, Rupert's Bluecoats, more than half a mile behind the Royalists' original line. When Fairfax threatened a second charge, Rupert's remaining men left the field. So too did Charles, after being prevented from joining the battle as it meant certain death. When the Parliamentarians captured his abandoned personal baggage, they found letters showing the king was seeking the support of Catholic nations in Europe. It was a damning piece of propaganda put to full use against him.

But as well as his reputation, the battle also destroyed his fighting power. His infantry were broken, his horse scattered, 500 officers dead or captured. He would - could - never raise an army of that size again. It remained only for Parliament to mop up the last pockets of resistance. In this Rainborowe played a leading role.

Fairfax wasted no time. His first port of call was Leicester. Within two days of Naseby, on June 16, the bulk of the NMA was at the gates of the East Midlands town, summoning it to surrender. Its governor Lord Hastings refused and, after a council of war, Fairfax called in ladders, carts, hay, straw and other equipment to storm the town. Hastings rapidly despatched a trumpeter to Fairfax announcing his surrender. Fairfax appointed Rainborowe and Pickering as his commissioners to handle the terms. In talks lasting until midnight on June 17, terms were hammered out with Parliament again granting Hastings and his men quarter.

Now Fairfax and his 13,000-strong army[16] headed south west. His destination was not clear. The king and Rupert, with some 3,000 cavalry salvaged from the wreckage of Naseby, had moved to South Wales. Here they could both regroup and recruit. Fairfax could either move into Wales and finish off the king or go to the West Country. Here the king's one remaining army, under General Lord George Goring, was besieging Taunton. As Fairfax and his men moved towards Amesbury, the Committee of Both Kingdoms ordered Fairfax to attack Goring.

Lord George – it was a courtesy title after Charles made his father earl of Norwich but Parliament refused to recognise it – was not a man to be trusted. Dissolute, often insubordinate and "unquestionably fond of the bottle", there seemed always to hang over him a doubt that he would strike out as an independent commander or, worse, defect to Parliament. But he was also a "brave and skilful officer",[17] an able match for Fairfax.

Goring told Charles that his siege would last three weeks and then he would join him further north.[18] But when Fairfax reached the north west Dorset town of Beaminster on July 4, he heard the surprising news that the unpredictable Goring had abandoned his siege. He was now heading for Ilminster and that night was quartered in Somerton. His 10,000-strong force was fewer than 20 miles north of Fairfax.

A raiding party sent out by Fairfax captured a handful of Goring's men who told the Parliamentary commander that their general planned to head west to Langport. The two armies began to stalk each other. As Fairfax marched north to Crewkerne and on to Petherton where he found the bridge over the River Parrett smashed by the Royalists, Goring moved his men around, setting up garrisons at Ilchester and Langport.

But Fairfax would not attack. He reasoned the canny Goring's position on the river was too strong. After more cat and mouse moves, Goring pulled his masterstroke. Intelligence reached Fairfax, now in Ilchester, that his quarry was in Langport, six miles northwest of him, but that he had sent the "great part" of his army to Taunton. In fact it was about 1,500 men under his commissary-general George Porter.[19] Fairfax immediately despatched Major General Edward Massey's brigade of horse as well as a "considerable strength"[20] of his own army in pursuit of them.

Porter, displaying a damaging lack of initiative, holed up in the village of Isle Abbotts, just four miles west of Langport. Massey caught him there and in a skirmish on July 9, with the help of 2,000 musketeers from Colonel Edward Montagu's regiment, bested Porter's men, killing about 30 and taking 300 prisoners.[21] But Goring and his main body of men remained constantly elusive.

After a council of war on the evening of July 9, the Royalists opted to retreat to Bridgwater. Goring decided to withdraw his guns and infantrymen first, leaving the horse to mount a "delaying action...just east of Langport."[22] When Fairfax, no doubt exasperated by Goring's slipperiness, saw the retreat, he decided to attack. The chosen battlefield was ground to the east of Langport. Goring's forces were deployed on Ham Down. Across the Wagg Rhyne stream which runs north to south, were Fairfax's men, stationed on Pibsbury

Down. He opened fire with his cannon, stationed on the ridge above the stream. Within an hour, the few Royalist guns not withdrawn to Bridgewater were silenced. It was time for the foot to attack.

Rainborowe led 1,500 musketeers, backed by Colonel Ralph Weldon's foot, down to the Wagg Rhyne to fire on the Royalists. "With admirable resolution [they] charged the enemy from hedge to hedge, till they got the pass."[23] Some reports say the Royalists musketeers crumbled without a fight. Others reported that "a hot and stubborn contest developed, lasting a good hour before the Roundheads affected a crossing of the stream and a firm lodgement on the far side to the north of the road."[24] Either way, Rainsborowe's success enabled Cromwell to send in his cavalry. About 120 horse, under the command of Major Christopher Bethell, rode along the narrow path, wide enough for just four horses, across the stream and into the enemy positions. They were quickly followed by three troops – about 180 cavalrymen – led by Major John Desborough, from Fairfax's regiment.

"Instantly they put them [the enemy] to a disorderly retreat and our musketeers came close up to our horse, firing over the enemy whereupon their regiments...marched away apace."[25] A spirited counter attack by Goring forced Bethell back but with Desborough's horse arriving on the scene, "Royalist resistance speedily collapsed."[26] The combined attack of Bethell and Desborough's horse and Rainborowe's musketeers "proved too much for the Cavaliers; after a fierce and fairly prolonged hand-to-hand contest they gave way, split up into small parties and dissolved."[27] Some of Goring's men fled to Bridgwater – the general himself reached the town that evening. But they were pursued most of the way by Parliament's horse and many died or were captured on route.

Fairfax in his letter to Commons Speaker William Lenthall reporting the victory, said he, Cromwell and other seniors officers watching from Pibsbury down singled out the charge by Bethell and Desborough as "the most excellent piece of service that ever was in England."[28] But others make the valid point that it was Rainborowe's "surprise attack" that "drove the Royalists from their position" opening the way for the cavalrymen's charge. Langport was won "as much by the efforts of Rainsborough's men driving back the Royalist foot, opposing them from hedge to hedge and then breaking into the ranks of the earl of Cleveland's brigade of horse, as by the more spectacular eruption of three troops of New Model cavalry into the midst of Goring's army."[29]

Within nine days of his victory at Langport and the dispersal of Goring's army, Fairfax was closing in on Bridgwater, a town ten miles to the north. After a council of war, Fairfax decided to storm the town which was sheltering remnants of the Royalist army. The attack began at 2am on July 22 and ended 36 hours later with the town's surrender. Rainborowe's regiment was part of the forces deployed on the eastern side of the town and which did most of the attacking. But there is no record of what his role was or what he actually did.

As Fairfax moved eastwards, he despatched a bridge of horse and foot under Pickering to take Sherborne Castle. The Tudor mansion, immediately south east of the Dorset town of the same name, had been a Royalist stronghold throughout the war. Its commander in 1645 was Sir Lewis Dyve. He had served with Rupert at the relief of Newark in 1644 and was now serjeant-major general of Dorset. One of the reasons for his presence was that his mother had married into the Digby family who owned the castle and substantial tracts of the surrounding land.

Rainborowe's regiment, part of Pickering's brigade, was given the dangerous job of guarding the artillery train. This left it more exposed to enemy fire than other regiments. First his captain lieutenant, Flemming, was shot dead on August 6. Then at dusk on the same day, Captain Horsey, also from his regiment, died from a shot from a birding piece, a small bore sporting gun, fired by a sniper from one of the castle towers. Both were buried in the church at Sherborne. John Rushworth, Fairfax's secretary, wrote an anguished letter to Speaker Lenthall: "The greatest hurt they do us is by two keepers of parks they have in the garrison who in long fouling piece take aim through the loopholes in the wall - for the most part at commanders. Captain horsey, a valiant gentleman was shot dead by one of them, likewise Captain Lieutenant Fleminge to Colonel Rainesboroughe who is also dead."[30]

The siege, which began on August 2, did not go well and casualties mounted. Dyve refused a summons to surrender and, after a council of war, the Parliamentarians decided to press on while waiting for more cannon from Portsmouth and miners from the Mendips to dig a tunnel under the castle wall. The cannon arrived on August 11 and the miners the next day. After Dyve again refused to surrender, they began digging. The Royalists retaliated by raining down "fiery faggots" on the miners and managed to set fire to a bridge the soldiers were building.

Within a day the miners were within two feet of the castle wall. But the new guns were now in place and at 11am on August 14, began pounding the castle. "Before six [they] had made a breach in the middle of the wall, that ten abreast might enter, and had beaten down one of the towers, which much disheartened the enemy." Then Colonel Richard Ingoldsby led soldiers to capture one of the castle towers.[31] Seeing his plight was hopeless, Dyve offered to surrender on honourable terms. "No terms but quarter," was the curt reply as Dyve "had slipped and slighted the opportunity" and he would not get even that unless he surrendered speedily.[32]

A day later Dyve surrendered without terms and he and his men were granted quarter. For Rainborowe, the cost of this short, nasty siege mounted. Two more officers died, Major Done and Captain Crosse while another, Captain Creamer was injured. Dyve was sent to the Tower of London where he stayed until 1647, fostering an unlikely friendship with John Lilburne, the Leveller leader and frequent resident. He was among 400 prisoners taken at Sherborne along with 18 pieces of ordnance. A further bonus was that the Parliamentary victory reduced the attacks of the Clubmen[33] who, spurred on by the castle, had been causing havoc in the region. Many of them were among the 400 captured and sent to London.

After two days rest, Fairfax continued his breathless pursuit of the enemy in the West. But as the bulk of his men marched eastwards towards Bristol, Rainborowe was sent to the village of Somerset village of Nunney, two miles south west of Frome. The prize there was Nunney Castle, yet another stronghold holding out for the king. Built in the French style in the 14th century, the castle had four towers and was surrounded by a moat. When Fairfax visited it, he remarked that it was a "very strong piece."[34] The castle was owned by Colonel Richard Prater, a staunch Roman Catholic who had declared for Charles from the start of the war. His family had owned it since the middle of the previous century and had installed a Catholic altar. As Royalists towns and strongholds fell in the spring and summer of 1645, both Catholics and Royalists sought refuge in the Castle. It was, expecting an assault from Fairfax's troops, also well garrisoned.

Rainborowe took his own regiment and that of Colonel Hammond plus two pieces of ordnance to reduce Nunney. After Prater refused a summons to surrender, he began his battery of the castle's north wall on August 18. As he did so, Prater ran up a flag with a Catholic crucifix on it. This is likely to have incensed his strongly anti-popish attackers. The castle wall was soon breached and Prater and his followers surrendered on August 21. Rainborowe allowed those inside to return unharmed to their homes.[35] While the castle was damaged in the siege, it was not destroyed as other strongholds were. But the Praters did not get their property back until the restoration of Charles II in 1660.

By the time Fairfax got the good news about the fall of Nunney Castle, he was well advanced in his preparations for the storming of Bristol, the greatest prize in the south west. There was much debate after the victory at Sherborne as to whether Fairfax should go west. There were good reasons for doing so. It would stop Goring drawing recruits from Devon and Cornwall to boost his shattered army. It would so enable Parliament to relieve Plymouth. Finally the plague was raging in and around Bristol with a hundred people dying each week.

But the reasons to march on Bristol were more compelling. Prince Rupert had mustered a formidable army there. There were 3,000 he could put in the field, still leaving enough to defend the city with the help of Clubmen. The king's nephew could also call on new recruits from Wales, who could arrive unhindered over the River Severn, and from the Midlands. The latter, if they timed their arrival correctly, could block off Fairfax's men from London. Bristol was the only major port in the country held by the king. It was through here that his ammunition arrived. If, Fairfax and his senior officers reasoned, they could take the city, it would prove "fatal" to Charles's cause.[36]

While Rainborowe began his battery of Nunney Castle, Fairfax's main army set up headquarters in Shepton Mallet, a town 15 miles south of Bristol. His first move was to send Henry Ireton with 2,000 horse and dragoons to protect the towns around Bristol. As he moved nearer to his target, Fairfax then sent a message to vice admiral Robert Moulton, patrolling the waters off Milford Haven in South Wales, to send ships up the Bristol Channel to block off Bristol. Then he sent a "strong party of horse" to the north of Bristol to alarm the enemy.[37]

By this time Rainborowe and the two regiments under his charge were back with the main body. They were soon in action again. About noon on August 24, Rupert sent out a body of both horse and foot from near Prior's Hill Fort which surprised a party of Parliamentary dragoons. These were rescued by cavalrymen and Rainborowe's men who beat them off, killing a major and "some others."[38]

The skirmishing intensified and on September 1, in wet and misty weather, again at noon, "Prince Rupert, with one thousand six hundred foot, sallied out the sixth time… and came upon our horseguards with much fierceness; but the horse instantly came up, and, with the assistance of the foot of colonel Rainsborough's brigade, forced them to as hasty a retreat." The attack cost Parliament dearly. Captain Guilliams, "a captain of horse, a valiant, faithful, and religious man" was killed and Colonel Okey, head of the dragoons, got lost in the mist and was taken prisoner.[39]

Finally, amid news that the king was approaching from Oxford,[40] Fairfax drew up his final battle plans. These mark a significant promotion for Rainborowe. Largely unknown to Fairfax at Naseby, Rainborowe had since risen steadily in his estimation. He fought bravely and vitally at Naseby, Langport and the siege of Sherborne Castle. At Nunney Castle, Fairfax had put him in charge, for the first time, of two regiments and saw him complete what he himself saw as a tough assignment in three days. Rainborowe's reward was to be put in charge of a brigade. This consisted of five regiments: his own, Skippon's, Hammond's, Birch's and Pride's. It was his highest command yet.

His formidable task was to storm Prior's Hill and take the fort. Bristol was defended by a triangle of fortifications around the city with the River Avon as its defensive guard on its south side. Prior's Hill Fort was at the apex of the triangle, to the north of the city. There and the fortifications running down the north west of the city to the Avon was the area Rainborowe was ordered to attack and take. It consisted of five forts linked by earthwork ditches. The Royalists had captured the city from Parliament in July 1643 and their chief military engineer, Sir Bernard de Gomme had strengthened some of the outer defences. This included the Royal Fort which lay to the south of Prior's Hill but not Prior's Hill Fort or, slightly to the south, Colston's Fort where Rainborowe was due to focus his attack. Under Fairfax's battle plan, two hundred men were to approach the Water Fort, the defence furthest to the south west, in boats with seamen. A regiment of horse and one of foot were to move in the closes beneath the Royal Fort Hill to create alarm. A regiment of dragoons and two of horse were to carry ladders to attack the enemy line and works at Clifton and Washington breach.[41]

While Rainborowe attacked from the northwest, Colonel Weldon's brigade was to storm three points on the Somerset side of the city. Fairfax's brigade, under Colonel Montagu, were to storm both sides of Lawford's Gate which lay on the east side. As Rainborowe's guns opened up on Prior's Hill Fort on September 9, Parliament summoned Prince Rupert to surrender. With Cromwell arriving with 2,000 extra men recruited in the area, Rupert played for time, asking that he be allowed to consult the king. Fairfax said 'No' and demanded a speedy answer to his summons. Rupert refused it.[42]

At 2am on September 10, the attack began. The signal to move was a great fire of straw and faggots on one of the hills and the unleashing of four great guns against Prior's Hill Fort. Immediate progress was made around Lawford's Gate where 22 guns and many prisoners were quickly captured. To the northwest, Rainborowe with his and Hammond's regiment began his advance on Prior's Hill while those of Skippon and Birch moved towards the city near the River Frome. Pride's regiment was divided: half joined the assault on Prior's Hill, with the help of the seamen and the rest moved around the Royal Fort to alarm it.[43]

Parliament's cavalry made good progress on the Royal Fort and Colston's. But Rainborowe, despite the cover of darkness, faced strong resistance on Prior's Hill. The enemy "very obstinately held out, playing fiercely with great and small shot upon our men for two hours after the line was entered." But the attack was halted as the ladders brought up to scale the fort walls proved too short and were knocked back by the defenders. "Notwithstanding, this disheartened them not, but up they went again upon greatest danger and disadvantage; some at last creeping in at the portholes, and others got on the top of the works." A Captain Lagoe, of Pride's regiment, was the first to grab the enemy's colours.[44]

At last Rainborowe's men forced the Royalists to retreat. They moved back to the fort's inner rooms and asked for quarter. "But our soldiers were so little prepared for to show mercy, by the opposition that they met withal in the storm, and the refusal of quarter when it was offered, that they put to the sword the commander, (one major Price, a Welshman,) and almost all the officers, soldiers, and others in the fort, except a very few, which, at the entreaty of some of our officers, had their lives spared."[45] It was a bloody end to a bitter battle.

Prior's Hill Fort, the key to the city of Bristol had been taken before daybreak. Even though the Royalists had repelled other Parliamentary attacks, Rupert sued for peace within four hours. Fairfax appointed Rainborowe, Pickering and Montagu as his commissioners to negotiate the peace. Rupert, his officers and others were allowed to march out of the city. All forts, fortifications, ordnance, arms, ammunition and provisions were surrendered to Parliament. Hostages were also taken to ensure no Royalists did damage to the city as they walked out. Rupert was banished from England[46] with many of his followers. He was, however, back with the king within a few months.

In the siege Rainborowe lost another officer, Captain Sterne. Another of the heroes of Langport, Major Bethell who led the cavalry charge, was also killed. But casualties were surprisingly low, numbering fewer than 40 men for both Rainborowe's and Montagu's regiments. As part of the terms of surrender, Colonel Okey and other prisoners were released.

The dazzling success of the siege of Bristol raised Rainborowe further in the eyes of the senior officers. One contemporary observer wrote of the action: "The service was hot, especially at the prince's fort where Rainsborough performed very bravely; they cut in pieces most of the soldiers within the fort, with their Captain Pride, and took four pieces in the fort and two more in a redoubt."[47] Another reported: "Colonel Rainsborough's brigade, who with a party of his forces, spent three hours in the storming of Pryor's Fort, a place of great advantage, which piece of service was as bravely performed as ever thing was done by man, in regard they were put to the utmost, by scaling ladders to win the Fort."[48]

But it was Cromwell who heaped the most praise on Rainborowe. Writing to Speaker Lenthall to report the victory, the lieutenant-general said: "colonel Rainsborough, who had the hardest task of all at Priors Hill Fort, attempted it, and fought near three hours for it, and indeed there was great despair of carrying the place, it being exceeding high, a ladder of thirty rounds scarce reaching the top thereof.

"But his resolution was such that notwithstanding the inaccessibleness and difficulty, he would not give it over. The enemy has four pieces of cannon upon it, which they plied with round and case upon our men; his lieutenant-colonel Bowen and others were two hours at push of pike, standing upon the Palizadoes, but could not enter." The arrival of a troop of horse, led by a Captain Ireton, forced a gap, allowing Rainborowe's and Hammond's men to enter the fort "and immediately put almost all the men in it to the sword," Cromwell wrote.[49] It was in this melee that Bethell was mortally wounded.

Despite his victory, Fairfax had no intention of resting on his laurels. Within days he had despatched Cromwell with a brigade to take Devizes, a town 20 miles south east of Bristol and Rainborowe, also with a brigade, to take Berkeley Castle, 12 miles north of the city. The castle, dating back to the 11th century and owned by the Berkeley family, was the last major Royalist stronghold in Gloucestershire. Fairfax had sent, in June 1645, Colonel John Butler and his regiment of horse to keep guard on the castle. The main aim was to keep its commander, Sir Charles Lucas, inside the castle.

Lucas, then 32, was a born soldier. His sister described him as "having a natural genius for the warlike arts as natural poets have to poetry." He was one of the most successful cavalry men in the war, rivalling both Cromwell and Rupert. He had been engaged in the war from the start, fighting in the very first cavalry encounter at Powick Bridge, near Worcester in September 1642. There he forced terrified Parliamentarians to jump in the River Severn to escape his charge. At Marston Moor, he had "utterly routed" Fairfax, who was lucky to escape with his life. But despite his undoubted brilliance, there was another side to him which Clarendon noted: he was on occasions "of a nature not to be lived with, of an ill understanding, of a rough and proud nature." Fairfax did not want such a dangerous enemy at large as he moved west.[50]

Now Fairfax needed to capture the castle. Rainborowe with his own regiment and those of Skippon, Colonel William Herbert and Pride, began his furious assault on September 23. This was after Lucas had insultingly rejected Rainborowe's two summons to surrender. He would, he replied, rather eat horse flesh or man's flesh before he would yield. After cannon fire, the infantry stormed the castle and its church with scaling ladders. They fought "with so much resolution and gallantry (both officers and soldiers) as quickly made them masters of the place." Ninety prisoners were taken and a further 40 men put to the sword, including a major and a captain. Lucas, sensing the hopelessness of his position, "was glad to sound a parley."[51]

But it was another bloody affair. A Lieutenant John Freeman who took part in the siege, wrote: "The work was difficult, the Castle strong and the enemy within especially the Governor Sir Charles Lucas, as obstinate as an enemy could be, yet as soon as our forces were joined with those of Sir Thomas Fairfaxes, whereof valiant Colonel Rainsborough had the command, we made no long stay but fell presently upon their works." Freeman, possibly part of Butler's regiment which had been guarding the castle for three months, said many men were drowned and "some few slain" in the assault. He added: "We planted our great guns against the tower, and battered it much, and they returned the like, roaring resolutions at us, with case shot of bullets, nails and such like manner, and killed some of our men." As the end of the assault neared, Lucas ordered a flag of defiance to be flown from the top of the castle's tower. When the victorious Parliamentarians tried to pull down the flag, part of the tower collapsed, killing at least one of them.[52]

Not all Lucas's men took surrender well. One of his lieutenant colonels "swore to colonel Rainsborough, he could be content to go to hell, and be a major there to plague the Roundheads" while another officer remarked: "He thought God was turned roundhead, the king's forces prospered so ill." Surprisingly Rainborowe allowed Lucas and the remaining 500 men to march away. Rainborowe's brigade suffered the loss of one captain and "not many" soldiers, although many were wounded.[53] Rainborowe and Lucas would meet again.

Rainborowe and his brigade re-joined the main army, now at Warminster, a town about 30 miles south east of Berkeley on September 27. While Fairfax led his army around the west country in Somerset and Devon, Rainborowe's men do not appear to feature in any of the actions. During this time Tiverton Castle was taken, Exeter besieged, Royalists defeated at Bovey Tracy and Dartmouth taken.

But by December he was involved in the siege of Corfe Castle which stood on a peninsula called the Isle of Purbeck in south Dorset. By the time Fairfax's army had mopped up much of the remaining resistance in the West Country, this was one of the last Royalist strongholds. It had been owned by Sir John Bankes, chief justice to Charles. When he left to fight for the king, he put his wife, the formidable Lady Mary Bankes in charge of the castle. She successfully fought off a six week Parliamentary siege in 1643. Bankes himself died in 1644.

Rainborowe, now an established siegemaster, seems to have begun his assault sometime in December. But greater duties called.[54] Fairfax got intelligence around Christmas Day, 1645 that the king's cavalry were making regular sallies out of Oxford "doing much mischief." Rainborowe was ordered to march to Abingdon, five miles south of Oxford "to attend the motion of the king's horse, and guard the associated counties, as also in relation to the straitening of Oxford." He was accompanied by the horse regiments of Colonel Charles Fleetwood and Colonel Edward Whalley and Fairfax's own foot regiment with orders "to lie about Islip" just north of the city.[55] It was the run up to the crucial siege of Oxford.

Charles had arrived in the city in November 5, 1645. After his council of war in Cardiff in July and his subsequent falling out with

Rupert, the king had meandered around the country. First he rode northwards with the intention of uniting with the earl of Montrose's army in Scotland. But he halted at Chester where the Royalist defence of the city was nearing collapse. He came off worse in a clash with NMA cavalrymen which saw the death of his cousin, Lord Bernard Stuart.

The chastened king then rode eastwards to Newark where he had an unexpected confrontation with a furious Prince Rupert. This resolved nothing and Rupert and his men rode off still in a state of anger with the king. Throughout his travels, Charles suffered the repeated hammer blows of bad news. The defeat at Langport, the loss of Bristol and Sherborne Castle; Cromwell's victories in Hampshire and Wiltshire; the failure to raise fresh troops in Wales; the retreat of his favoured counsellor, Lord Digby, to the Isle of Man; and finally the destruction of Montrose's army by Sir David Leslie's Covenanters at Philiphaugh on the Scottish borders on September 13. Even his own courtiers were now thinking in terms of peace.

In a mood close to despair, the king began his journey southwards in September to Oxford, the city he had made his capital after his flight from London in January, 1642. The winter brought little relief. Hopes of reinforcements from Ireland were dashed and plans for Queen Henrietta to bring troops from France were abandoned through the lack of a safe port. In March he received the bitter blow that the army of Sir Jacob Astley, which was due to join him in Oxford, had been defeated by Parliament's Sir William Brereton at Stow-on-the-Wold. The king had lost one of his last armies.[56]

During these months, he had also heard the ominous news that substantial Parliamentary forces were gathering. There were troops from "London under Col Rainsborough" as well as forces from Coventry, Gloucestershire and Northampton "which will in all make no less than 8,000 and 4,000 horse and dragoons and are designed to block up Oxon. from a distance."[57] In fact Rainborowe seems to have been around the Oxford area since January. In March, Fairfax was sufficiently confident of him to give him not only the command of all forces in Banbury but also the power of martial law.[58] Fairfax clearly saw Oxford as a critical arena and Rainborowe as his main player.

A steady stream of reinforcements was called up as Fairfax began to move his troops around. Rainborowe was ordered to tighten the cordon around Oxford to stop anything getting in. Ireton was ordered to take three regiment of horse and one of dragoons to join the burgeoning siege. Colonel John Venn, commander in Northamptonshire, sent 1,100 men to Whalley with the hope of a further 600 to be despatched soon. He also sent 700 men, "mustered, armed, and clothed" to Rainborowe. But he warned that he had not seen these men recruited in Lincolnshire and that as counties "press the Scum of all their Inhabitants", they were likely to include former Royalists and "men taken out of prison, Tinkers, Pedlars, and Vagrants that have no Dwelling, and such of whom no Account can be given." It would be no surprise if they ran away, Venn grimly warned.[59]

Rainborowe moved his men from Banbury to Witney, west of Oxford, where he picked up his new recruits, and then to Woodstock, north of the city. It was here that Rainborowe was involved in two bizarre incidents, one supposedly regarding the king's surrender to him, and the second, his only real set back as a soldier. In the first incident, a man named as Ffontaine came to Rainborowe's quarters offering some inside information about conditions in Oxford. He was a barrister from Lincoln's Inn, London who had once been imprisoned by Parliament for failing to pay his contribution to the support the trained bands and for speaking out against the Parliamentary cause. But Rainborowe was wary of him and packed him off to Aylesbury for further questioning.

Rainborowe's next move was to besiege Woodstock Manor. This was a substantial building, owned by Philip Herbert, earl of Montgomery, a supporter of Parliament. In 1643, the king had granted the manor to Montagu Bertie, earl of Lindsey. Rainborowe opened up with his cannon on April 15 and in the early evening about 6pm, his soldiers stormed the manor. Without precedent for Rainborowe they were driven back with looses of about 100 men. Many others were wounded and in the aborted attack, they lost their scaling ladders. Whitelocke recorded: "Colonel Rainsborough's men received some loss attempting to storm Woodstock Manor."[60] Nonetheless he pressed on but it was not for another 11 days that Woodstock surrendered.

John Rushworth, one of Fairfax's army secretaries, reported that Rainborowe and Fleetwood had "for some time" besieged Woodstock before the defenders sought a parley. Four of the king's top advisers arrived from Oxford to negotiate the terms of surrender, the earls of Southampton and Lindsey, Sir William Fleetwood, and Colonel John Ashburnham, the king's secretary. The agreed peace saw the surrender of the manor with its arms and ammunition but the field officers were to "march away with their swords, the other officers and soldiers without arms, to have a convoy to Oxford."[61]

It was during these peace talks that the second bizarre incident happened. In a letter to Speaker Lenthall, signed by both Rainborowe and Charles Fleetwood, they reported that Southampton had put a proposal to them. This, Southampton said, "might not only give us the possession of this [Woodstock] but other garrisons." If Parliament was sincere as it had said it was in protecting the king's life and honour and if Rainborowe and Fleetwood would stand by this promise, "then the king would come into our quarters (there to remain, or where else you please to direct) and do what you should require of him." The two officers replied they would have to pass the offer to Parliament.[62]

It is not likely that this was a genuine proposal. It is even possible that Charles did not even know his counsellors were making it. After the steady stream of military setbacks in the last months of 1645, Lindsey and Southampton and others had earlier approached the king to suggest suing for peace. They had been firmly rebuffed.

Given Charles' deep mistrust of the NMA and its officers, it stretches belief that he was going to hand himself over to them. But Oxford was alive with rumours that the king was planning exactly that: to surrender to Fairfax and demand to be taken to London where, Royalists believed, an exuberant welcome awaited him. Clarendon confirmed many years later that the king had no intention of surrendering to Fairfax. He wrote that one thing the king was resolved to avoid "to be enclosed in Oxford and so to be given up, or taken, when the town should be surrendered, as a prisoner to the Independents' Army; which he was advertised from all hands, would treat him very barbarously."[63] The third and most obvious explanation is that the offer was a ruse to put Parliament off the scent and the rumours were put about by his close confidants. The aim was to gain time for his real intentions. Whatever the truth, it was all theoretical. Within two days the king had escaped.

Disguised as a humble servant with trimmed hair and a false beard under a flat hat with a flap at the back and answering to the name of Harry, Charles slipped out of Oxford on the night of April 27. Travelling with just two companions, a chaplain and Jack Ashburnham, a groom of his bedchamber, he rode northwards by night, "eating and drinking in strange taverns and ale-houses." Nine days later he reached the Saracen's Head in Southwell, near to the Scots army headquarters near Newark. He put himself in the care of the Scots.[64] It was what he had been minded to do for several months.

Fairfax heard the news surprisingly quickly on April 28 while he was in Newbury. He struck camp and immediately marched on Oxford. Rainborowe also heard the news immediately but far more dramatically when the Duke of Richmond, Lindsay and others came to his quarters and "cast themselves upon the mercy of Parliament."[65] Again he scrupulously passed the information to Parliament. Its angry reaction was to demand that no more people be allowed to leave Oxford. It is likely that this whole incident hardened Rainborowe's views against Charles the man and king and possibly against the institution of monarchy itself. He had been at least used, possibly also flattered, by Southampton's silky enticement, only to find himself duped. It helps explain Rainborowe's uncompromising attitude to the king when next their paths crossed in the summer of 1647. Fairfax and other senior officers saw the incident differently, citing Rainborowe's and Fleetwood's decision to tell Parliament immediately of the proposal as a mark of their high honour. It would have been "inconsistent with their trust and duty, being the servants of the state, to own or entertain any such thing, they certified the Parliament thereof, and understanding this to be their sense also, they absolutely refused to be tampered with concerning that matter."[66]

Fairfax arrived in Oxford on May 1 and straightaway began preparation for the siege of the city. After a general rendezvous on May 2, Fairfax and his senior officers, including Rainborowe, began a survey of the city. What they found was not encouraging. It stood between two rivers, the Isis, the name for the Thames where it flows through Oxford, on the west and the Cherwell, a major tributary of the Thames, on the east. It was surrounded by a series of small garrisons loyal to the king. The Isis ran close to the city wall which provided the city with a "great defence" on the west while on the east, the Cherwell had overflowed into adjacent meadows. It meant the city was surrounded on three sides by water. Only the higher north side was dry. Within the city were 5,000 good infantrymen while there was a "plentiful magazine of victuals, ammunition and provisions." It looked impregnable. At the very least, Fairfax calculated it would be a long siege.

Fairfax decided to build his headquarters on Headington Hill, to the east of the city with space for 3,000 men. Skippon was charged with this work. Rainborowe was ordered to build a bridge over the Cherwell at Marston, two miles to the north east, and a line between the Isis and the Cherwell. On land here between the two rivers, Fairfax planned to station the bulk of his foot. As other officers were assigned to block off the various garrisons, a call went out across the county for spades and pickaxes. Parliament was asked to send more ammunition and tents for the soldiers. Fairfax was taking no chances.[67]

The preparations complete, on May 11 Fairfax sent the standard summons to surrender to the governor of Oxford, Sir Thomas Glemham, the man who had sent Charles on his way with a cheery "Farewell Harry" as he made his escape. To Fairfax's surprise and possible relief, Glemham sent out two commissioners, Sir John Mounson and Philip Warwick to meet with Fairfax's commissioners, Rainborowe, Lambert and Colonel Harlow.[68] The Oxford men played for time, asking to send to the king for a decision on surrendering. Rainborowe and his colleagues grudgingly gave them a day.

While the Royalists discussed surrender, Rupert rode out of the city with 100 cavalrymen, ostensibly to take the air, more likely to espy the enemy's strength and deployment. The prince, riding without boots and in his shoes and stockings, rode towards Rainborowe's men who, evidently less concerned about his health, fired on him. He got a flesh wound in his shoulder and beat a hasty retreat. In another sally out of the city three days later, two Parliamentarians were killed.[69]

But it was mere play acting. On May 17, Glemham announced he would discuss terms of surrender and called on Fairfax to name his commissioners. Rainborowe was not on the list. The talks were prolonged and Fairfax called a council of war of June 9, attended by Rainborowe, to discuss alternatives in case negotiations failed. In the event, the city surrendered on June 24.

But Rainborowe had little time to enjoy the triumph. He was sent immediately to Worcester where the siege of the city was not going well. Colonel Whalley had been sent there after the fall of Banbury in May following a four month siege. He had a few troops of horse "but there was a great want of foot for a regular and close siege." It was enough men to hinder the enemy but not enough to storm the fort. Rainborowe was sent westwards with a brigade and got to work straightaway. He "no sooner came before the town, but he laid his foot quarters close to the enemy's works, and in two or three nights (according to much judgment and resolution) raised a work which much annoyed the enemy's great fort."[70]

Rainborowe arrived outside the city in early July and set up his headquarters in Barbourne House, to the north of the city and mustered his brigade on Rainbow Hill overlooking Worcester from the east. On July 10, he drew a new siege line from the top of Perry Hill in the east southwards Red Hill which he reinforced with two cannon with a range of 1,000m which had great success in bombarding the city.[71]

A report in London painted a similar picture of no nonsense haste: "Major General Rainsborow being come before Worcester and made his approaches very high, that so terrified them within, that in a kind of mutinous way, they pressed the governor to surrender, whereupon he sent this ensuing letter to Major General Reinsborow." The mere threat of an assault by Rainborowe created panic. His reputation had clearly gone before him.

The letter of the governor, Colonel Henry Washington appealed for fairness on both sides. "We do not decline the rendering of this city upon honourable and equal conditions." On receiving the letter, Rainborowe "yielded to a parley which was carried on with very much gallantry, and wisdom, and the result thereof produced an agreement for the surrender of the city of Worcester." The treaty was signed on July 19, 1646.

The city with all its forts, ordnance, arms, ammunition, stores and provision of war, were surrendered to Parliament. The soldiers were allowed to walk away but most had to surrender their arms and horses. All had to promise "never to bear arms any more against the parliament of England."[72]

The war was now largely over. There were a few remaining strongholds still to fall, like Raglan Castle in South Wales. This finally surrendered after months of siege in August after Fairfax and Rainborowe moved their big cannon to within firing range. In little over 15 months, Rainborowe had risen from a new and unknown colonel, with a background more suited to the sea than land, to a highly respected, brave and essential commander on whom Fairfax increasingly relied. By the time of Worcester, he was regularly put in charge of a brigade. In four major operations, at Nunney Castle, Berkeley Castle, Woodstock and Worcester, Fairfax appointed him as the chief commander. He never let his general down and it is clear Fairfax held him in high regard. His methods were a compelling mix of sheer professionalism, raw courage and when necessary a streak of ruthlessness. Few soldiers did more individually to ensure Parliament's success.

Notes for Chapter Four

1. Peacock, *Archaeologia*, p. 15.
2. Austin Woolrych, *Britain in Revolution 1625-1660*, (Oxford, 2002), p. 290.
3. This is the version of the famous words used by Woolrych in *Britain in Revolution*, p. 291.
4. Woolrych suggests it might have been that his "gentle, humane nature" was shocked by the "slaughter and suffering he had seen." *Britain in Revolution*, p. 290. But Manchester, a Presbyterian, may also have strongly disliked the increasing influence of the more belligerent Independents in the Parliamentary cause.
5. Ian Gentles, *The New Model Army*, (Oxford, 1992), p. 16.
6. *Commons Journal*, iv, p. 105. Grey is probably James Gray who later became adjutant-general of foot in the NMA and was killed in Ireland in November 1647.
7. Prince Rupert (1619-1682) was a younger son of Charles I's sister Elizabeth and her husband Frederick V, Elector Palatine. In the Civil War, he was commander of the Royalist cavalry and ultimately its senior general. He was banished from England after his surrender at Bristol but returned within a few months. He later fought as a senior naval commander for his cousin Charles II in the Anglo-Dutch wars. His nephew became George I of England.
8. Firth and Davies, *Cromwell's Army*, pp. 418-9.
9. Calendar of State Papers Domestic 28/34, fos. 365, 463-4 in The National Archives. See also Gentles, *New Model Army*, p. 35.
10. *Lords Journal*, viii, p.170. In a petition to Parliament in February, 1646, Westminster, Southwark and Tower Hamlets claimed they had provided men for 10 regiments, compared with 17 by the City. But "our regiments being much fuller...your petitioners have sent out double the number with the City."
11. Dr John Fell (1625-1686) was an undergraduate at Oxford by the age of 11 and protégé of William Laud, Archbishop of Canterbury. He served as an ensign in Charles's army. After the Restoration, he became Bishop of Oxford and vice-chancellor of Oxford University.
12. Joshua Sprigge, *Anglia Rediviva*, (London, 1647), p. 22. Sprigge was a retainer of Fairfax and kept an almost daily if somewhat slanted account of the action.
13. Sir Bulstrode Whitelock, *Memorials of the English Affairs*, (Oxford, 1705), i, p. 441. Whitelock was a lawyer and MP used by Parliament in some of its attempts to negotiate with the king during the war. After the war, he was ambivalent about the return of the Royals but remained on good terms with Cromwell.
14. Keith Roberts, *Cromwell's War Machine: The New Model Army 1645-1660*, (Barnsley, 2009), p. 90.
15. Sprigge, *Anglia Rediviva*, pp.36-7
16. Gentles estimates that 4,000 infantrymen deserted Fairfax after the battle of Naseby. *New Model Army*, p. 36.
17. Alfred Higgins Burne and Peter Young, *The Great Civil War: A Military History of the First Civil War 1642-1646*, (London, 1959). P. 54.
18. Sprigge, *Anglia Rediviva*, pp. 47-8.

19. John Barratt, *The Battle of Langport 1645*, (Bristol, 1995), p. 11.
20. Sprigge, *Anglia Rediviva*, p. 63.
21. Ibid., p. 64.
22. Barratt, *Battle of Langport*, p. 13.
23. Sprigge, *Anglia Rediviva*, p. 65.
24. Burne and Young, *Great Civil War*, p. 213.
25. Sprigge, *Anglia Rediviva*, p. 65.
26. Barratt, *Battle of Langport*, p. 18.
27. Burne and Young, *Great Civil War*, p. 214.
28. Letter, dated July 10, written at Fairfax's headquarters to the Speaker Lenthall and read to Commons on July 12, quoted in Barratt, p. 18.
29. Malcolm Wanklyn and Frank Jones, *A Military History of the English Civil War 1642-1646*, (Edinburgh, 2005), p. 256 and p. 268.
30. Portland MSS, 13th report of the Historical Manuscripts Commission, p. 242. The letter was dated August 9.
31. Sprigge, *Anglia Rediviva*, p. 84. Sprigge called him Inglesby but it is almost certainly Ingoldsby to whom he is referring.
32. Ibid., p. 85.
33. Ibid., p. 86. Clubmen – so called because they carried clubs - were ostensibly neutrals who wanted an end to the fighting and peace and stability for the country. They were particularly active in the West Country in 1645. But they were not always as neutral as they claimed. They tended to favour the King in Dorset but Parliament in Somerset. See Diana Purkiss, *The English Civil War A People's History*, (London, 2006), pp. 435-441.
34. Sprigge, *Anglia Rediviva*, p. 89.
35. Ibid., p. 90.
36. Ibid., p. 88.
37. Ibid., p. 89.
38. Ibid., p. 90.
39. Ibid., p. 93.
40. This was unlikely as Charles and Rupert had had a major row which was disastrous for the royal cause. At a Royal council of war in July near Cardiff, the king had promised his nephew to join him in Bristol to boost royal morale after the Langport defeat. Charles changed his mind, rode northwards and in his letter to a devastated Rupert stupidly said he did not have time to give him his reasons for his change of mind but that one of his courtiers, a rival of Rupert's, would do so. It is not clear if Fairfax knew of this falling out.
41. Sprigge, *Anglia Rediviva*, p. 95.
42. Ibid., pp. 94-100.
43. Ibid., p. 106.
44. Ibid., p. 107.
45. Ibid., p. 108.
46. Rupert achieved a unique double here as Charles, on hearing of the defeat at Bristol, supposed his nephew to be guilty of treason and expelled him as well.
47. Whitelock, *Memorials of the English Affairs*, i, p. 512.

48. Vicars, *The Burning Bush not Consumed*, in his *Englands Parliamentary Chronicle*, vol iv, p. 266.
49. Sprigge, *Anglia Rediviva*, p. 115.
50. Williamson, *Four Stuart Portraits*, pp. 115-6. Clarendon, *Great Rebellion*, xi, p. 388.
51. Sprigge, *Anglia Rediviva*, p. 125.
52. Quoted in Vicars, *The Burning Bush not Consumed*, pp. 283-4.
53. Sprigge, *Anglia Rediviva*, p. 125.
54. The siege seems to have been taken over by Colonel John Bingham, governor of nearby Poole. Lady Bankes resolutely held out for 48 days until February 1646 before one of her own men, a Colonel Pitman, betrayed her. Promising to bring in 100 recruits to boost her defiance, he in fact brought in 100 Parliamentarians in disguise. The castle soon surrendered but Lady Bankes and her garrison were allowed to walk away. Recent research suggests that Lady Bankes might never actually have been a Corfe Castle during the final siege. See Patrick Little, *History Today*, vol. 65, 2 (February, 2015).
55. Sprigge, *Anglia Rediviva*, p. 174.
56. Sir Charles Lucas who had surrendered to Rainborowe after the siege of Berkeley Castle and was released just six months before was again captured. This time he was also released again but pledging never to take up arms against Parliament again. It was in effect his death warrant.
57. From the Clarendon State Papers, quoted in Samuel Rawson Gardiner, *The History of the Great Civil War* (London, 1886), 11, p. 198. No specific reference is given.
58. Whitelock, *Memorials*, i, p. 584.
59. Lords Journal, viii, pp.267-9.
60. Whitelocke, *Memorials*, ii, p. 9.
61. John Rushworth, *Historical Collections*, vi, pp.249-76.
62. Tanner MSS, lix, i. Quoted in full in Peacock, *Archaeologia*, p. 89.
63. Clarendon, *Great Rebellion*, x, p. 192. The reference to the Independents' Army suggests hindsight assisted Clarendon in his labours. The expulsion of Presbyterian officers from the NMA was not until 1647.
64. Christopher Hibbert, *Charles I*, (London, 1968), p. 239.
65. Whitelocke, *Memorials*, i, p. 202. Quoted in Peacock, *Archaeologia*, p. 19.
66. Sprigge, *Anglia Rediviva*, p. 247.
67. Ibid., pp. 249-50.
68. Probably Colonel Edward Harley who, though appointed in early in 1645 with the other new officers of the NMA, did not take up his post until a late in the year due to injury. Lt. Colonel Pride commanded the foot regiment in his absence.
69. Sprigge, *Anglia Rediviva*, p. 256.
70. Ibid., pp.284-5.
71. Malcolm Atkin, *The Civil War in Worcestershire*, (Stroud, 1995), pp. 114-6. The vantage points of Perry Wood and Red Hill were also used by Cromwell at the Battle of Worcester in 1651.
72. Worcester Archives, Parcel 1, xxvii, document BA 3669, Ref: 899.31.

Chapter Five: The Army's Great Radical

As the New Model Army mopped up the last pockets of Royalist resistance in the summer of 1646, the majority of the population yearned for peace and a political settlement. After four years of bloody conflict, England was in deep discontent. Out of a population of fewer than five million, an estimated 190,000 had died in England and Wales, including 84,000 in battles, with many more dead in Scotland and Ireland. Thousands more were injured or maimed.

The 1640s and 1650s saw a steady stream of petitions to the quarter sessions by men crippled in the war and by women whose husbands had perished in Parliament's cause.[1] But the malaise went deeper than just the war. England was still prey to killer diseases such the plague, typhus and smallpox. While there had been no major plague epidemics since 1625, when the death rate soared to 43% above average, there were few years when the country was free of the disease. In 1643-4, the middle of the war, the death rate was 29% above average.[2] To add to the gloom, a series of bad harvests in the 1640s had caused widespread hunger. The first half of the century ended with some of the worst harvests since the 1590s, inevitably forcing food prices rising to the highest they had been for 50 years.[3]

The presence of thousands of both Parliamentary and Royalist troops, demanding or just taking free quarter, exacerbated this already desperate situation. For many ordinary people, it was a struggle for survival. "By the time Marston Moor was fought, the men and women of England were fighting a grimmer battle, a battle to find enough food to stay alive. Not just the battered armies but the whole country was getting hungry. Harvests had been poor because of the cold, wet summers, and there were fewer men to get in the crops."[4] Amid this bleak landscape, trees were chopped down for siege equipment and fuel, furze faggots, normally used for feeding animals, were requisitioned for gun emplacements, while unruly soldiers, unpaid and unfed, plundered what they could.

England was also suffering a crisis of authority. County committees, set up by Parliament, imposed swingeing taxes. But these bodies were not composed of the men who normally ran local affairs, the gentry and the squirearchy, but of newcomers often picked for their religious zeal. It left not only the traditional rulers demoralised but with a strong sense that old orders and values were slipping away. "Between the first and second Civil Wars, indeed, the country was smouldering with discontents which flared into open disorder often enough to arouse fear that the very fabric of society was threatened with dissolution."[5]

If, socially, England was heading for breakdown, many thought that, politically, it was in a vacuum. Charles I was in the custody of the Scots in Newcastle, while the Commons, backed by its successful New Model Army, held a fragile, uneasy sway over the rest of the country. The vast majority of people wanted a quick peace settlement and expected the king to return to his throne. But for many, the terms of any return were crucial. It was the discussions, debates and increasingly heated arguments on this critical point that produced an extraordinary period in English history, culminating in the Putney Debates of October and November 1647 where Rainborowe made his unprecedented call for one man, one vote.

The national debate was not just among the Parliamentarians who had waged war with Charles. The MPs were certainly vocal and animated as the union of the war years disintegrated and new, though more fluid, allegiances formed. But there was also a flourishing and increasingly loud chorus from those outside Westminster. The victorious Army, its radical backbone stiffened by agitators from within its ranks and by extremists from London, took an ever greater and ultimately dominating role in national politics. At the same time, in the background but inexorably moving to centre stage, men such as John Lilburne, Richard Overton and John Wildman – later to be derided as "Levellers" – incessantly drummed out their arguments and ideas for fundamental change.

The result in the summer, autumn and winter of 1647 was a frantic and frenetic crescendo of differing views. It was a "period of glorious flux and intellectual excitement, when, as Gerrard Winstanley put it, 'the old world... is running up like parchment in the fire.'"[6] At a time when absence of authority had left the press gloriously and unprecedentedly free, thousands of pamphlets appeared in London promoting all shades of religious and political views. Everything was questioned, nothing was sacred. What was the true religion, what was the proper role of Parliament, should the people be sovereign, were kings no more than tyrants and men of blood? And what, if any, was their future role? Nothing was out of bounds.

It was against this shifting and dangerously unstable background that Rainborowe took his first steps into politics. After the success of the siege of Worcester, Fairfax recommended to Parliament that his most successful siegemaster be made governor of the city. In his letter of August 1, 1646 to Commons speaker Lenthall, Fairfax praised Rainborowe's "discreet carriage" in the taking of Worcester and asked Parliament if he "may have the charge of it...seeing you have found him very faithfull, valiant, and successful in many undertakings since you put him under my command."[7] There is no record of any reply or confirmation by the MPs but there are two references to Rainborowe holding the post.

One is from John Winthrop, governor of Massachusetts. Rainborowe's eldest sister, Martha, had married Winthrop while his younger one, Judith had married his son Stephen. Winthrop senior told another of his many sons that "your brother [Stephen] has again sent for his wife [Judith] and it seems he means to stay with his brother Rainsborow, who is governor of Worcester."[8] The second is more political in tone. It comes from Richard Baxter, a leading Puritan scholar and churchman of the 17th century, who wrote "Two or three days before it yielded, Col Rainsborough was sent from Oxford (which was yielded) with some regiments of foot, to command in chief; partly that he might have the honour of taking the city and partly that he might be Governour there (and not Whalley) when the City was surrendered; and so when it yielded, Rainsborough was Governour to head and gratify the Sectaries, and settle the City and Country in their way: But the Committee of the County were for Whalley, and lived in distaste with Rainsborough and the Sectaries prospered there no further than Worcester City itself (a Place which deserved such a judgment); but all the Country was free from their infection."[9]

It needs taking with a pinch of salt as Baxter, nauseously sanctimonious and breathtakingly self-important, was, in 1646, chaplain to the regiment of Col Edward Whalley, a cousin of Cromwell, a former major in his regiment and a religious orthodox. Fairfax, in his letter of recommendation, said it was the "earnest desire of the committee and gentlemen of Worcester" that Rainborowe be governor[10] and Thomas Fairfax, himself a religious moderate, did not promote men on the strength of their godly convictions.

But there had been a hint of this dislike towards Rainborowe just a year before in 1645 when Presbyterian MPs and Lords were unhappy with his appointment as an officer in Fairfax's New Model Army. But there were no formal objections in either House. Those to whom there were objections were mainly men who were seen, or later emerged, as religious or political radicals. The Lords alone cited 58 men, among then Henry Ireton, Rainborowe's great opponent at Putney, and Rainborowe's brother, William. While the Commons scored a success in temporarily stopping Nathaniel Rich, brother-in-law of John Hampden and in the 1650s a probable republican, becoming an officer, Fairfax otherwise ignored the Lords' objections.

Rainborowe's second step up the political ladder was a much larger one. In January 1647, he was elected as "recruiter" MP for Droitwich. These were men picked to replace members who had died since the Long Parliament was first called in November 1640 or were Royalists who had left to join Charles's Oxford Parliament in 1643. By mid-1646, around 150 of these newcomers had entered

Parliament. The majority were men like Rainborowe, Army officers and religious Independents. Some also became political radicals. Their number included Ireton, Thomas Harrison, Edmund Ludlow and Charles Fleetwood. With a House of Commons numbering 489, the new arrivals considerably altered its political make up. But this was changing anyway.

When war broke out in 1642, the Commons was broadly united against the king. But this unity began to fade by 1644 as peace and war parties began to emerge. The first group trusted the king and wanted to negotiate with him rather than defeat him totally. The second sought victory, the king's unconditional surrender and a dictated peace. These were the two parties that shortly re-invented themselves, respectively, as Presbyterians and Independents. But the groups were extremely loose and neither in early 1647 had a guaranteed majority in the House.

Of the two, the Presbyterians were more solid. The county or borough was still the main focal point for most people in the 1640s and any attempt by Parliament at centralisation was firmly opposed. The countrymen saw exactly this happening in the county committees set up during the war which effectively displaced the traditional authority of the usually Royalist gentry. Added to this was a growing resentment of the Army and its endless need for quarter. It was from these disaffected men who longed for a quick peace that the Presbyterians drew their support.

They were led by Denzil Holles, MP for Dorchester, a childhood friend of the king and brother-in-law of the doomed royal favourite, the Earl of Strafford. Holles was a firebrand in his youth, one of the two members who held down Speaker Finch in the Commons in 1629 while Sir John Eliot's *Protestations* were read out against the king's wishes. The incident led directly to the dissolution of Parliament and Charles's 11 years of personal rule. Holles was also one of the five members Charles tried, notoriously and unsuccessfully, to arrest in the Commons in January, 1642. Age had mellowed Holles although it had not improved his political judgement.

The Independents were a far looser and more fragile alliance. The largest faction was the "middle group" led by the lawyer and judge Oliver St John, MP for Totnes. St John, an austere and aloof man, was a firm supporter of John Pym and Hampden in the heady years of 1640-2 when the Long Parliament imposed reforms and restraints on the King and, later, a close ally of Cromwell in the bitter fall out between Parliament and the Army in 1647.

The other groups within the Independents were the Commonswealthmen, led by Sir Arthur Haselrige, Edmund Ludlow and Sir John Pyne, uncle of Maximilian Petty, one of the main radical speakers at Putney, the religious zealots such as Sir Henry Vane, MP for Hull, who championed freedom of worship, and "a small handful of until 1648 still covert republicans led by Henry Marten."[11]

It was this tiny faction that Rainborowe joined. Marten, MP for Berkshire in the Long Parliament, was the son of the extremely rich Sir Henry Marten, a lawyer and diplomat. Marten spent much of his father's inherited fortune on wine and women. According John Aubrey, the 17th century antiquary, Marten was "a great lover of pretty girls to whom he was so liberal that he spent the greatest part of his estate." Charles took a less generous view, describing him as "an ugly rascal and whore-master." Marten also made substantial financial contributions to the Parliamentary cause.

The classical education he had at Oxford University may have been the source of his republican views. Marten became increasingly strident in his opposition to both king and the concept of monarchy. In August 1643 he was "disabled" from Parliament for supporting the views of a preacher, John Saltmarsh who said that it would be better if one family suffered (the Royal family) rather than the whole country.

Allowed back in Parliament in January 1646, Marten continued to push his republican agenda and supported Thomas Chaloner, MP for Richmond, Yorkshire and a fellow republican, in his notorious

"Speech without Doors." In this, Chaloner called Charles a "dog" and urged Parliament to make peace agreements without him. Rainborowe took his oath as an MP in February, 1647 but made no discernible impact in his first months in Parliament. The first mention of him in the Commons Journal for that year refers to him as a soldier. This sounds feasible as Rainborowe was still largely engaged with the Army and was now, thanks to his exploits in the last year of the war, one of its major figures.

But in the aftermath of the fighting and mopping up, the unity of the New Model Army began to fray at the edges. There were some 22 mutinies in English regiments alone between May and September 1646 and "several" more in Wales.[12] The chief grievances were a chronic lack of pay, no indemnity for acts committed during the war and no provision for the widows and children of slain colleagues. About £3m, a phenomenal sum in those days, was owed to Parliamentary soldiers by early 1647, with about half that being owed to the New Model Army, including its officers.[13] Up to March 1647, there was little overt political activity by the Army, although with about 20 of its senior officers also MPS, it would be naive to assume there was no political awareness that the wind at that time was blowing in the Presbyterian direction.

What changed the Army, politicised it almost instantly, was a crass political move by Holles. By the end of January, the Scots army, after agreeing adequate compensation, was on its way home. It had handed Charles over to Parliament and the king was now in its safe custody at Holmby House, Northamptonshire. Better still, from the Presbyterian point of view, peace proposals, the revised Newcastle Propositions, were again on the table for talks between king and Parliament.

It was part of the programme of Holles and the Presbyterians that the now largely redundant Army should be disbanded, a rump kept for service in Ireland and a more compliant force established, formed from the London trained bands but purged of their Independents. Fairfax and his senior officers were not completely opposed to this disbandment with the fighting all but done. The general actually wrote to Parliament on March 6, 1647 stating his willingness to talk about the formation of a new force for Ireland.

But by this time the Lords had already voted not to raise any more taxes to pay for the Army and, on the same day as Fairfax wrote his conciliatory note, they voted to ban the Army quartering in the area of the Eastern Association, regarded as the likeliest hotspot for unrest. It was into this delicate situation that Holles jumped both feet first.

He persuaded the Commons on March 29 to pass a motion which condemned the soldiers as "enemies to the state and disturbers of the public peace."[14] It became known as the Declaration of Dislike and "transmuted the Army's already sharp political consciousness into revolutionary militancy."[15] Holles must have thought he could have got away with it; after all, the country people, who supported his faction, resented the Army, their violent soldiers and the cripplingly high taxes they had to pay to keep them. They wanted nothing better than to see the back of them. But the soldiers themselves, far from seeing themselves as enemies of the people, believed they were the common people in uniform, the ones who had risked their lives to save the social order from the tyranny of a wayward king.[16] What Holles did not reckon on, or discounted, was that his insulting words would sting the Army into political action.

Overnight, the Army, officers and rank and file, united and within days had produced the first of many declarations of grievances and demands. For Rainborowe, the politicisation of the Army played inexorably into his hands. He was already a member of its innermost councils through his military prowess. But now the discussions within these councils slowly turned from military tactics to political strategy. Unlike in Parliament, where he had no power base and few allies, he found both among the officers and men of the Army, many who listened to and empathised with his radical views. As the highest ranking officer with pronounced radical views, he inevitably became their leader and spokesman in the Army's inner councils. With equal inevitability, it put him on a collision path with the more moderate and conservative Cromwell.

The Army and the Presbyterian-led Parliament had already been circling around each other in the early weeks of March 1647. As parliamentary commissioners arrived at the Army's current headquarters at Saffron Walden in Essex to organise a 12,600-strong force for service in Ireland, a petition was already doing the rounds among regiments in nearby Norfolk demanding their arrears of pay before they went anywhere. The first two of what would become an almost constant stream of radical pamphlets on the Army's rights had emerged anonymously from clandestine presses in London. The first, *A Warning for all the Counties of England*, spoke of the soldiers' birthright, while the second, *An Apologie of the Souldiers to all their Commission Officers in Sir Thomas Fairfax his Armie*, called for the officers to stand firm with their men.

As the petition gathered signatures, it also won the support of officers after its wording was toned down. Besides the original three grievances, it now added demand for payment for quarter and that no soldier should serve abroad against his wishes. Fruitlessly, Parliament demanded its suppression and an outraged Holles pushed through his calamitous motion. Now the two protagonists locked horns. Parliament spoke darkly of mutiny and corralled Presbyterian officers in the Army to lead its force to Ireland. Those who refused to go, mainly Independent officers, were ordered back to their regiments – exactly those now threatened with disbandment. The upper echelons of the Army were split, although the rank and file stayed solid. Men of Ireton's regiment – one of those facing disbandment – threatened to draw up a second petition and select two men from every troop to deliver it to Parliament. It was the first hint of the imminent rise of the agitators.

Within a month of the Declaration of Dislike, five officers of the Army delivered the Army's response to Parliament. *The Vindication of the Officers of the Army* was presented on April 27 and was read to the Commons three days later. It confirmed the Independent officers' solidarity with their men and, significantly, claimed they had concerns for the country that stretched beyond their grievances as soldiers. On the very same day, April 30, Major General Philip Skippon[17], the new commander-in-chief of the force for Ireland and an MP, presented to the Commons the first manifesto from the agitators. The document, later published as The *Apologie of the Common Soldiers of Sir Thomas Fairfaxes Army*, was signed by 16 men from the eight cavalry regiments at Army HQ. Among them was Edward Sexby, later a prominent speaker at the Putney Debates, William Allen and Thomas Shepherd who all accompanied Skippon to Westminster for the presentation of the manifesto.

At this time, Rainborowe seems to have kept a low profile. Little is known of his activities from the autumn of 1646 to spring 1647. There is no record of any contribution in the Commons. He did not attend Fairfax's Council of War on March 21-22 in Saffron Walden to discuss service in Ireland, although his brother, Captain William Rainborowe, was there on the second day. He was not present at the subsequent meeting called by Fairfax on April 15 again to discuss service in Ireland with a new group of parliamentary commissioners who now included his former business associate, the Earl of Warwick. Two of his junior officers, Captains George Drury and Thomas Creamer did attend, with the former saying he was ready to serve in Ireland and claimed "that the rest of the said Regiment, Officers and Soldiers, will for the most Part engage therein."[18] In the light of what shortly happened, this may have been wildly optimistic.

It is likely that for much of this time, Rainborowe, still very much the soldier, was drawing up plans for the reduction of Jersey. Royalists under the bailiff George Carteret, who, incidentally, served as a senior officer in Rainborowe's father assault on Sallee, had taken over the island in 1643. By May 1647, this Channel Island was the last part of the British Isles still under the King's control. While his fellow officers continued their meetings with their men and the commissioners, Rainborowe was appointed by Parliament on May 1 to take Jersey.

He was voted £6,700 for "his proposition...for the reducing of Jersey." The money was not just to pay his men six weeks arrears of pay once the job was done and the regiment disbanded. It was also to be used for equipment for the assault, including arms, coats, pickaxes, shovels, barrows and ladders. Rainborowe was to "command in chief" about 12,000 men on the expedition, including a troop of horse supplied by Fairfax.[19] Rainborowe's foot regiment numbered about 1,300 men including officers, but there is no indication from where the remainder of the force was to be drawn.

Rainborowe's regiment moved down to Portsmouth and Petersfield in Hampshire ready to embark for Jersey but the colonel did not join them, spending at least part of May in London, probably fine tuning his preparations. The Commons got wind of trouble brewing in the regiment in Hampshire and, on May 12, it ordered "That Colonel Whitehead and Colonel Norton do write (*sic*) down to Portesmouth and Petersfield, where Colonel Rainsborough's Soldiers are for present quartered; and to assure the Country, that these Soldiers will be, very suddenly, either shipped or removed."[20] The next thing that Parliament heard was that the soldiers had mutinied. On May 28, Rainborowe was ordered to "with all Speed, repair to his Regiment, and command all his Officers that are in Town, to repair down thither likewise with all Speed: And that he do take Course to stay his Regiment in the Place he shall find it at his coming down, until this House take further Order."[21]

While Rainborowe was away, his regiment had not only mutinied but marched north to Oxfordshire. What he found when arriving there was mayhem. The men were quartered in towns and villages around Abingdon; his officers were mostly at regimental headquarters not daring to be among the men. "They had not been long in their quarters ere the majors serjeant was almost killed by his own soldiers and his ensign if he had not exceedingly well defended himself against another company, he had been all cut to pieces, but in defending himself he hath wounded divers of them, two whereof I am confident cannot possible escape with life", he told Lenthall, the

Commons speaker. The men were also extracting a half crown each from local residents for their food. [22]

"I found no other way then to draw them to a rendezvous, where having acquainted them with your order to me and used all the Arguments I could to persuade them yield obedience thereunto, there was not any man returned the least word of answer whereupon I peremptorily commanded them to repair to gather no more unless by special order, but to keep their several quarters, and to offer to draw out or march any way without the said order, on pain of the highest and most severe punishment," Rainborowe told Lenthall.

But this is barely half the story – and Rainborowe probably knew much more than he told Parliament. The MPs' order that he keep his regiment where he found it betrays, correctly, that they thought something was going on. There was a magazine including artillery and siege equipment, stationed near Oxford and, amid the deteriorating relations, both sides wanted to secure it for themselves. A party of dragoons that Parliament had sent to Oxford to give Colonel Richard Ingoldsy £3,500 to pay off his regiment was then ordered on May 31 to bring back the magazine to London. But they were too late. The Army by then had already seized it.[23]

Soldiers, led by Cornet George Joyce, a junior officer in Fairfax's horse regiment, probably with the approval of Cromwell and with the help of some of Rainborowe's men, had secured it by May 28 – the day Rainborowe was ordered to Oxford. By the time he wrote his soothing letter, the magazine was safely in Army hands. Worse was to follow for Parliament. Realising it had lost the magazine, it ordered the hard-pressed dragoons on June 1 to go back to Oxford and retrieve the £3,500 from Ingoldsby. In a pitched battle outside All Souls College the dragoons were seen off. [24]

Parliament's bad weekend then got worse. On the same day it ordered Rainborowe to go to his troops, Lieutenant Edmund Chillenden,[25] a radical officer in Whalley's regiment, wrote to agitators that £7,000 was being sent by Parliament to Chelmsford on the following Monday, June 1, to pay off Fairfax's foot regiment. The clear implication is that the money, which would be accompanied by the Earl of Warwick and four Presbyterian MPs, be seized. In the same letter Chillenden, who conspiratorially signed himself as "102", revealed he knew Rainborowe had been ordered to Oxford and advised "Let two horsemen go presently to Colonel Rainborow to Oxford, and be very carefull not to be overwitted."[26] It seems Rainborowe was in touch with the agitators.

Not surprisingly Rainborowe's version of events around Oxford was not universally accepted, especially by Royalists and Holles. This came out in manuscripts by the Earl of Clarendon[27] and Holles' *Memoirs*, both published after the war. The former cited a Royalist Newsletter that said Rainborowe claimed his regiment had marched north "to participate in the fortune with the rest of the soldiery." Rainborowe allegedly told the Commons that he did not know what this meant and that he had been more of a solicitor than colonel to his men in the past three months.

He is said to have added that his soldiers' behaviour had injured the local people of Hampshire so they were "constrained to dislodge, and was now marched towards Oxon which gives much jealousy to the Parliament that there is some design in hand."[28] Holles had already worked himself into a lather at the conduct of MPs who were also senior officers, including Rainborowe, Cromwell, Ireton and Fleetwood. These men, he charged, had stayed around the Commons so "that the soldiers might be left to themselves to fire the more, run-up to extremes, and put themselves in a posture to carry on their work of Rebellion."[29]

After the non-event of the assault on Jersey, Holles accused Rainborowe of not just disobeying Parliament but of staying in London and "pretending" to prepare for the expedition to "give his soldiers an opportunity to mutiny." Holles said Rainborowe had deliberately held back news of his regiment's revolt from the House which was finally informed by another MP, Sir William Lewis, early in the evening of May 28. Holles accepted that Rainborowe "immediately" left to join his men but added that he then "put himself at the head of them but instead of taking care for Jersey, marched to Oxford first and so to the Army."

Widening his attack to include his fellow MPs and Lords, Holles sarcastically concluded: "None was more violent in the Rebellion than he [Rainborowe]; for which good service, and joining with the Agitators in their highest exorbitances, for the destruction of the king, and altering the Government, and particularly in a Petition for taking away the House of Lords, the House of Commons afterwards made him Vice-Admiral and the Lords, to the eternizing of their honour for their gentle, tame dispositions, consented."[30]

But is there any value in Holles' charge that Rainborowe connived in the mutiny of his regiment? Certainly Rainborowe's radical views made him broadly sympathetic to the plight of his men. They were owed considerable money in arrears of pay, they faced disbandment without indemnity for any acts committed during the fighting and there was a chance that they would be sent to Ireland against their will. But if he was an impetuous man, he was also an honourable and scrupulous one. His Army career shows he was a man who followed orders rather than acted as a maverick. He was also conscientious in his dealings with Parliament, his masters. His letter to Lenthall, although obviously putting the situation in the best possible light, also honestly relates a clearly lawless situation.

Furthermore as a professional soldier contemplating a difficult assault on an island across the Channel, he would have been well aware of the essential need for detailed planning. As the son of a national naval hero, he would have known the preparations his father William made for his successful expedition to Sallee in 1837. He would also, as a naval man, have been aware of the catastrophic expedition of the Duke of Buckingham to besiege the French fortress on the island of Rhe off La Rochelle during the Anglo-French war of 1827-9. This failed humiliatingly through lack of planning. Not only were the Duke's cannon too small to breach the fortress walls but his ladders were too short to scale them. This came two years after the equally embarrassing expedition to Cadiz, where more of the Duke's men died from hunger than enemy gunfire.[31] It is unlikely in the extreme that Rainborowe wanted a repeat of such fiascos. Holles's charge, remains, at the very least, unproven.

The most likely scenario is that Rainborowe had a good idea of what was going on regarding the magazine. As a specialist in siege warfare he would undoubtedly have realised the value of such ordnance to the Army if fighting resumed.[32] But it is equally unlikely that he expected his regiment to have fallen into the chaotic state in which he found it. With his men largely out of his officers' control, he acted in the best and possibly only way he could to prevent further lawlessness by accompanying them to Oxford rather than trying to force them to go to Jersey. Rainborowe's whole career as a seaman and soldier made him the ideal man to carry out the seaborne expedition and assault on Jersey. Success in such an expedition would have added enormously to his reputation. He would not have abandoned it without good reason.

But there is one intriguing aspect of this clouded affair. Just what happened to the money Parliament voted Rainborowe? After all, £6,700 was a considerable sum in the 17th century. If his men had been sent to Hampshire to prepare to embark, it would suggest some at least had both been received and spent. Nothing in the *Commons Journal* of the time suggests any of it was ever returned or indeed throws any light on what became of it. Interestingly a newsletter in London reported on June 3 that Rainborowe's men had received a fortnight's pay.[33] Whatever the extent of Rainborowe's involvement it seems to have done him little if any harm with Fairfax or Cromwell. He remained a senior member of Fairfax's Council of War.

But these incidents were just part of a whole, rapid series of events in May and early June which finally severed any bond between the Army and the Presbyterians in Parliament. Relations between the two sides were deteriorating from the end of April. Any doubt that Parliament was bent on breaking the Army disappeared when, on May 4, it handed control of the London Militia to the fiercely

Presbyterian City Corporation.[34] This became, in effect, a potentially rival force to the Army.

Two more decisive and divisive votes followed. First, Parliament voted on May 18 to accept the king's latest response to the Newcastle Propositions. These would have restored Charles to the throne but also, just as crucially, made Presbyterianism England's established religion for three years. Then, on the strength of a prospective settlement with the king, it voted on May 25 finally to disband the Army.

Taken in tandem, the two events convinced not just the Army radicals but senior officers like Cromwell that this was a Presbyterian plot to destroy the Army. One scenario held that Charles would be taken to Scotland, where he would head an army ready to fight the New Model Army. Cromwell, who was in London and still attending Parliament in the hope of a settlement between the two sides, was keenly alive to the threat. He immediately held a series of meetings with Army officers and civilian radicals at his home in Drury Lane at the end of May. The attendees included Cornet Joyce. Not only was the capture of the Oxford magazine by Joyce discussed but also, far more momentously, the securing of the king. This discussion took place on the evening of May 31, after the magazine had been seized, with Cromwell agreeing that Joyce should only secure the king at Holmby House, not take him away.

By now, the radicals were in the driving seat, with men such as Joyce presenting their daring plans to senior officers like Cromwell rather than awaiting orders. The radicals had grown quickly in strength and boldness during May and built up, with remarkable speed, an effective network of communications between each regiment. They planned the manoeuvres that both secured money meant for disbandment and the valuable magazine. Then, with no more than Cromwell's connivance, they grabbed the greatest and most essential prize of all, the king.

These swirling events presented Fairfax with an unenviable dilemma. Should he defy the obviously angry mood of his men and obey Parliament - and if so with what consequences? - or should he defy his masters at Westminster and back his men? He chose to summon on May 29 around 100 officers to a Council of War in Bury St. Edmunds. Each officer was asked to vote individually on two pivotal points: on the first, they decided overwhelmingly that Parliament had not granted enough concessions to ensure that any forced disbandment would not cause riots. Second, they voted, equally decisively, that, against Parliament's specific orders to disperse their regiments around the country, they would gather them together. On a third question, they decided without even voting that Parliament's decision to disband the Army should not be relayed to the men.[35] Equally significantly, they accepted a *Humble Petition of the soldiers of the army*, requesting a general rendezvous. It was signed by 31 agitators from 16 regiments, a marked rise in the 16 who signed the first petition just a month before. The rendezvous was arranged to be held near Newmarket on June 4-5.

But events were now moving at breakneck speed. The king was residing at Holmby under the protection of a Parliamentary guard led by the Presbyterian Colonel Richard Graves. Taking 500 men from the force that captured the Oxford magazine, the ever bold Joyce rode to Northampton and by the early morning of June 4 had secured the king. He wrote triumphantly at 8am that day: "We have secured the king. Graves is run away, he got out about one o'clock in the morning and so went his way." Joyce went on to say that he and his soldiers were "resolved to obey no orders but the General's." The probability is that this letter, addressed only to 'Sir', was sent to Cromwell.[36] With the die now cast, Cromwell abandoned Parliament and London, probably on June 3 as Joyce was moving towards Holmby, and returned to Army HQ, now at Newmarket. He arrived in town about the same day as Charles. Probably the fear of a return by Graves with soldiers to rescue the king had persuaded Joyce to move Charles to Army HQ.

While the king was being brought to Newmarket, the general rendezvous began on June 4. Later that same day, Parliament, fearful that events had slipped out of its control, made a last ditch attempt to rein in the Army. Full arrears of pay would be handed over and the Declaration of Dislike erased from its records. It was too little, too late. The Army was bent on a course that intensified the confrontation. On the second day of its rendezvous, it issued *A Solemne Engagement* which was probably written by Ireton. Its preamble said it was agreed "by all officers and soldiers of the several regiments." [37] It said the Army would "cheerfully and readily disband" or serve in England or Ireland – provided its grievances were settled first. It spoke ringingly of how its soldiers and other citizens as "free-born people of England" should not be subjected to oppression, injury or abuse that had recently been attempted – a basic call for the Presbyterian leaders to quit. Ominously it added: "That without such satisfaction and security...we shall not willingly disband, nor divide, nor suffer ourselves to be disbanded or divided."

The last few words were almost a challenge to Parliament: the Army wanted to promote "an establishment of common and equal right and freedom to the whole, as all might equally partake of, but those that do by denying the same to others, or otherwise render themselves incapable thereof."[38] The Army had moved into politics.

Under the terms of the *Solemne Engagement*, the Army had set up a new body, the General Council of the Army, which was formed of senior officers, plus two junior officers and two soldiers elected by each regiment. As it hammered out its new course of action, the Army had unprecedentedly given a voice to the rank and file.

From May 18, when Parliament believed it was close to settling with Charles, to June 5, when the Army issued its provocative *Solemne Engagement*, were 19 days that changed the political landscape of England. It was far more the fear of a giveaway deal with the king and the imposition of Presbyterianism than a failure to settle the soldiers' grievances that spurred the Army to action. In the course of those few frenetic days, it seized from Parliament ordnance, money, the king and, most of all, the initiative. In the aftermath of the *Solemne*

Declaration, it was Parliament that was on the back foot and the Army looking to push home its burgeoning dominance. It wasted little time.

After the general rendezvous in Newmarket, the Army began its march on London. Fairfax called another rendezvous on June 10 at Triploe (now Thriplow) Heath near Royston, in Cambridgeshire, where the Army now had its headquarters. The outcome of this was a letter sent to the still defiant City Corporation explaining the advance on London. The Army charged that a party in the kingdom was seeking the destruction of the Army and the overthrow of the privileges of Parliament and People. Rather than fail in this design, this party was ready to plunge the country into another war, "putting the kingdom into blood." The Army said it did not want to interfere in the government of England but "Only we could wish that every good Citizen, and every Man that walks peaceably in a blameless Conversation, and is beneficial to the Commonwealth, may have Liberties and Encouragements." It added: "for the obtaining these Things, we are drawing near your City."

It ended with an unmistakable warning: "If, after all this, you, or a considerable Part of you, be seduced to take up Arms, in Opposition to, or Hindrance of, these our just Undertakings, we hope, by this brotherly Premonition...we have freed ourselves from all that Ruin which may befall that great and populous City, having hereby washed our Hands there of."[39] If the City resisted, any blood would be on its hands. It was signed by 13 senior officers among them Rainborowe, Fairfax, Cromwell and Ireton. The wish for "every man" to have his liberties was echoed by Rainborowe at the Putney Debates.

But the letter had little effect. Both Parliament and the City's Common Council[40] sent new commissioners to assure Fairfax that they did not want another war at the same time setting about raising troops. The Army for its part continued its intimidating march on London, reaching St Albans on June 14 where it issued the famous *Declaration*[41] of its political aims, probably written by the senior officers in the Council of War. As long as the Army pursued the redress of grievances relating purely to the welfare of its men, unity was largely assured. But once it strayed over that line into the minefield of national politics, and worse still, the politics of change, a variety of different views and solutions were bound to spring up. A split became inevitable.

After a preamble setting out how it wished England's Freeborn people might live "under the glorious administration of Justice and Righteousness and in full possession of those fundamental Rights and Liberties", the *Declaration* emphasised the Army was "not a mere mercenary army hired to serve any arbitrary power of a state" but one that had been formed to defend "our own and our peoples just rights and liberties."[42] This was a crucial and essential plank in the Army's case. It resented the idea that it was made up of hired men ready to fight for any reason rather than of principled men who had signed up voluntarily to defend their rights and those of the country.

It then listed its eight political demands, among which were the purging of corrupt members from Parliament, the removal from power of those who had abused the Army and Parliament, fixed length Parliaments that could not be dissolved by the king, the right to petition and a reduction in the powers of county committees. But almost half hidden in the fourth political aim was a paragraph that called for a settlement of grievances, relating both to the Army and the country, *before* any deal with the king. The crucial sentence read: "We shall then desire that the rights of his Majesty and his posterity may be considered of and settled in all things so far as may consist with the Rights and Freedom of the Subject, and with the security of the same for future."[43]

In other words, any deal with Charles was not only to come after the settlement with the country but also in terms that did not impinge upon people's rights and security. If Charles returned to his throne, it would be as a monarch whose powers were limited by the set rights of his people. This was a far more radical approach than that set out in the letter to the City Corporation. This had talked of hopes and aspirations but the *Declaration* went some way to show how these could be achieved. But in stating, effectively, that the powers of the king should be limited, it also created for itself the same dilemma that had afflicted the opposing Independents and Presbyterians in Parliament: just how and to what extent should those powers be curtailed.

On the same day as it issued its *Declaration*, the Army sent an indictment of 11 MPs both to Parliament and the commissioners with them in St Albans, calling for their impeachment. Among the 11 were Holles and his Presbyterian co-leader Sir Philip Stapelton.[44] The charge claimed that the 11 had "jointly and severally invaded, infringed or endeavoured to overthrow the Rights and Liberties of the subjects of this Nation, in Arbitrary, violent or oppressive ways."[45] This drew little response from Parliament, inducing the Army to send it a long 11-page *Remonstrance* [46] complaining that its *Declaration* had never been answered and the 11 MPs not suspended. Intriguingly the *Remonstrance* also demanded that the rights of the king be respected.[47]

Charles had lately been in talks with the Scots, and Parliament was still hoping to reach an agreement with him. It clearly was not in the Army's interests to alienate him. Two days later, on June 25, Fairfax increased the pressure on Parliament by moving his Army to Uxbridge. The tactic worked as Parliament softened its line towards the Army, allowing Fairfax, as he had promised, to move back to Reading when tensions eased.

If the Army's aim in impeaching the 11 MPs was to destroy the Presbyterian leadership in the Commons, it was also looking at the wider picture of its own deal with the king. A subtle process of soothing Charles, almost a charm offensive, had begun in June as officers took copies to him of the *Declaration* and then the *Remonstrance*. They, no doubt, pointed out the passage about protecting the monarch's rights to him. Cromwell met him on July 4 and Fairfax asked Parliament that Charles, a strong family man, be allowed to see his children - a move also certainly made known to the king - as well as keeping his chaplain and courtiers.[48] By this time

Ireton and Colonel John Lambert, probably with imput from Lord Wharton[49] and Lord Saye and Sele[50], were drafting the early stages of what became the Army's plan for a national settlement: the Heads of the Proposals.

But London radicals were also coming more forcefully onto the scene. In a period where the press was unprecedentedly free, thousands of pamphlets promoting all shades of both political and religious views flooded through London. These included tracts from radicals like John Lilburne, Richard Overton and William Walwyn that increasingly challenged the political status quo and advocated a shift of power from the monarch to the people. Overton and Walwyn, in their pamphlet, *Remonstrance of Many Thousand Citizens (1646)*, wrote that the nation's sovereign lord was not the king but its people, while Lilburne claimed in his savage attack on monarchy, *Regall Tyrannie Discovered(1647)*, that there was no difference between a king and a tyrant.

Radicals such as this were a tiny majority but sufficiently part of the London scene in the summer of 1647 for Cromwell, who dabbled in radical ideas, to invite them to his London home in Drury Lane. Among the visitors were Walwyn, who in the 1640s "conducted a weekly discussion group on republican politics" among his friends[51], John Wildman, a brilliant young lawyer, and Maximilian Petty. Wildman was born in Berkshire in 1623 and studied law at Cambridge and the Inns of Court. He seems to have become involved in radical politics in London by late 1646 and may have written two influential pamphlets, *Londons Liberties*, published in October, and *The Charters of London*, published in December. The first said every free man in London should have a vote in city elections, that rotten boroughs should be abolished and that representation should be fixed according to taxes paid.[52] *The Charters* called for the abolition of the property qualification for voting, supporting the argument with the claim that "The poorest he that lives has as true a right to give a vote as well as the richest and greatest."[53] The clear similarity to the famous words of Rainborowe at the Putney Debates is unmissable.

Petty hailed from a long established Oxford family. His uncle was Max Petty, a radical MP for Westbury in 1628. He was a long standing friend of Edward Sexby, one of the original agitators, who was apprenticed to the Grocers' Company in London in 1632. The pair met in 1634 when Petty also joined the company. By 1647 both Wildman and Petty were moving towards republicanism, although it is likely that their views were based more on the events of the previous years than on classical republican theory. However, by the late 1650s, both were members of James Harrington's[54] republican society, The Rota Club.

Walwyn, Wildman and Petty were all subsequently invited up to Army HQ in Reading in July 1647 - probably by Cromwell - for political discussions. These talks embraced not only the officers but also the agitators and the soldiers. While the politicisation of the Army had taken place without outside help, both officers and men had developed growing contacts with the radicals of London. Sexby was almost certainly the linkman. Rainborowe and his brother, Londoners themselves and widely known for their radical views, were part of this network. While there is no record of any meeting, it seems likely that they would have met both Petty and Wildman while they were in Reading.

The strategy of softening up the king bore fruit when Queen Henrietta Maria arranged for one of his secretaries Sir John Berkeley to travel to Army HQ to meet Cromwell, Rainborowe and Sir Hardress Waller, also a colonel in the New Model Army, to sound out a possible deal.[55] The meeting, on July 12, went sufficiently well for Berkeley to hold further talks with Cromwell and Ireton.

With the situation between Parliament and its Army seemingly improving, Fairfax called the first ever recorded meeting of the new General Council, which included agitators from each regiment. It met on July 16 in Reading. Fairfax and Cromwell seem to have been aware from the start that the rise of the agitators posed a threat not only to Army unity but also to discipline. This new body was an obvious ploy to control the agitators by giving them the semblance of a say in the Army's policies.

But, from the grandees' point of view, the first meeting, the General Council got off on the wrong foot. Fairfax and his senior officers had planned to talk about the Proposals but were sidetracked by a petition from three officer agitators. *'A humble petition and representation'* was put before the Council by Major Daniel Abbot and Captains John Clarke and Edmund Rolf[56] but it had almost certainly been drawn up by other agitators and probably London radicals. Its main thrust was for an immediate march on London. But it also called for, among other demands, the removal of the 11 MPs from Parliament, the removal of the London militia from the command of the Presbyterian City and the release from prison of Lilburne. Rainborowe joined Cromwell and Ireton in opposing the petition.

But while the latter two were understandably concerned about the Army seeming to grab power in the run up to the delicate negotiations with the king, Rainborowe's objections were of a more practical nature. He called for the debate to be put off until "five or six a clock" that evening and observed that "in a business of such weight as this is, that if there can be more reasons given, action will be so much better accepted." He successfully demanded that "we may have some little time to satisfy our judgements in it."[57] A committee was set up, which included Rainborowe, to discuss the petition.

When Cromwell reported back to the Council in the evening, he said the senior officers accepted that the militia should be taken from Presbyterian control – Fairfax had already begun this process – and that the radical leaders should be released from prison. The only other issue was the march on London. Cromwell pleaded for time, for a chance for the Army's Proposals to be put to Charles. For this it needed the support of its friends in Parliament. An advance on the capital would scare them off. Cromwell and Ireton narrowly won the day. The Council agreed to petition Parliament to put the militia under its former commanders within four days – but not to threaten a march on London.

From the start it seems the grandees had underestimated the agitators. These ordinary soldiers were highly organised, determined and articulate. They had sent letters and emissaries to the sailors in the Royal Navy and other Parliamentary soldiers across the country explaining their views and seeking support; they also proved, when necessary, to be ready to fight for their beliefs in stark defiance of most senior officers; and, perhaps most disconcerting to the officers, proved to be remarkably fluent in doing so. From the start, it was not only differing opinions that were splitting the Army but also tactics. At some meetings, crucially the Putney Debates, it was the soldiers' agenda which was discussed. They also had a champion at senior level in the equally articulate Rainborowe, a man whose sharpening radicalism often chimed exactly with theirs.

On the second day of the General Council meeting, Ireton's Proposals, still at this stage in draft form, were finally discussed. Only one agitator spoke on them: William Allen, an immensely articulate soldier from Cromwell's regiment. He said he and his fellow soldiers were "but young Statesmen" and asked that a committee be formed to discuss Ireton's settlement plans.[58] This was duly done, with Rainborowe among 12 officers and 12 agitators appointed to "perfect" the Proposals.[59]

But Berkeley was by now pressing to see them. He had already discussed the draft form in detail with Ireton and a more complete version was shown to both him (and therefore the king) and the parliamentary commissioners by July 23. By then, Charles was installed in Woburn Abbey, home of the Duke of Bedford and Fairfax was planning to move his Army HQ to Bedford, just a few miles away. Talks were just a matter of time.

But events, quickly and decisively, began to move against the Army's carefully laid plans. All seemed well at first. On July 19, Parliament acceded to Fairfax's request that he be made commander of all forces in England. The next day the 11 MPs, still in the Army's sights, were given permission to withdraw, despite the presence of Presbyterian demonstrators in the grounds of Westminster Palace. But two days later Presbyterian discontent in the City boiled up. Thousands of apprentices, militiamen, reformadoes (soldiers dismissed from the Army and seeking arrears of pay) gathered in the City to sign the *Solemn Engagement,* which called for the immediate return of the king.

The next day, July 22, as Fairfax's Army arrived in Bedford, Charles held secret talks with the Earl of Lauderdale. This leading Scots Covenanter was ready to provide an army to invade England in return for Presbyterianism becoming the established religion. In London, nearly 3,000 demonstrators met in St James's Field – near the current St James's Square – to persuade the City to petition Parliament to restore Charles. In the face of the increasingly aggressive stance of the City, Parliament stuck to its guns and, on July 24, denounced the *Solemn Engagement* and put the militia back in the hands of its former commanders.

This merely further enraged the Presbyterians who, on July 26, marched on Westminster and occupied the Palace. First they forced the Lords to reverse its vote on the control of the militia and then forced the Commons to do the same. More crucially, they then made the MPs vote to invite Charles back to London. This was sheer intimidation: no MPs were allowed to leave until they had met the mob's demands. Some reports said that members of the mob even voted. As soon as the demonstrators dispersed, the speakers of both Houses, Lenthall and the Earl of Manchester, the latter a moderate with little sympathy for the radicals, 58 MPs and eight peers fled to the protection of the Army.

As each side took stock of the now dangerously volatile situation, Charles again met with Lauderdale at Bedford on July 27. The next day, Ireton, Rainborowe and Colonels Thomas Pride and Nathaniel Rich rode out of Army HQ formally to present the king with the Heads of the Proposals. These were surprisingly moderate and the best that Charles had so far been offered. The Proposals ranged from the settling of the soldiers' grievances to the grander intent of re-structuring the government of England.

There were to be biennial Parliaments, sitting for 120 days and which could be adjourned only by their own consent; a fairer distribution of seats in the Commons so that more populous areas got more MPs; no one was to be above the law, including any advisers to the king; Parliament was to be responsible for the armed forces for 10 years and have the right to raise money for them; a council of state would control the militia and handle foreign policy; the great offices of state were to be filled by men proposed by Parliament for the next 10 years; all laws enjoining the use of the Book of Common Prayer were to be repealed and no one was required to sign the Covenant; the king was to be restored to his throne in a condition of safety, honour and freedom.[61] This was a reforming document but not one that was emphatically radical. There was something in it for the king, the people and the country and the terms were more lenient than the Newcastle Propositions that Charles had previously been offered.

But events had made the timing of the meeting hopelessly wrong for the Army. Despite its attempts to soften his attitude to them, Charles still did not trust the senior officers. From the king's view, the Army was just one of three possible options. Besides the NMA, there were the Scots and their offer to invade; and now with the unrest in London, there was the chance the Presbyterians might regain the ascendancy and offer improved terms. These choices gave Charles, a man who lacked both the intellect and flexibility to handle the intricate give and take of negotiations, another opportunity to indulge his favourite but ultimately fruitless game of playing his opponents off against one another. Charles had a reasonably strong hand to play that day, although he held no trumps. In the event, he disastrously overplayed it.

In the mid-17th century Woburn Abbey was still essentially an old monastery. Some work had been done in the 1630s and this included a new state bedroom on the first floor. It is possible the fateful meeting took place there.[61] Besides the king and the four officers, two royal secretaries, Berkeley and Sir John Ashburnham, were present. While Berkeley saw the possibilities of the Proposals,[62] the snobbish Ashburnham made little attempt to hide his disdain for the soldiers. Surprisingly the meeting lasted three hours.

But Charles effectively ruled out any deal from the start. Adopting his most haughty and arrogant demeanour, he told the four men: "You cannot do without me; you will fall if I do not sustain you."[63] Berkeley described what happened at the meeting: "his Majesty (not only to the astonishment of Ireton and the rest, but even to mine) entertained them with very tart and bitter discourses, saying sometimes, that he would have no man suffer for his sake, that he repented nothing so much as the Bill against the Lord Strafford;[64] (which though most true, was unpleasant for them to hear;) that he would have the Church established according to the Law by the Proposals."[65]

Despite Charles subsequently softening his tone, Rainborowe had heard enough. He got up and walked out of the meeting. Berkeley again described the drama: "but it was now of the latest. For Col. Rainsborough, (who of all the Army, seemed the least to wish the accord,) in the middle of the conference stole away, and posted to the Army, which he inflamed against the king, with all the artificial malice he had." When the conference ended, the distraught Berkeley pursued Rainborowe to Army HQ at Bedford. "I met with some of the Adjutators, who asked me what his Majesty meant, to entertain their Commissioners so harshly? I told them that Rainsborough had delivered it amiss to them, as indeed, he had, by adding to the truth."

Worse was to follow for Sir John. He spoke to Ireton and other senior officers about what would happen if the king accepted the Proposals and they replied that they would offer them to Parliament. "But if they (Parliament) refused them, what would they do then? They replied they would not tell me" although they were certain they would prevail over Parliament.

"When I appeared not fully satisfied with this reply, Rainsborough spoke out these words: 'If they (Parliament) will not agree, we will make them'; to which the whole company assented." [66] This sounds ruthless but was in fact little more than Cromwell had told the agitators at the General Council meeting in Reading earlier in the month. There Cromwell had said he would not be opposed to a "purged Parliament" which saw not only the 11 members barred but also 20-30 more.[67] On the face of it, Rainborowe was merely repeating the views of his senior officer. More deeply, there was ominous intent to his words.

There was clearly something afoot. Tantalisingly, Berkeley does not say what it was that made him feel Rainborowe seemed to want an agreement less than his colleagues. This was the Colonel's second encounter with His Majesty. The first, a year or so before at the end of the siege of Oxford, was an indirect one. Charles told Rainborowe, through his courtiers, that he wished to surrender but then slipped away in disguise. From deceitful behaviour, the defeated king had now, in Rainborowe's view, adopted the pose of an aggressive and arrogant monarch. What had the war been about if the king could still behave in this imperious way? If he was already harbouring doubts about the value of a settlement with a man like Charles - and Berkeley clearly thought he was - this encounter can only have strengthened his opinion. It was a crucial awakening for him. But were the doubts simply about the wisdom of a settlement with a man like Charles - to which Cromwell and Ireton were still committed - or did they run more deeply, questioning whether England needed a king at all? His exasperation at Charles's conduct, which he lost no time in passing onto the soldiers, did Charles's cause immense damage. But just as clearly, it strengthened Rainborowe's position as a leading radical. More crucially, it also confirmed a growing split in the Army, with Rainborowe and Cromwell on opposing sides.

But events in London were now becoming urgent. Brushing aside the abortive meeting with Charles, Fairfax the next day moved his men nearer London to Colnbrook. The Presbyterians in

Parliament, still recklessly rattling their sabres, recalled the 11 members, appointed Edward Massie as their new commander in chief of all forces in the City and ordered Fairfax not to come within 30 miles of London. Meanwhile, Charles, who also seemed to have closed his eyes to reality, tried to arrange another meeting with Lauderdale. His guards had other ideas and threw the Scotsman out. Then on August 2, when further violence broke out in London between Independents and Presbyterian factions, Fairfax decided enough was enough. The next day, he sent his troops in.

After a rendezvous on Hounslow Heath on August 3, attended by at least 20,000 men, 14 peers and about 100 MPs,[68] Fairfax sent a brigade under Rainborowe to march over Kingston Bridge into Surrey, ready to move into Southwark. This was a shrewd choice by the general. Southwark, along with Westminster, was among the more radical areas of the capital and likely to be more accommodating than the Presbyterian-inclined City. But Rainborowe was also well known in the borough. He had property there and had recruited much of his regiment there. For his soldiers it was more a homecoming than an occupation.

At two the next morning, a 4,000-strong force of horse and infantry, comprising the regiments of Rainborowe, Pride and Colonels John Hewson and Edmund Rossiter,[69] entered Southwark without any opposition. They were greeted by Sir John Hardwick, leader of Southwark's trained bands. He had prepared the way by blocking the southern end of London Bridge, preventing access to the City but allowing any radicals from there to join them in Southwark. Rainborowe's soldiers behaved "very civilly without doing hurt to any; and finding the City Gate on the Bridge shut, and the Port-cullis let down, as also a Guard within; they planted Two Pieces of Ordnance against the Gate, and set a Guard without, and in a short time after the great Fort was yielded to them."[70]

An Army newsletter of August 5 triumphantly reported: "The forts in Southwarke were yesterday delivered up to Col Rainborow."[71] Clarendon, the Royalist, gave a similar picture: "They sent Col. Raynsborough with a brigade of horse and foot and cannon, at Hampton Court, to possess Southwark, and those works which secured that end of London Bridge; which he did with so little noise, that in one night's march he found himself master, without any opposition, not only of the borough of Southwark but of all the works and forts which were there to defend it; the soldiers within (the City) shaking hands with those without, and refusing to obey their officers which were to command them." When the City woke in the morning, it found that London Bridge was "possessed by the enemy."[72] The Army was master of London. Rainborowe had taken the City without a shot being fired. He was the hero of the hour.

Fairfax next increased his pressure on the City's Common Council. Having secured all the forts to the east, the general demanded the surrender of all those in the west by 6pm.[73] Clarendon said the Council "humbly submitted."[74] On August 5, Fairfax sent three regiment of foot and two of horse into London while marching the rest of his Army up to Hammersmith. Rainborowe's brigade, with laurel leaves in their hats, and Fairfax's lifeguard next escorted the Commons speaker, Lenthall, back to Westminster. The great procession included civilians, ministers and, in carriages, the Army's main supporters from the Lords, among them Lord Saye, and the Earl of Manchester.[75]

But Fairfax was not done. Two days later, he ordered a grand Army parade through the City. Lifeguards, trains of artillery and 20 regiments gathered at Hyde Park and, to the accompaniment of music, marched eastwards to Cheapside. From there, the soldiers spread out through the streets until eight in the evening gathering the applause and support of the people of London. Their job done, the men crossed London Bridge and went to their quarters in Surrey and Kent. This blatant show of force served two purposes: the Army's "friends" in Westminster were reminded just how much they needed its protection, while the Presbyterians were forcefully made to face up to their total defeat by the Army they so hated.

Rainborowe, in his hour of triumph, seems to have made little attempt to capitalise on his new found status as deliverer of London. He stayed in the capital but slipped from view emerging only at the end of the month living with his brother, William, in the latter's cottage in Fulham to the west of the City. Fairfax rewarded him, however, with an eminent place on the Committee of Officers. Rainborowe was one of the 12 officers on this committee that Fairfax ordered was to "receive and take into consideration all businesses which shall be by me referred or shall otherwise be tendered unto you, that are of public and common concernment to the Army or Kingdom." The general further decreed that if only three of this committee sat, one of them had to be Cromwell, Ireton, Rainborowe or Robert Hammond. The committee also had the power to appoint any sub-committee, made up from officers and agitators at headquarters.[76] Despite the rumblings of discontent about the Proposals, Rainborowe remained firmly at the Army's top table.

There is no evidence that Rainborowe took part in the recriminations in the City after the Army's occupation which saw many Presbyterians, including the Lord Mayor and three aldermen, thrown in the Tower of London accused of treason. Many of the senior officers retreated from the City when the Army set up its new headquarters in Putney. Five miles from London, it was near enough for the Army to move quickly back in if there was further opposition but also close enough for the London radicals to keep in touch with the soldiers. It also helped the officer MPs, such as Cromwell and Rainborowe, to get to Westminster more easily.

The part that leading Presbyterian MPs played in the unrest towards the end of July is cloudy. Sir William Waller, one of the 11 accused MPs, admitted that he knew about the petition and even spoke to apprentices about its presentation. Holles, on the other hand, denied all knowledge of events preceding the Army occupation. Although he admitted attending a dinner with others of the 11 in an inn near the Commons on July 22, he said he "did not hear the hubbub at the House" and "resolved not to go." This considerably stretches belief.[77] It is far more likely they were lurking with intent, in the hope the disturbances and the intimidating pressure on the Independents might give them a way back to their former ascendancy. It was not to be. In the light of the Army's occupation, many of the 11 slipped away by boat in the next few days to the continent. This was to have repercussions for the Navy's vice-admiral, Sir William Batten.

It was a sign of the growing influence and confidence of the radicals, both in and outside the Army, that the taking of London and the conquest of their Presbyterian persecutors were not enough. In fact the occupation of London marked the start of an intensification of the radicals' campaign. Even as the subdued Parliament redressed many of the soldiers' grievances, radicals called three times for the expulsion of all MPs who had continued to sit in the House after July 26.[78] They were unsuccessful but it merely emphasised the burgeoning split. Nor were things much calmer between the Army and Parliament. When the Army issued its *Remonstrance*, which called for both a friendly attitude to the king and for the MPs who had sat after July 26 to be brought to heel, the Lords quickly approved it. Not so the Commons which needed the menacing presence of Cromwell, Ireton, Rainborowe and all the other officer-MPs before it would sanction it. This echoed Rainborowe's frank admission to Berkeley in the aftermath of the disastrous meeting with the king that the Army would make Parliament bend to its will.

Outside the Army, radicals were adopting an increasingly strident anti-monarchism. Lilburne, Overton, now also in prison, and Wildman had become openly critical of both the Proposals and the Army's grandees. While he said nothing publicly, Rainborowe had also moved away from the Army's aim of a deal with the king. Two distinct camps were forming in the Army: those who supported the Proposals and those who opposed them and any deal with the king. In the Commons something similar was happening, with a split among the Independents between those who backed a deal with Charles, the 'royal' Independents, and those who opposed one, the

Commonwealthsmen. The latter were led by the republican Henry Marten, Rainborowe's ally. It was perhaps inevitable that when the Army set up its HQ in Putney at the end of August, the agitators pointedly set up a rival centre across the Thames in Hammersmith. Rainborowe probably joined his fellow officers in Putney. But the home of his similarly radical brother, William, in Fulham, where he was staying, was also just a short distance from Hammersmith.

Criticism from the radicals grew sufficiently loud for Cromwell to go to the Tower of London in early September to see Lilburne. The offer was release from prison and a place in the Army in return for Lilburne shutting up. The cantankerous and irascible Lilburne not only refused point blank but, a few days later, put out a savage pamphlet entitled *The Juglers Discovered*.[80] In it, Lilburne excoriatingly wrote: "But above all the rest be sure not to trust your great officers at the Generalls quarters, no further than you can throw an Ox." These men, Lilburne claimed, had "by their plausible yet cunning policies, most unjustly stolen the power both from your honest Generall, and your too flexible Agjutators."[80]

From the standpoint of Cromwell, Ireton and most other senior officers, an Army-inspired settlement with the king remained by far the best option. The other options were a settlement based loosely on the terms of the Newcastle Propositions, which would have delivered Presbyterianism as the national religion, or a deal with the Scots, which could have involved an invasion of England and renewed fighting. The matter was urgent as Parliament, despite being relieved of its Presbyterian leaders, had, on August 27, approved a new set of terms for a settlement. These were due to be put to Charles on September 7.

To reach their goal, the Army grandees had to move fast. But radicals, already suspicious of too lenient a settlement with the king, had good reason to be wary of Cromwell and Ireton. According to Berkeley, after the July meeting with the four officers and the subsequent occupation of London, his colleague Ashburnham was sending daily messages from the king to Cromwell.[81] Huntingdon, in his letter explaining why he resigned his commission, claimed to have been the go-between for many of these missives. He wrote that both Ireton and Cromwell assured the king that Parliament's Propositions were likely to come to nothing. The latter claimed they were nothing more than an attempt "to satisfy the Scott, which otherwise might be troublesome." Both, said Huntingdon, sent the king frequent assurances that the Army would stand by its own Proposals, which were far more lenient than Parliament's.

On one occasion, Ireton allegedly told Charles: "That they would purge, and purge, and never leave purging the Houses, till they had made them of such a Temper as should do His Majesty's Business; and rather than they would fall short of what was promised, he would join with French, Spaniard, Cavalier, or any that would join with him, to force them to it." The king made clear he did not believe a word of this by replying: "That if they do, they would do more than He durst do." [82] The Royalists were not slow to cash in on this falling out of their enemies, putting about a rumour that a deal was done with Cromwell who would be made Earl of Essex and captain of the King's Guard.[83] It merely increased the radicals' suspicions.

By mid-September, as Cromwell was fervently pushing the Proposals as a basis for a settlement, Rainborowe had reached the opposite conclusion: there was no further point in doing business with a slippery and deceitful man like Charles. To exacerbate the situation, the two had also got into a personal row during the month over the appointment of a new vice-admiral for the Navy. It resulted in a bitter and heated exchange in which Rainborowe said one of them must die.

Sources differ as to where this clash took place and over which of their disagreements. But most suggest it happened on September 16. On that day, there were meetings of both the General Council of the Army and the Commons and Lords Admiralty and Cinque Ports committee. However there was also a second meeting of the Admiralty Committee on September 17. It is possible the row took place there.

The General Council was held in the morning in Putney to discuss the Heads of the Proposals. By this stage many of the radicals supported Rainborowe in opposing a deal with Charles. These included the Army chaplain Hugh Peter,[84] who accused Cromwell of being too much the royal courtier. At the meeting, Cromwell managed to push through a process for the adoption of the Proposals by Parliament. This envisaged a series of Bills to secure the liberties of the people and privileges of Parliament and also to settle the issue of control of the militia. As soon as these measures received the Royal Assent, Parliament would then pass an Act to secure the rights of the king.

But Rainborowe strongly opposed these plans and, during the heated debate, is said to have told Cromwell "one of them must not live," according to a Royalist Sir Edward Ford.[85] Gardiner gives a similar account, saying Cromwell "exposed himself to a fierce attack from a vigorous minority which had come to the conclusion that it was useless to negotiate further with Charles. In the course of the discussions, Rainsborough, by whom this minority was led, so far lost his temper as to tell Cromwell that 'one of them must not live.'"[86] In his version, Clarendon merely speaks of "high language" between the pair, including the death threat but does not say where the exchange took place. But he adds with perception: "Cromwell grows distasteful to the Army" and that "regiments of the Independents have much complaint of the great officers."[87]

But a more detailed and believable account of the row comes from Sir Lewis Dyve, a Royalist prisoner in the Tower. From his cell, Dyve was sending regular bulletins to the king, made up of gossip, speculation and the odd fact while also developing an unlikely friendship with Lilburne.[88] It seems to have been an open secret that Rainborowe, not always the most discreet of men, had set his sights on the post of vice-admiral in the Navy and Dyve, like others, sensed it would lead to a clash with Cromwell. As early as September 5, Dyve wrote to Charles: "Cromwell, of a long time having had a strict league of friendship with Rainsborough, whose credit with the common soldiers is not inferior to any officer of the army, hath lately put such a slur upon Rainsborough for the Vice Admiral's place, whereof he thought himself secure, as hath quite cancelled the bond of their former friendship." This suggests the argument between Rainborowe and Cromwell over the vice-admiralship began at least in early September and Cromwell had made his opposition known to Rainborowe's appointment right from the start.

Dyve went onto suggest a plan to stop Rainborowe was drawn up by his foes. "And the subtlety done, to bestow the place upon some other man whose disposition was observed by some to look with an eye of jealousy upon Rainsborough as having too great a power already in their militia, who knowing him to be a man of such a temper as would rather act according to his own than other men's principles, conceived it might be dangerous to trust him with a place of so great a command at sea."

Cromwell, according to Dyve, wanted someone more flexible in the role but wished to avoid offending Rainborowe. He apparently agreed that Lord Northumberland, a prominent Army supporter in the Lords, to propose this other man. Cromwell could then support his "old friend Rainsborough" knowing the vote would go to the more biddable man. In the end, Dyve said the conspirators decided unanimously to appoint one man so that no one offended Rainborowe and he and Cromwell could remain friends. This seems wildly farfetched, especially as the man to be appointed was named as Deane, "a meane person, formerly a servant to Rainsborough's father."[90] Not the least problem with this entertaining scenario was that the vice-admiral's job, at that time, was not vacant.

It was a few days later - and Rainborowe, as suspected, meant to grab it for himself. The incumbent was Sir William Batten who had served Parliament well in the war. But in these changing times, his position was now precarious. He was not only known to have Presbyterian leanings but also a wish for a moderate, negotiated settlement with the king. When there was evidence of Charles's planned escape in November 1646 from the Scots who were holding him in Newcastle, Batten was sent with a squadron of ships to Tynemouth. His orders were to make sure two ships which had mysteriously arrived in the port, a Dutch man of war and a Dunkirker (a ship belonging to privateers in the Channel) did not leave and that all other ships were searched as they left to make sure the king was not aboard.

But while there, his chaplain Samuel Kem preached a sermon to the king calling for a negotiated truce. It seems likely that Batten was sending a personal message to the monarch.[90] This was bad enough in Independent eyes but worse followed. His next and far graver mistake was to help five of the 11 members to escape the country. He had been told by the Admiralty and Cinque Ports committee on August 13 that the 11, who also had passes from Speaker Lenthall, could leave England. Batten had stopped the ship in which the men were travelling but, on the strength of his orders, had allowed them to continue.

But by the time the Committee met again on September 16, its membership had substantially changed. Cromwell and Ireton remained members but they had now been joined by Rainborowe, his Parliamentary ally, Marten, Sir Henry Vane, Sir Henry Mildmay and Nathaniel Fiennes, son of Lord Saye. The new committee was basically packed with radicals ready to back Rainborowe. Batten was duly stitched up. At the meeting on September 16, the same day as the General Council meeting, it ordered Batten to appear before it the next day "that some matters objected against him may be then imparted to him."

Batten guessed what was in the wind and at the meeting the next day, held in the home of Sir Abraham Williams in Westminster, resigned before the case against him was put. He told his foes that he had "served the Parliaments commands faithfully" and that he would "still do so if they shall please to continue him in that charge."[91] After Batten's resignation, the Admiralty minutes recorded that Rainborowe was then nominated captain of the *Happy Endurance* and commander-in-chief of the winter guard. He had got his job.

Batten had no doubts as to why he had been targeted. He later claimed: "I was displaced by a committee at the head-quarters at Putney, with the advice of the adjutators though nothing was objected, but my suffering some of the 11 members to go beyond the seas, when all of them had the Speaker's pass: this, and because I was not of the temper of the army, were judged sufficient to have me dismissed."[92]

But Batten, although he had a point, was being disingenuous. By the late summer, early autumn, he was "already scheming to turn the navy against the army and its Independent allies." There were constant rumours of strong links with the Scots through his staunch Presbyterianism. He had in fact contacted the Scottish earl of Lauderdale saying he would declare for the Scots and bring both English Presbyterians and 22 ships with him, provided the Scots could victual them. The Scots could not mange this so Lauderdale contacted the French ambassador to Scotland to ask if he could help.[93]

Perhaps equally damning for him, the Lords had received on September 14, two days before the admiralty committee met, two sworn statements. One was from an Andrew Gosfright, sworn at Sandwich in Kent, that "That he had heard Captain Batten ... say that the Army, notwithstanding they did hold the King in suspense, would in the conclusion take off His Head." The second was from John Springham who said he heard Batten say "That he feared the Army would not deal fairly with the King."[94] Despite the political chaos of mid-1647, this was far beyond what Parliament could tolerate from its senior admiral. His "conduct was treasonable by any normal standards"[95] and that was what sealed his fate. The incident of the five MPS merely confirmed Parliament's darkest thoughts. Batten was no longer with them.

However it was perhaps not so much the dismissal of Batten that created alarm among the Presbyterians and Royalists as the installation of Rainborowe in his place. Putting aside Rainborowe's naked ambition for the post, it was, without much doubt, a political appointment. With hindsight, it is easy to conclude it was a calamitous choice. But at the time, the politics of the country were fast moving. The Royalists were stirring; the Presbyterians were increasingly resentful at being pushed aside; the Scots were, as ever, threatening to invade. It was not farfetched to imagine an alliance of the Presbyterians Scots and the Presbyterian Navy. There was little to stop Batten defecting and it would have done the Independents' cause - as well as that of the NMA - serious damage.

If the Independents really believed that Batten was about to defect - and they had good grounds to think so - they had to act quickly. The only means they had was to remove him and replace him with one of their own. This indicates why there were rumours of Batten's dismissal well before the meetings on September 16 and 17. The obvious choice to replace him, perhaps the only one, was Rainborowe. He was both a competent mariner and proven leader.

But the sharp difference between Rainborowe's politics and those of the seamen, made it an obvious risk. It was perhaps the lesser of the two evils facing the Independents, losing the fleet or risking a naval revolt. Probably it was this calculation that persuaded Cromwell and Ireton to go along with the appointment rather than the bluster from Rainborowe. It is noteworthy that throughout Rainborowe's time as vice admiral, Fairfax invariably referred to him as Colonel. Perhaps the general and others always saw it as a temporary post. Whatever the fine calculations, Batten's dismissal and Rainborowe's appointment exacerbated the differences between the army and the navy. The new vice admiral was not likely to have an easy run.

Dyve rather gleefully added the colour to Rainborowe's appointment in a letter to the king the next day. "That business between Rainsborough and Crumwell which I formerly mentioned unto your Majesty, has been so happily managed as has set Rainsborough in defiance against Crumwell." Dyve sets the scene by telling Charles that when the Juncto - the committee - met, Cromwell, Ireton, Vane and Oliver St. John were all present. "And as they were there in consultation Rainsborough came thither and went into the chamber where they were, where after they had continued for some time with great silence, the doors being shut, Crumwell was heard to be very loud by a captain that sat in the next room, who came along with Rainsborough, and Rainsborough thereupon clapping his hand upon the table with violence rose from the board, and told Crumwell aloud that he would no longer be abused by him under the colour of friendship, and vowed unto him that he would have the place or make him repent it."

After this, Dyve reported that the others calmed the two antagonists down. But it did not last long. "Rainsborough again flew from the board and told Crumwell flatly that it should cost one of them their lives but that he would have the place, for that he had better deserved it than Crumwell had done to honour he took upon him, so as the company were enforced again to interpose, fearing they would have fallen unto blows." Dyve said the committee then agreed that Rainborowe should get the job he wanted "and so the Juncto broke up in a seeming friendship one all sides." Dyve went on to reveal that his source, the captain in the next room, was Captain Thomas Creamer from Rainborowe's regiment and "a great friend to Rainsborough."[96]

It is not clear exactly what Cromwell's objections were to Rainborowe getting the commander's job. It may be – although this seems unlikely – that Cromwell was trying to protect Batten in his job. More likely, Cromwell feared that Rainborowe's increasingly extreme views would have made him a liability in a Navy predisposed to the Presbyterians. In the event Cromwell's fears proved all too right. But there seems also to be a measure of personal animosity and rivalry between the two men. They were Parliament's two most successful soldiers now on different and irreconcilable paths in pursuit of a settlement of the kingdom.

More clashes were bound to occur, and the next one came six days later. On September 21, the Commons had concluded that Charles's latest response to their peace proposals amounted to a rejection. The following day, as the House discussed its future relations with the king, Marten proposed a vote of No Address, that Parliament should have no further dealings with the king. His followers were a small minority and the vote was duly lost by 84 to 34 but Cromwell acted as a teller for the majority group while Rainborowe, bringing out both their political and personal hostility, was a teller for the minority. Marten tried to get his motion through the following day but again lost heavily, 70 to 23.[97] But by that time both Cromwell and Rainborowe had returned to Putney for a meeting of the General Council. Nothing of their rows was mentioned at this meeting.

The vote was proof of the split in the Independent party. It was now "two factions, the one under its old leaders still desirous of an understanding with the king; the other, which may fairly be styled Republican, aiming under the guidance of Marten and Rainsborough at the abolition of monarchy."[98] Cromwell himself remained bitter and angry at the conduct of Rainborowe. According to Huntingdon, Cromwell wanted Rainborowe out of both the Army and Parliament and even saw him and his allies as a threat to the safety of the king.

Huntingdon wrote: "After this, the Delay of the Settlement of the Kingdom was excused, upon the Commotions of Colonel Martin and Colonel Rainsbrough, with their Adherents; the Lieutenant General saying, 'That speedy Course must be taken for outing of them the House and Army, because they were now putting the Army into a Mutiny.'" Cromwell, according to Huntingdon, accused Rainborowe of having a hand in the printing of a provocative pamphlet, *An Agreement of the People*, and in league with new, even more radical agents who had attached themselves to the cavalry regiments.

Huntingdon claimed Cromwell often said of the radicals that "These People were a giddy-headed Party, and that there was no Trust nor Truth in them." The lieutenant-general had followed up his views by writing to Colonel Whalley, who was guarding the king at Hampton Court, "That His Majesty's Person was in Danger by them, and that he should keep Out Guards to prevent them;" which Letter was presently shewed to the King, by Colonel Whaley."[99]

This conversation probably took place weeks after the No Address vote as *An Agreement of the People* was not written until the end of October. But it suggests the lieutenant-general was in no mood to compromise. Battle lines were drawn between Cromwell and his "old friend Rainsborough."

Notes for Chapter Five

1. James A. Sharpe, *Early Modern England: A Social History 1550-1760*, (London, 1987), p. 23.
2. Paul Slack, *The Impact of Plague in Tudor and Stuart England* (Oxford, 1985).
3. Donald. C. Coleman, *The Economy of England 1450-1750*, (Oxford, 1977), p. 94.
4. Diane Purkiss, *The English Civil War: A People's History*, (London, 2007), p. 340.
5. Austin Woolrych, *Soldiers and Statesmen*, (Oxford, 1987), p. 3.
6. Christopher Hill, *World Turned Upside Down*, (Penguin, 3rd edition, 1991), p. 14, quoting from G.H. Sabine (ed.), *The Works of Gerrard Winstanley*, (Cornell, 1941), p. 252.
7. Tanner MS lix (ii), f. 444.
8. John Winthrop, *History of New England*, vol ii, pp. 428 and 458-60.
9. Richard Baxter, *Reliquiae Baxterianae*, ed. Matthew Sylvester, (London, 1696), p. 56.
10. Tanner MS lix (ii), f. 444.
11. David Underdown, *Pride's Purge*, (Oxford, 1971), p. 71. I am indebted to Underdown for his deep analysis of the shifting allegiances of the post war Parliament.
12. Woolrych, *Soldiers and Statesmen*, p. 3.
13. Gentles, *New Model Army*, pp. 49-52.
14. *Commons Journal*, v, p.129.
15. Gentles, *New Model Army*, p. 151.
16. Hill, *World Turned Upside Down*, p. 25.
17. Philip Skippon became an MP at the same time as Rainborowe but held more moderate views. Parliament called him down from Newcastle, where he was governor, to suppress the first petition circulating among the soldiers. He was well respected by the Army but terrible wounds suffered at Naseby rendered him unfit for further field service. He shortly resigned his commander-in-chief role.
18. *Lords Journal*, ix, pp. 151-7.
19. *Commons Journal*, v, p. 158.
20. Ibid., p. 169.
21. Ibid., p. 193.
22. Rainborowe's letter to Lenthall from Culham, dated June 1: Tanner MS vol. 58 (i), fol. 125; Edward Peacock, *Archaeologia*, vol 46, pp. 22-3.
23. *Clarke Papers*, i, p. 112.
24. Ibid., p. 114N.
25. Edmund Chillenden was one of the five officers who presented *The Vindication of the Officers of the Army* to Parliament. He was also the man who tipped off the Army of Parliament's plan to seize the magazine at Oxford. In the late 1630s, he was a religious radical and close associate of John Lilburne, one of the emerging "Leveller" leaders.
26. *Clarke Papers*, i, pp.105-6. See also Woolrych, *Soldiers and Statesmen*, p. 100-1.
27. The Earl of Clarendon during the war years was Sir Edward Hyde, a staunch supporter of Charles I. Had Rainborowe ever got to Jersey, he would have found Hyde in residence writing his great work *The History of the Rebellion and Civil Wars in England*.
28. Clarendon MS 29, 2522.

29. Denzil Holles, *Memorial of Denzil Lord Holles* in Francis Maseres, *Select Tracts Relating to the Civil Wars,* (London, 1815), vol i, p. 239.
30. Ibid., pp.245-6.
31. Barry Coward, *The Stuart Age: England 1603-1714*, (Harlow, 1994), p. 161.
32. H. N. Brailsford, *The Levellers and the English Revolution*, (London, 1961), p. 199.
33. *Clarke Papers*, i, p.119.
34. *Commons Journal*, v, pp.160-1.
35. The two votes were, respectively, were 86-3 with four abstentions and 82-5 with six officers absent. *Clarke Papers*, i, pp.108-9.
36. *Clarke Papers*, i, pp. 118-9.
37. *Army Book of Declarations*, (London, 1647), p. 23.
38. Ibid., pp. 26-7.
39. *Lords Journal*, ix, pp. 252-9.
40. The Common Council is, in effect, the City's 'parliament' where the main decisions on governance are made.
41. *Army Book of Declarations*, pp.36-46.
42. Ibid., p. 37.
43. Ibid., p. 44.
44. Ibid., pp. 47-50.
45. Ibid., p. 47.
46. Ibid., pp. 57-67. It was issued on June 23.
47. Ibid., p. 64.
48. Ibid., pp. 72-5. It was sent from Reading on July 8.
49. Philip, 4th Baron Wharton (1613-1696) came from a staunch Puritan family, which backed Parliament in the war. He was a close associate of Cromwell, served on the Committee of Both Kingdoms and supported the Army in 1647.
50. The first Viscount Saye and Sele (1582-1662) was a long-term opponent of both James I and Charles I. He had business interests in New England with the Earl of Warwick, Lord Brooke and John Pym – all prominent opponents of Charles. He emerged in 1647 as a strong supporter of the Army.
51. Samuel Dennis Glover, 'The Putney Debates: Popular versus Elitist Republicanism', *Past and Present*, 164, (Oxford, 1999), p. 59.
52. *Londons Liberty in Chains* (London, 1646) E359(17); quoted in David Wootton, 'The Leveller Movement' in J.H. Burns and Mark Goldie (eds.), *The Cambridge History of Political Thought 1450-1700*, (Cambridge, 1991), pp. 428-9.
53. *The Charters of London* (London, 1646), E366(12) p. 4; quoted in Wootton, 'Leveller Movement', pp. 428-9.
54. James Harrington (1611-1677) was a gentlemen groom of the royal bedchamber during 1647-8 but his views subsequently changed to those of a republican. He published *The Commonwealth of Oceana* in 1656, despite Cromwell's initial attempts to suppress it; this envisaged an ideal, Utopian republic. Blair Worden, the best historian on republicanism in the 1640s and 1650s described Harrington as "the most distinguished thinker of English Machiavellianism." See Worden, 'Classical Republicanism and the Puritan Revolution' in Hugh Lloyd-Jones, Valerie Pearl and Worden (eds.), *History and Imagination: Essays in honour of H. R. Trevor-Roper*, (London, 1981), p. 184.

55. Woolrych, *Soldiers and Statesmen*, p. 153..
56. Abbot, Clarke and Rolf came, respectively, from the regiments of Colonel John Okey, Colonel Sir Hardress Waller and Colonel Robert Hammond.
57. *Clarke Papers*, i, pp. 178-9.
58. Ibid., p. 213.
59. The 12 agitators on the committee are not named in Clarke.
60. For full text see John Rushworth, *Historical Collections*, vii. p. 731.For a summary, see Gentles, *New Model Army*, pp.182-4.
61. I am grateful to Chris Gravett, curator of Woburn Abbey, for this information.
62. Berkely later wrote: "never was a Crown (that had been so near lost) so cheaply recovered, as his Majesty's would be, if they agreed upon such terms." *Memoirs of Sir John Berkeley*, Maseres, i, pp. 366-7.
63. Ibid., p. 368.
64. Thomas Wentworth, Earl of Strafford, a leading counsellor to the king during his personal rule of 1629-40, was condemned by an Act of Attainder after Parliament's attempts to impeach him failed. Despite promises to the contrary, Charles signed his death warrant and Strafford was executed in May, 1641.
65. Berkeley, *Memoirs*, Maseres, i, p. 368.
66. Ibid., p. 369.
67. *Clarke Papers*, 1, p. 192 and pp.205-6.
68. Rushworth, *Historical Collections*, vii, pp. 731-800.
69. In this operation, Rossiter's regiment was commanded by Lt. Col. Philip Twistleton. Rossiter, a Presbyterian, had left the Army by this stage.
70. Rushworth, *Historical Collections*, vii, pp.731-800.
71. *Clarke Papers*, 1, p. 220.
72. Clarendon, *History of the Great Rebellion*, book x, p. 247.
73. *Army Book of Declarations*, p. 109.
74. Clarendon, *History*, p. 248.
75. Clarendon MSS, 30, fo. 33.
76. Clarke Papers, i, pp. 223-4. Fairfax issued his notice of this new committee on August 29, 1647.
77. Holles, *Memorial* in Maseres, *Select Tracts*, vol i, pp. 273-9. Patricia Crawford, *Denzil Holles 1598-1680 A Study of his Political Career*, (London, 1979), p. 156.
78. The first attempt was the 'Humble address of the Agitators on August 14, followed by the 'Resolution and Protestation' on August 23 and a third plea to Fairfax on September 2.
79. Cromwell met Lilburne on either September 5 or 6. *The Juglers Discovered* was published on September 8. Long excerpts from the pamphlet also appeared in *Mercurius Pragmaticus*, a new publication by Marchamont Nedham, later a leading republican.
80. John Lilburne, *The Juglers Discovered*, (London, 1647), pp. 10 and 12. E409 (22).
81. Berkeley, *Memoirs*, Maseres, i, p. 370.
82. Sir Robert Huntingdon, 'Sundry Reasons inducing Robert Huntingdon to lay down his Commission, humbly presented to the Honourable Houses of Parliament', *Lords Journal*, x, pp. 406-14.
83. Berkeley, *Memoirs*, Maseres, i, p. 371.

84. Hugh Peter (1598-1660) was an unorthodox preacher who left England during the Personal Rule for Holland and later New England. He returned in 1641 and got involved in the politics of the time. He later became an Army chaplain. He was executed in 1660 for his part in Charles' death.
85. Letter from Sir Edward Ford to Lord Hopton, dated September 20 in Clarendon MS 30, fo. 67. Ford was a Royalist who served in the war in a regiment of horse under Hopton, a prominent Royal commander in the south west. It is not clear how Ford came about this piece of information.
86. Samuel Rawson Gardiner, *History of the Great War*, (London, 1884-6), vol iii, pp. 364-5.
87. Clarendon MSS, vol 30, 67.
88. Caution is needed. Dyve, in his letters to the king, was certainly currying favour by passing bits of inside information about the enemy, while Lilburne was probably deluding himself about his eminence in the radical hierarchy of autumn 1647. Both may well have been gilding the lily.
89. Sir Lewis Dyve, *The Tower of London Letter-book*, ed. H. G. Tibbutt, (Bedfordshire Historical Society, 1958), vol 38, pp. 84-5.
90. Bernard Capp, 'Naval Operations' in John Philips Kenyon and Jane Ohlmeyer, *The Civil Wars A Military History of England, Scotland, and Ireland 1638-1660*, (Oxford, 1998), p. 178.
91. Minute Book of the Committee of the admiralty 1646-8, Admiralty Papers 7/673, 379, 381-2, 413.
92. A Declaration of Sir William Batten Late Vice-Admiral for the Parliament, 1648. Quoted in D. E. Kennedy, 'The English Naval Revolt of 1648', *English Historical Review*, 77, 303, (April, 1962), pp. 248-9.
93. Capp, 'Naval Operations', p. 178.
94. Lords Journal, ix, p. 433.
95. Capp, 'Naval Operations', p. 179.
96. Dyve, *Letter-book*, p. 89. This is the same officer previously referred to as Captain Cramer.
97. *Commons Journal*, v, pp. 312-5.
98. Gardiner, *Great War*, vol iii, pp. 200-1.
99. Huntingdon, "Sundry Reasons", *Lords Journal*, x, pp. 406-14. He is conflating events which happened over several weeks.

Chapter Six: The Attempted Army Coup

The weeks after the failure of the vote of No Address were the lull before the storm. For Rainborowe it brought the good news that the Commons had approved his appointment as captain of the *Happy Endurance* and as vice-admiral of the fleet for the winter guard. On the same day, September 27, 1647, it voted him £1,000 as part of his arrears in pay for his service in the Army.[1] Just over a week later the Lords confirmed the appointment and both Houses then agreed he should also be appointed commander-in-chief of the fleet.[2]

Rainborowe had got his wish but it was still the Army, not the Navy, which occupied his immediate thoughts. Fairfax had called meetings of the General Council in St Mary's Church by the Thames in Putney on September 30 and October 7 and 14. All had passed quietly, apparently, with discussions of arrears and quartering. On the first, at least, Parliament was beginning to act. It set up a committee on October 22, which included Rainborowe, and ordered it to meet the next day and report "with all convenient speed" on how the problem of arrears could be resolved.[3]

But the split in the Army remained. The discontent, now focused far more on the prospect of Cromwell and Ireton reaching a settlement with Charles than on the soldiers' grievances, rumbled on. If Cromwell still retained the support of Fairfax and most of the senior officers, the rank and file were firmly against any deal. The men who had emerged as their leaders were a tightly knit group far more opposed to the monarchy than the Levellers' leaders, Lilburne and Overton. The pivotal figure was Henry Marten, the avowed republican. His followers included Wildman, his Berkshire neighbour and "intimate friend"[4] and Petty. The latter had known Sexby, one of the original agitators since the early 1630s.

It is probable that Wildman and Petty met as members of radical circles in London in the mid-1640s. Rainborowe was a close ally of Marten in Parliament – he had backed the latter's motion of No Address while Marten had championed his case for the vice admiralty. Rainborowe would almost certainly have met Sexby in the General Council meetings and also Wildman and Petty when they attended Army HQ. According to an earlier biographer by this time Rainborowe "was considered to be the most active and prominent among those who now hardly disguised their desire for a republican form of government."[5]

Wildman, Petty and Rainborowe also appeared on an intriguing secret code Marten drew up in the autumn of 1647.[6] Walwyn was also listed, as were adversaries, such as the king, Cromwell, Ireton and Fairfax, as well as many of the Army's regiments. But neither Lilburne nor Overton were on it which says a lot about the attitude of Marten's cronies to them. They were clearly not in his inner circle. In the code, Marten referred to Wildman as A, Rainborowe as W, Petty as E, Cromwell as L and the king as G. What it was actually for is difficult to say as no letters between the main players survive even if they existed.

The safest surmise may be that when Marten, Wildman, Petty and Rainborowe corresponded or perhaps even spoke, they referred to themselves and others on the list by their given code letter. The one certain thing is that the republican Marten saw Wildman, Petty and Rainborowe as his close allies. They with Sexby, were the leading radicals who spoke at the Putney Debates. They were not followers or disciples of Lilburne or Overton. Their views were different from them. They could be described, in differing degrees, as quasi-republicans. What united them at Putney was their opposition to Charles.

The man very much out of this loop was Lilburne. As he and Overton remained in jail - the Army did little to free them after its occupation of London - they were effectively marginalised. It made Lilburne more irascible than ever. He loudly complained that the agitators were basically in the pockets of the senior officers and that Rainborowe was not to be trusted because of the £1,000 Parliament had voted him. Lilburne's solution was to appoint five new agitators to spur on the existing ones. These newcomers, often referred to as the London agents, were in touch with the original agitators, probably through Sexby, but they never sat on the General Council nor replaced any of the originals.

The lull ended on October 18 when the Agitators presented Fairfax with their latest pamphlet. *The Case of the Armie Truly Stated* had some Leveller influence but it was first and foremost an Army document - eight of its 10 sections dealt with Army issues. Only two dealt with external matters, including some measure of political reform. The likely author was Sexby, an Army man, with the political section possibly written by Wildman.[7] It was signed by some of both the original and new agitators and claimed to speak for the five regiments of horse who were said to be represented by the new agitators.

It is an angry document, a brutal and personal attack on the senior officers not only for moving away from the commitments of the June 14 *Declaration* regarding a settlement with the king but also for doing nothing since the Army's Newmarket rendezvous in June, 1647. One of the strongest charges against them was that they had broken their pledge at the Kingston General Council meeting to purge Parliament. It was a "massive indictment of the senior officers, not only for having rendered the army odious to the people, but also for failing to care adequately for the wants of the rank and file, maimed soldiers and the widows and orphans of the slain."[8]

Fairfax, as careful as ever, laid the document before the next meeting of the General Council on October 21. Cromwell and Ireton, no doubt furious at the charges against them, successfully stopped it being read out. They accused the authors of bringing anarchy and disruption to the Army and began what amounted to a witchhunt to find them. Cromwell believed that Marten and Rainborowe were somehow helping the new agents with their propaganda. As ever, the General Council set up a committee, led by Ireton, to examine *The Case* and summon anyone they wished – that is, flush out the authors. The committee was to report to the next meeting of the General Council on October 28.

Events overtook them. Ireton almost immediately climbed down from his high horse and suggested his committee read *The Case* to see just what just was in it. A statement was then written by the committee about the points to which it objected. Sexby and two other agitators on the committee were sent up to London to talk with the new agents about the statement. It no doubt also gave them the chance to talk with their fellow radicals while in the capital.

But what was next laid before the officers on October 27 was far more than they bargained for. Robert Everard, an agitator in Cromwell's regiment, was sent to Putney not just with the new agents' reply but also with a completely new document. *An Agreement of the People* had been written late in October after a meeting of agitators, agents, soldiers and civilians. Wildman, who wrote it, later told the General Council that "divers country gentlemen" had asked him to "be their mouth."[9] The short, three-page pamphlet, has become one of the most famous documents in English history. Wolfe described it as "a landmark in the history of constitutional theory" and of "anticipating the fundamentals of the American constitution" more than a hundred years later.[10] It was both revolutionary and republican.

It proposed a written constitution and the sovereignty of the people, for whom there should be set, inalienable rights that no Parliament could take away. It proposed that Parliament must be reformed to create more equal constituents, that there should be a parliament every two years and that the power of the parliaments was to be "inferior only to theirs that chose them." Further the pamphlet said there should be religious freedom, no impressment for military service and that everyone should be subject to the law. It ended with a flourish: "These things we declare to be our native rights." The only mention of the king is in the last phrases, which bemoan the fact that the people, despite earning their rights, "are yet made to depend for the settlement of our Peace and Freedom, upon him that intended our bondage, and brought a cruel War upon us."[11] The disdainful tone of the sole reference to Charles as "him" suggests that Wildman had finally joined Rainborowe in seeing no prospect of a settlement with that deeply distrusted man.

There is no evidence that Lilburne had any hand in drawing up the pamphlet or even knew about it. Like *The Case*, its writing stemmed purely from the meetings of the agitators, Wildman and Petty, and drew on both the radical and republican ideas that had been circulating for years. "It is hard for us, at this distance of time, to grasp how revolutionary this document was."[12] When Rainborowe read it for the first time at the Putney Debates (at least he said he did), he immediately gave it his support.

But there was more to come. A day or so before the Debates opened, an anonymous but blistering attack on both the grandees and the monarchy appeared. *A Cal to all the Souldiers* was "overtly republican", with Wildman the probable author.[13] It started with an incitement for soldiers in effect to mutiny and join "the free people of England" to establish the "just liberties and peace of this nation."[14] It accused Cromwell and Ireton of having "become one"[15] with the king and called on soldiers to "avoid them as the most venomous serpents." Officers and Parliament, it said, just wanted to please the king "who hates you and us with an inveterate hatred."[16]

But its most damning indictment was of kingship and of Charles: monarchy was "but the gilded name for tyranny"[17] while Charles himself was described as a "man of blood." This last phrase must have struck a chilling chord with the many who knew their Bible well. It came from Psalms 55, verse 23. The King James' version reads: "bloody and deceitful men shall not live out half their days." The Elizabethan version was: "Men of blood shall not live out half their days." Was Wildman calling for the death of Charles? But there is also more than a hint that Cromwell also should go. "You [the soldiers] have men as fit to govern and others to be removed."[18] Cromwell, Wildman was telling the ranks, was dispensable.

Once again, the grandees were outmanoeuvred, even ambushed, by the agitators. When what became known to history as the Putney Debates began in St Mary's Church on October 28, *An Agreement*, not

The Case was the subject for discussion. Worse, Cromwell and Ireton had again had their reputations publicly shredded by a spokesman for their men. It was not the best start for them. The first exchanges in the Debates made this clear. Brushing aside Ireton's wish that *The Case* be debated, Edward Sexby, the plain-speaking soldier, continued Wildman's theme in *A Cal to all the Souldiers*. The men had, Sexby said, made three mistakes which had caused them misery: they had tried to satisfy all and ended up satisfying nobody, they had tried to please a king and "except we go about to cut all our throats, we shall not please him" and they had tried to please a Parliament of "rotten members."

For this, he blamed Cromwell and Ireton's pursuit of a settlement with Charles. Instead he urged them to study the paper the agitators had put before them – *An Agreement* – to see what was good in it and what could be done to ease the kingdom and quieten the soldiers.[19]

Cromwell insisted he had behaved honourably and that there should be a new attempt to settle with the king. For once, Rainborowe backed him, confirming that Cromwell had indeed been speaking for himself and not the Army in the Commons on the vote of No Address. The Commons had believed it was the wish of the Army that further approaches be made to the king when it had rejected the motion of no Address for a second time. This, Rainborowe said, was not the case.[20] He was not going to let Cromwell forget that he and Ireton were about the only two men in the Army who still wanted a settlement with Charles.

Rainborowe's speeches at the Putney Debates were the only time he stated his political beliefs. There are no letters to family, friends or fellow radicals or indeed any other documents that set out his views. Their origins, therefore, remain unclear. As the son of a wealthy mariner, Rainborowe probably went to a grammar school, though he did not go on to university. At school he would have learned Latin and, as he told the Debates, he read history books. He knew of the many occasions in English history when authority had been challenged. "If writings be true there has been many scufflings between the honest men of England and those that have tryrannized over them" he told the Council.[21]

Like many men in the 1640s, he saw nothing wrong in challenging the power of a king who had behaved badly. He also came from a community with strong Puritan beliefs. For him this meant a code of morals and obedience to his conscience. Again he told the Council: "For my part I think I shall never do anything against conscience, and I shall have those hopes of others." But perhaps strongest of all was his belief in liberty, not just for himself but for all men in England: "That which is dear unto me is my freedome,"[22] he said at Putney. He also believed that the laws of the country should come from the people and if the people did not like laws that they have been under for years, there was no reason Rainborowe could think of for not changing them.[23]

However, his belief in the sovereignty of the people did not translate into full blown republicanism, as it later did for Wildman and Petty. He made that clear on two occasions in the debates. First he said: "It may be thought that I am against the King; I am against him or any other power that would destroy God's people, and I will never be destroyed until I cannot help myself."[24] Later, Rainborowe declared: "I do very much care whether (there be) a king or no, Lords or no Lords, property or no property; and I think if we do not all take care we shall have none of these very shortly."[25]

It seems clear that Rainborowe's quarrel was with Charles the man, not monarchy itself. His opposition to Charles is based on his belief that he is a tyrant not that he is a king. In this sense he differed from John Lilburne who believed all kings were tyrants. Rainborowe's method for combating kings who degenerated into tyrants was to give all men the vote, so making them sovereign of the country. He was proposing a form of constitutional monarchy which the country adopted after the 1688 Revolution which forced James II, Charles's second son, from the throne.

Rainborowe was a leading light among a small group of men, mainly called Levellers by historians but more accurately identified as radicals of various varieties. They sought a more equal society where the people or their representatives were supreme, where the power of kings or lords was checked, where free men had a say in who formed a government and where, perhaps of most importance, there was liberty of conscience - the freedom to worship as you pleased.

The origins of these beliefs are more difficult to pin down. A grammar school education in the 17th century meant a study of the classics but Rainborowe never identified the books he read at school. It may have been classical authors like Aristotle who, like Rainborowe, did not accept that all kings were necessarily tyrants, or Tacitus or even Niccolo Machiavelli, the great propagator of classical republicanism. Closer to home it is possible that he read the radical tracts of men like Lilburne, Overton and Walwyn. His famous defence of the rights of the poor bear a strong resemblance to a passage in the pamphlet *The Charters of London*, probably written by Wildman. This called for the abolition of the property qualification for voting, supporting the argument with the claim that "The poorest he that lives has as true a right to give a vote as well as the richest and greatest."[26]

Just as likely is that Rainborowe's radical views had their origins in his religious beliefs. The Puritans were far more inclined to liberalism and a loose democracy than the stiff, hierarchical Church of England. If there could be religious freedom, why not secular freedom as well? Again Rainborowe is very likely to have been influenced by the men who returned from New England to fight for the Parliamentary cause, several of whom served in his regiment. While some had left England for economic reasons, many had also been spurred to leave by fears that the increasingly autocratic Charles and his Archbishop Laud were taking the church back towards Rome.

But more intriguingly they were, in New England at least, setting up a new kind of society which was more open and free than that of old England. It was where men had a say on how the community was governed, where the power of the most powerful man was controlled and where if this man offended, he could be voted out. This theme echoes through Rainborowe's speeches.

But it is likely that Rainborowe's views were also in part formed by what he saw going on about him. These were epic times with epic events taking place. Political mayhem had degenerated into civil war and the cause, in Rainborowe's eyes, was one man who had oppressed his people. It was this that probably forged his belief that a tyrant like Charles had to be opposed if liberty were to be preserved.

Rainborowe's next intervention in the Debates ranged from a heartfelt plea to some straightforward common sense of which even Cromwell approved. Rainborowe told the Council he had received a letter since his appointment as vice-admiral that told him his regiment had been taken away from him.[27] This raises the unanswered question as to how he was allowed to attend a General Council meeting when no longer in the Army. But Rainborowe clearly saw it differently, telling the Debates: "I am loath to leave the Army with whom I will live and die, insomuch that rather than loose this Regiment of mine the Parliament shall exclude me the House, (or) imprison me; for truly while I am (employed) abroad I will not be undone at home."

He next turns his attention to *An Agreement* in which "many things have engaged me, which, if I had not known they should have been nothing but Good, I would not have engaged in." Next he warned of two dangers facing the Army. The first was division: "Truly I think we are utterly undone if we divide, but I hope that honest things have carried us on thus long, and will keep us together." The second was difficulties where Rainborowe gently mocked "unhappy men" who thought taking up arms against a king would be straightforward. If the cause was just, it was worth pursuing. And, far more seriously, he reminded those who stalled at changing the government of the kingdom that all laws now well established were once new and entrenchments on the power of kings and lords.

Warming to his theme, Rainborowe said he was in favour of any measure that gave power to freeborn men rather than to governments. He urged that two or three days be set aside to consider *An Agreement*. "All that is to be considered is the justness of the thing - and if that be considered then all things are - that there may be nothing to deter us from it, but that we may do that which is just to the people." If *An Agreement* was a just document, Rainborowe said, then the Council should adopt it.

Cromwell answered in placatory tones, saying he was glad Rainborowe was present and that the meeting would enjoy his company longer than expected. Rainborowe, half in jest, half in uncertainty, butted in to say: "If I should not be kicked out."[28] Even by the first session of the debates, Rainborowe had marked his concern both for the rights of free born men and the possible value of a new, written constitution. If Ireton emerged as the best debater at Putney despite his personal unpopularity and his longwinded style, Rainborowe quickly became the radicals' most articulate champion.

But Rainborowe's apparent belief that he could be vice-admiral and still stay in the Army betrays a rather large element of naivety. There is no doubting his ambition. His promotion of the doomed expedition to Jersey which, if successful, would have considerably enhanced his reputation in the Army was an earlier example of this. His determined pursuit of the naval post which included having to face down and even threaten his superior officer Oliver Cromwell indicates not just ambition but an element of ruthlessness. However, it is difficult to see how Rainborowe can have imagined he could keep his regiment despite his obvious attachment to it. As a professional solider he would surely have recognised that Fairfax needed a full time commander rather than a mainly absentee officer to run the regiment at a time of intense uncertainty.

Rainborowe's firm intent on becoming vice-admiral – in addition to his colonelcy in the Army also throws doubt on his commitment to radicalism. The Navy he wished to join was markedly Presbyterian in nature and its men had rejected or ignored overtures from the agitators to join their cause. By going to sea, Rainborowe was effectively cutting himself off from the main action of a settlement of the kingdom. He would be unable to attend either General Council meetings, even if allowed, or Parliament. His say in events would have been greatly curtailed and his absence would have robbed radicals of one of their main spokesmen. That Rainborowe was, at the very least, willing to risk this self-exclusion from centre stage suggests his ambition came before his radicalism.

However, it would not be fair to conclude that his course of action devalued his radical views. Austin Woolrych wrote in his masterly book on the General Council, that Rainborowe's "active support of the Leveller interest lasted less than two months."[29] This is inaccurate. First, Rainborowe was known for his radical views at least as far back as 1646 when Richard Baxter referred to the "distaste" many people in Worcester felt for him when he was appointed governor of the city.[30] Secondly, there are no grounds to claim his views were ever voiced in the "Leveller interest." His quasi-republican views, or, more strictly, his anti-Charles views, were personal. They did chime with those of Lilburne and Overton on this single matter but he never spoke or showed any interest in other Leveller views, for example, on de-centralisation.

But there is the further difficulty of how active Rainborowe actually was in pursuit of his views. He was not always a regular attendee at the Army's Council of War nor later of the General Council. He probably missed all the three held in October before the Putney Debates. In his defence, Rainborowe could fairly claim that he was otherwise engaged. For the Council of War meetings, he was occupied in organising his aborted expedition to Jersey when his regiment rebelled and took part in the seizure of the Oxford magazine in May 1647. For the October meetings, he was no doubt preparing for his new post in the Navy.

Historians have argued that the main reason for his attendance at the General Council meeting which began on October 28 was to complain that his beloved regiment had been transferred to another officer. But it seems highly unlikely that he did not know what was afoot. His brother, William, with whom he was living in Fulham at the time, was an active radical who did attend the meetings. It stretches belief that two brothers with similar views did not discuss what was happening. But it also seems surprising, after Robert Everard, one of the new London agents from Cromwell's regiment, read out *An Agreement* at Putney, that Rainborowe remarked that he had never seen him before.[31] There may just have been a touch of disingenuousness in Rainborowe's stance.

After Wildman and Ireton got themselves bogged down in an argument of what engagements the Army had made and in what circumstances these promises could be broken, Rainborowe called them back to what he saw as the main business: the Army had engaged with Parliament and for the liberties of the people. Its soldiers had beaten the king yet "they shall still be masters of our Houses." He added for clarity: "For my part it may be thought that I am against the King; I am against him or any power that would destroy Gods people, and I will never be destroyed till I cannot help myself." A pilot who ran his ship against a rock or a general who turned his cannon on his own men would be resisted, Rainborowe declared. Similarly, he said, the king should not be offered terms, let alone by this Army. "That which is dear unto me is my freedom. It is that I would enjoy, and I will enjoy as I can." He concluded by claiming there was not as much difference between the two sides as they might think.[32]

At the end of the first day, Cromwell resorted to his usual ploy when there was a mix of opinions and set up a committee, which included Rainborowe, to consider *An Agreement*. By the next day, Rainborowe had had second thoughts. He arrived late and missed the prayer meeting, claiming "the ill disposition of my body caused me to go to London last night, and (hindered me) from coming so soon this morning."[33] It seems more likely that Rainborowe, not known for illness, attended a meeting of radicals. His view was that the General Council should get on with debating *An Agreement*, a plea he made twice without success.

It was not until after several more, often rambling, speeches, that *An Agreement* was read. Over hastily, Ireton seized on a point with which he disagreed: that the size of parliamentary constituencies should accord with the number of inhabitants. This meant, the commissary-general objected, "that every man that is an inhabitant is to be equally considered, and to have an equal voice in the election of the representors."[34] He had played right into the hands of Rainborowe, Wildman and Petty.

So began one of the greatest debates in English history. Petty[35] was first to strike, claiming that all men who had not lost their birthright should have an "equal voice in Elections." But it was Rainborowe who then made the Debates' most arresting speech. "For truly I think that the poorest he that is in England hath a life to live as the greatest he; and truly Sir, I think it's clear, that every man that is to live under a government ought first by his own consent to put himself under that Government, and I do think that the poorest man in England is not all bound in a strict sense to that Government that he has not had a voice to put himself under."[36] H. N. Brailsford called it "the straightest and simplest plea for equality ever made in English history."[37] He might have added it was also the most elegant and eloquent.

It cut no ice with Ireton, who stuck to the solid conservative line that it was only men of property who should have the vote. "No person hath a right to an interest or share in the disposing or determining of the affairs of the Kingdom, and in choosing those that shall determine what laws we shall be ruled by here, no person has a right to this, that has not a permanent fixed interest in this Kingdom; and those persons together are properly the Represented of this Kingdom." There was no objection, he solemnly told the Council, to men born in England having access to air, or ground or the highways, but being born in England was not "sufficient ground" for him to have a share in power.[38]

Rainborowe dismissed this out of hand. It was either the law of God or the law of man that stopped the "meanest man" in England having a vote. "I do not find anything in the law of god, that a Lord shall choose 20 Burgesses, and a Gentleman but two, or a poor man shall choose none." It was, therefore, Rainborowe argued, the law of man that denied poor men a say in the government of their country. There were also the cases of many men who previously had the right to vote but had spent so much on Parliament's cause that they now were too poor to vote. Did they no longer have an interest in the country? He ended: "When those that are to make their laws are called by the King, or cannot act but by such a call, truly I think that the people of England have little freedome."[39]

The argument, hitherto cold but polite, then took on a more personal edge. Ireton, without any justification, in effect accused Rainborowe and his supporters of wanting to see the end of property. If every man had a right to vote, then he also had a right to another man's meat, drink, clothes and land. Where will it end, he demanded to know. But Rainborowe, determining to be "a little more free and open with you", scornfully rejected the charge that his views would lead to anarchy. Having a right to vote did not mean the end of property but currently men without a vote were subject to all laws be they right or wrong. This was the "greatest tyranny that was thought of in the world."[40]

The atmosphere was now hot and Cromwell as chairman stepped in to try and calm matters. He assured Rainborowe that no one thought he wanted anarchy but argued that his views might cause it. Ireton disingenuously said he could not understand why Rainborowe was so offended. Rainborowe brushed them aside to return to the matter of the vote. He could understand that men had property but why should the franchise be the property of one but not another? This law was the "most tyrannical under heaven." Rainborowe, caught between the patronising blandishments of

Cromwell and the sharp epee of Ireton, was buoyed by the intervention of Petty. There was nothing in *An Agreement* to suggest anarchy. It was about the power of the king and the lords, about changing how the representatives of the people were chosen. "Every man is naturally free," Petty said and wondered aloud if the law on the franchise were to be drawn up now, would people say "'you have not 40s a year, therefore you shall not have a voice?'"[41]

As the debate progressed, seemingly getting nowhere, an exasperated Rainborowe intervened to say: "Truly I think we are still where we were; and I do not hear anything argument given but only that it (the franchise) is the present law of the Kingdome." He said the Army could not proceed unless it took heed of the liberty of the people. "If we can agree where the liberty and freedom of the people lies, that will do all." Though not Ireton, who refused to accept this. He could not agree to what he saw as the destruction of the constitution.

Sexby, the straight forward soldier, quickly and forcefully disabused him. "We have engaged in this Kingdom and ventured our lives, and it was all for this: to recover our birthrights and privileges as Englishmen, and by the arguments urged there is none. There are many thousands of us soldiers that have ventured our lives; we have little propriety in the Kingdom as to our estates, yet we have had a birthright. But it seems now except a man hath a fixed estate in this Kingdome, he has no right in this Kingdom. I wonder we were that deceived. If we had not a right to the Kingdom, we were mere mercenary soldiers."[42]

This last sentence was a wounding riposte to Ireton who, in writing the Army's Declaration of June 14, had proudly proclaimed the New Model Army was "not a mere mercenary army hired to serve any arbitrary power of a state" but one that had been formed to defend "our own and our peoples just rights and liberties."[43]

Ireton's feigned hurt at Sexby's arrow and his continued defence of the rights of property owners brought a furious and sarcastic response from Rainborowe. "Sir I see it is impossible to have liberty but all property must be taken away. If it be laid down for a rule, and if you will say it, it must be so. But I would fain know what the soldier has fought for all this while? He has fought to enslave himself, to give power to men of riches, men of estates, to make him a perpetual slave." Rising to his assault on Ireton's intransigence, he claimed it was only poor men who were press ganged during wars. "When these Gentlemen fall out among themselves they shall press the poor shrubs to come and kill them." Ireton's response must have rendered Rainsborough incandescent. He – Ireton – felt himself to be so right in such matters that he would not be persuaded by such "flourishes."[44]

It was Rainborowe's last major speech on the debate on the franchise. Cromwell offered, as ever, to set up a committee and Rainborowe was content although he repeated he had heard nothing to change his mind. Sexby apologised for his "zeal" after being rebuked by Cromwell and, a little later, Rainborowe gave a half-hearted apology for his passion and reflections although he blamed Ireton for inciting him.[45] The debate closed with Rainborowe included in the committee to consider the franchise. But he did succeed in planting a ticking time bomb when he proposed that the Army call a rendezvous to settle matters.[46] It exploded a few days later.

Cromwell's latest committee duly met and reported the next day. Its conclusions were a substantial victory for Rainborowe and his supporters. It first recommended, in line with the proposals of *An Agreement*, that constituencies should be much fairer in size "so as to render the House of Commons as near as may be an equal Representative of the whole body of the people that are to elect." The vote was to go to all freeborn men including everyone who had fought for or helped Parliament's cause. It was not Rainborowe's ideal of a vote for "the poorest he" but the ordinary soldiers at least now had won something from the war.[47]

In the midst of these debates on Sunday October 31, Rainborowe took time to visit Lilburne in the Tower. The two men had never met before and Rainborowe had a clear purpose for his call. Would Lilburne, a fellow radical, support *An Agreement of the People* at the proposed general rendezvous of the Army? The only account of the meeting comes from the imprisoned Royalist, Sir Lewis Dyve, who may have remembered with mixed feelings that it was Rainborowe to whom he surrendered after the latter successfully besieged Sherborne Castle in Dorset in 1645. In the Tower, Lilburne apparently confided in this Royalist on a regular basis.

Dyve, in one of his frequent letters to Charles on November 3, wrote that Lilburne had told him that the five regiments "with many more in the army who have promised to adhere to them in this action" planned to purge the Houses of Parliament and to "secure" officers in the Army whom they disliked including "Cromwell and his faction." Dyve assured Charles there was no intention of "ill meaning" towards the king but nonetheless warned him to be on his guard. Dyve then reported that Rainborowe had come to the Tower last Sunday and "had a two howers discourse with Mr Lilburne unto whom he professes much friendship." Dyve identified Rainborowe as the "likeliest man to become head of this faction (which would purge Parliament) out of the hatred he bears to Crumwell and the general good esteem of him in the army."

Dyve went on to claim that Rainborowe disliked those who supported the purge of Parliament who "by a foolish zeal were transported to evil intentions towards your Majesty which he said he knew well the greatest part of the army abhorred to think of, and concluded that their own safety also lately depended upon your Majesty's preservation." Dyve's analysis was that the factions of Cromwell and Rainborowe mean "to break each others power" leaving the way open for a return of the king.[48] Charles must have been delighted to read of this falling out of his enemies but the scenario described needs to be taken with caution. Lilburne himself was living in a fantasy world where he saw himself as the great mover and shaker. He had previously suggested to Dyve that the king could charm such dyed in the wool radicals such as Captain John Reynolds,

Captain (later Major) Francis White, (the latter being thrown off the General Council for his extremism), and Sexby, an implacable opponent of the king.[49]

It also seems unlikely that Rainborowe would speak out in such a way against fellow soldiers to a man he did not know, or that he would tell Lilburne about their supposed evil intentions towards the king. It does not sound feasible. Dyve, in one paragraph of his letter, named Rainborowe as the leader of the faction intent on purging Parliament to deal with the king while later he depicted him as a man apart from those who bore the king evil. But what Dyve and perhaps Lilburne did get right was Rainborowe's intense opposition to Cromwell. That was to come to the fore again a few days. On the same weekend, in a spot of mischief, Royalists spread the rumour that Colonel Rainborowe was soon to become a general.[50]

The next day, Monday, November 1, after discussing, at Cromwell's behest, what advice the Council members had received from God – at one point Rainborowe intervened to suggest they get on with it – the debate centred on the crucial issue of a king's powers. Wildman wanted a clear answer on whether the king should have power to veto a law passed by the Commons. Ireton's lengthy replies suggested the problem did not really arise – neither the king nor the Lords had a right to veto. But Rainborowe feared there was no way to stop the king or the Lords from behaving in a destructive way. If they should act against the Commons, it had no way to help itself.

Rainborowe was arguing for not just a restriction on the power of the king and the Lords but, more forcefully, for the sovereignty of the people. Ireton's reply was that Lords were subject to the law like everyone else. But Rainborowe doubted if a "petty constable or sheriff" could arrest a Lord and get away with it. It was a rambling debate with point-scoring on both sides but the same committee which considered the franchise managed to get some sense out of it. It concluded that the Commons was the country's only lawmaker: no law could be made or repealed without its consent. Furthermore, all commoners were subject to the law, the king had no power to pardon anyone condemned by the Commons, but peers could still try fellow peers. On the crucial matter of religion, there was also to be a measure of freedom.[51]

By this stage, things were going better for Cromwell and Ireton than they could have hoped. Modest concessions had been made to the radicals but the greatest fear of the grandees - a split in the Army - had not come about. This dramatically changed at the meetings on November 4 and 5. They were the days when "Rainsborough's party...composed of the young men elected by the officers of each regiment and the soldiers' Agitators, was at its height."[52] On the first of these momentous days, they scrapped the report by the committee on the franchise and substituted the far more radical clause: "That all soldiers and others, if they be not servants or beggars, ought to have voices in electing those which shall represent them in Parliament, although they have not forty shillings per annum in freehold land." The hated property qualification was out. This was far nearer to the radicals' dream of manhood suffrage. Only three voted against the measure. The radicals had won the support of many senior officers.

But the next day was even more traumatic for the grandees. On the "second historic November 5 of this century",[53] with Cromwell attending the Commons and Fairfax taking the chair at the General Council, Rainborowe took his opportunity and pushed his advantage home. His motion for an Army rendezvous, proposed earlier in the Putney Debates - his ticking time bomb - was carried. He next persuaded the council not to hold any further talks with the king which meant that Henry Marten's motion of No Address, that had so ignominiously failed in the Commons just over a month before, had now been approved by the Army.

A shaken Fairfax, who was clearly unable to stop the process, refused to sign the ensuing letter to Speaker Lenthall. It was signed in his place by William Clarke, the Army secretary. The letter, acknowledging that the Commons favoured another address to the king, stated: "This night the General Council of the Army declared, that any such representation of their desires was altogether goundless; and that they earnestly desire no such consideration may be admitted into the house's resolution in that particular."[54] Ireton was so incensed by the outcome that he stormed out of St Mary's Church, refusing to return until the letter had been rescinded.

The Royalist press naturally reported these divisive events, although in a surprisingly restrained way: "Colonel Rainsborough, at a council of war held at the headquarters, intimated that the Army was not disposed to make any more addresses to the King, which produced the letter to the Speaker, now in print, to that effect, signed by William Clarke, dated the 5th of November from Putney. Ireton opposed the same all he could, and in testimony of his dissent left the council, protesting he could come no more there to be partaker of the high neglect and violation of reason and justice which he observed to reign amongst them. He hath been moved since to return but continues resolute."[55]

The agitators were far less circumspect. In a letter to the soldiers, dated November 11, relating the proceedings at Putney, they wrote: "At the next General Council our friends obtained a general rendezvous, and a letter from the Council to clear the Army from any desire or intent of constraining the Parliament to send new propositions to the King."[56]

With the initiative firmly in their hands, the radicals pressed on. The next day, Saturday, November 6, they tried to have a motion on "Whether it were safe for the Army or people to suffer any power to be given to the King" freely debated. In their letter to the rank and file, probably written by Wildman, the agitators claimed that Cromwell, now back at Putney, had agreed.[57] But it was to no avail. Fairfax, Cromwell, and certainly Ireton, had had enough.

The beast they had helped create in allowing agitators to promote the soldiers' views was now out of control. There was a serious chance the Army would split, ending any hopes of a settlement with the king. But there was also an equally disturbing issue developing over the person of Charles. Persistent rumours said that his Majesty was planning his escape from Army custody at Hampton Court. The grandees acted quickly. Over the weekend they decided to end the Putney Debates.

Fairfax retrieved what he could from the near wreckage. At the council meeting on Monday, November 8, members first agreed the agitators should return to their regiments. Then Fairfax agreed to an Army rendezvous. But this was not the hoped for mass meeting where Rainborowe and his allies assumed they could persuade the bulk of the soldiery to back *An Agreement*. It was to be three smaller meetings, which the grandees thought they would have a better chance of managing. Finally, yet another committee was set up to consider all the Army's engagements, *The Case*, *An Agreement* and all that had been discussed and argued over at Putney to see what could be salvaged.

Rainborowe and his brother, William, were on the committee. Surprisingly, so was Wildman. The next day, the Council agreed to send a letter to Speaker Lenthall saying the previous letter stating the Army's feelings about further talks with Charles did not mean to suggest it opposed Parliament talking to the king. Neither of the Rainborowes signed it. The General Council then dispersed, never to meet again in the same form.

Fairfax had snatched back much of the initiative. But Rainborowe must have been pleased with the turn of events. There were to be no more Army-backed addresses to the king and the three gatherings still gave them a chance to go over the heads of Cromwell and Ireton and win the soldiers' support for *An Agreement*. Cromwell, on the other hand, must have been both furious and disappointed. His rival had brought the Army to the brink of a split, which still might happen - this was the split that Rainborowe himself had warned at Putney would be a disaster for them – and in the process had also ended any further progress Cromwell and Ireton might make on a deal with Charles.

Cromwell's fear of a split was well founded. There were regiments that were all for *An Agreement*, but in others feelings against the agitators and for the king were equally strong. The unity of Cromwell's cherished Army was not so much in danger of splitting as disintegrating. However, he was rescued from an unexpected source.

The rumours regarding Charles's planned escape were circulating as the Putney Debates reached their climax. He was being guarded at Hampton Court by Col Whalley, Cromwell's cousin and Rainborowe's apparent rival for the governorship of Worcester in 1646. Charles seems to have decided to escape by the first week of November. The negotiations with the Army were going nowhere and to Charles the Scots still appeared a better bet. But more disturbingly for the king, there were rumours of a radical threat to his life, with Rainborowe possibly involved.

During the Debates at Putney, "letters of Intelligence written in London by Persons well-informed" were being sent to the king's secretary Sir Edward Nicholas who passed them on to Edward Hyde, later the Earl of Clarendon. Who the spy in the Army camp was is not known. The first, dated November 1, 1647[58] said that the General Council had passed a vote to extend the franchise to all men except servants and that many regiments in the Army were against the king, including those of Fairfax, Cromwell and Ireton. This was despite that "their commanders be his Majesty's greatest friends." It added intriguingly that the wives of Cromwell, Ireton and Whalley had attended a feast at court with "Mr Ashburnham taking Mrs Cromwell by the hand." It added more ominously: "How the agitators will take these things I know not: but next Thursday doth threaten strange business, a king or no king."[59]

The next letter, sent on November 4, before the climax of the Debates, set out the alleged mood among the radicals. "All things here are in a very sad condition. Colonel Rainsborough and Colonel Pride, with H. Martin, are so violent in the new way against the King, the Army, Parliament and all eminency that Cromwell and some of his party are like to side with them out of fear, and so, notwithstanding all former probabilities and possessions that they would in the end do well for the king, his Majesty's affairs, are grown more desperate than ever."

The letter went on to claim that Cromwell's opponents - no specific names were mentioned - were trying to have him impeached. Finally, the writer says he has been to Hampton Court but Fairfax had ordered that no one should see Charles.[60]

Then, in a letter dated November 15, the informant told Nicholas and Hyde: "Upon Friday last the king was certainly designed to have been murdered; but God, the preserver of all things sacred and just, prevented those hellish intentions by his Majesty's escape upon Thursday night, about five at night."[61] The informant was not the only one who knew of this alleged plot. Charles himself had received a letter on November 9 claiming that eight or nine agitators had met the night before and hatched a scheme. The letter was signed "E.R.", probably Lieutenant-Colonel Henry Lilburne.[62]

If a junior officer knew by November 9, senior officers like Cromwell must also have known by then. But Cromwell did not act until November 11 - the day Charles fled - and then not until the early evening, after first meeting of the committee Fairfax had set up three days before. Did Cromwell delay because he did not believe the rumours of a plot or was there another reason – that it suited him for Charles to escape? If it were the former what better piece of black propaganda than for the radicals to feed the story of a plot to a gullible young officer whom they knew would pass on the details to the king. Charles would believe it, or at least claim to, based on his long mistrust of the Army officers.

His real reason to escape was his determination to continue talks with the Scots. The "plot" gave him the perfect excuse to do what he planned to do anyway, and with the King's flight, the radicals would achieve their aim of having no further talks with him.

But if the delay was because Cromwell wanted Charles to escape, this was an altogether more risky strategy. It may have united his cherished Army through having their common enemy once more at large. But if the delay had led to the King being killed while in the custody of the Army, "it would prejudice their cause hopelessly before the country."[63] Cromwell did not usually play for such high stakes. Something must have happened at the committee meeting to rattle Cromwell into believing there may just be something in the rumours of a plot.

At this committee meeting Colonel Thomas Harrison spoke out strongly "that the king was a Man of Blood, and therefore the Engagement taken off, and they were to prosecute him."[64] It was the same damning phrase that Wildman had used earlier in his *A Cal to all Souldiers*. Was it this, with the phrase's chilling undertones of death to the king, that made Cromwell think the plot was real or did he pick up some unguarded gossip during the day?

Either way, as soon as the meeting was finished, he wrote to Whalley: "Dear Cousin Whalley, there are rumours abroad of some intended attempt on his Majesty's person. Therefore I pray have a care of your guards." The king's harm "would be accounted a most horrid act."[65] But it was too late. The king stole away sometime in the afternoon of Thursday, November 11, before Cromwell wrote his letter. Whalley did not realise he had gone until the early evening, by which time Charles was miles from Hampton Court, on his way to Carisbrook Castle on the Isle of Wight. There, on November 14, he placed himself in the hands of the startled young governor, Colonel Robert Hammond,[66] another of Cromwell's many cousins.

The escape dashed Cromwell's hopes of any future talks – he was working on new peace proposals when the king fled. But it sealed a day of great success for Rainborowe and his radicals. The king was gone and there would be no future talk of a deal with him. The allegiance of Harrison to their cause was also a great bonus for them. He did not speak at, and may not have attended, the Putney Debates, but he was a brave, accomplished and highly respected soldier, an immensely influential figure on the Parliamentary side and, up to that point, a friend and supporter of Cromwell. But it was not all good news for the radicals. If Charles's escape had "solved" the problem of a negotiated peace settlement, it created another, far more disturbing, scenario. A second civil war was now far more likely.

Fairfax had by now fixed the place and date for the first of the three Army rendezvous at Corkbush Field, near Ware in Hertfordshire as November 15. The radicals immediately began preparations for it. While denied their wish for a general rendezvous, their hand was strengthened by the king's escape and they were also counting on considerable support from London radicals and apprentices. As Charles contemplated the letter warning of a plot to kill him, the House of Commons was presented with *An Agreement of the People* for its consideration. It rejected it out of hand as "destructive to the Being of Parliaments, and to the fundamental Government of the Kingdom" and ordered Fairfax to tell them what on earth was going on in his Army.[67]

Meanwhile, the agents' letter was circulated in London in an obvious attempt to win the support of the people for the soldiers' fight for their rights. The radicals' plan was that the *Agreement* should be read out at the head of each regiment attending the Corkbush rendezvous. Rumours in the capital said that up to 20,000 weavers would march to Ware in support of the radicals.[68] It never happened.

When Fairfax and Cromwell arrived at the rendezvous, only the seven regiments ordered to attend were there.[69] There were no weavers or any other supporters from London and John Lilburne, given some measure of freedom from the Tower by Cromwell to prepare his case for release, had ridden up to Ware for the day but never emerged from the inn where he awaited news of the mutiny.

But trouble was brewing. Colonel Richard Eyres and Major Thomas Scott were haranguing the troops, attempting to whip up support for *An Agreement*. Fairfax ordered their immediate arrest, with Eyres to be court-martialled while Scott, an MP, was escorted to Westminster to answer to the Commons for his conduct. His escort was Lieutenant Edmund Chillenden, once a radical but now firmly in Fairfax's camp. Some others were also arrested for "dispersing sundry scandalous and factious papers, as the Agreement of the People, &, among the private soldiers."[70]

But then Rainborowe rode forward to present Fairfax with both a copy of *An Agreement* and a petition signed in its support. Fairfax disdainfully brushed him aside. While Rainborowe was not also arrested is a mystery. No longer a member of the Army, he should not even have been there. But Fairfax took no action against him.

It may have been because the seven regiments present all "behaved with great order and submission to Military authority"[71] that Fairfax felt there was no need to risk this control by arresting a popular officer. But he took no chances. A specially prepared *Remonstrance*, in which he threatened to resign unless dissent in the Army ceased, was read out to each regiment, followed by a personal address from the general. He would, he told his men, "live and die with them" while doing his utmost to have the grievances over pay and indemnity redressed. He was met with acclaim.[72]

But before the grandees could congratulate themselves on a successful day, two uninvited regiments appeared in the field, Colonel Harrison's horse and Colonel Robert Lilburne's foot. Men from both regiments had copies of *An Agreement* in their hats bearing the motto in capital letters 'England's Freedom, Soldiers' Rights.' It is not clear if Harrison or any of his officers, who included William Rainborowe, accompanied their men. It is more likely that they came without them, perhaps persuaded by the London agents.

Again Fairfax acted decisively, riding to Harrison's men and addressing them. His "severe Reproof" led to the men tearing *An Agreement* from their hats and pledging loyalty.[73] A second account gives a similarly bland description. The regiment "was no sooner informed by the general of their error, but, with a great deal of readiness and cheerfulness, they submitted to him, and expressed the same Affection and resolution of obedience with the other Regiments."[74]

Lilburne's foot however, "the most mutinous Regiment in the Army",[75] were a different matter. They had been ordered by Fairfax to Newcastle three weeks before but had stopped at St Albans after receiving copies of *The Case of the Armie Truly Stated*. They had subsequently "driven away their senior officers" and marched to Corkbush under the tenuous command of Captain William Bray. He was a young firebrand who had argued strenuously with Cromwell in the last days of the Putney Debates over what powers a king should have. On his way to Ware, he refused to obey Fairfax's order to stay where he was, claiming he was powerless to control the men. Bray was arrested on arrival and charged with disobeying orders. A Council of War was set up and "divers Mutineers, for example's sake were drawn-forth, three of them were tried and condemned to death, and one of them (whose turn it fell to by lot) was shot to death at the head of the Regiment; and others are in hold to be tried."[76] The man shot was Private Richard Arnold.

Having been pointedly asked just a few days before by the Commons about what exactly was going on in his Army, Fairfax understandably played down the events at Corkbush Field, presenting a picture of a minor disturbance that he had fully controlled. He blamed the London agents for stirring up the trouble and deliberately glossed over the size of the revolt.

A far more dramatic picture emerged from the account by Lieutenant-General Edmund Ludlow, which said that Cromwell, who had not been mentioned by Fairfax or Clarke, played a violent and decisive role. Ludlow claimed that Cromwell became angry when faced with the defiance of Lilburne's men and seized some of them. "To this end, being accompanied with divers officers whom he had preferred, and by that means made his creatures, he rode up to one of the regiments which had the distinguishing marks, requiring them to take them out; which they not doing, he caused several of them to be seized; and then, their hearts failing, they yielded obedience to his commands. He ordered one of them to be shot dead upon the place; delivering the rest of those whom he had seized, being eleven in number, into the hands of the Marshal; and having dispersed the army to their headquarters, went to give an account of his proceedings to the parliament."[77]

The spy in the Army camp writing his "letters of intelligence" to Nicholas and Clarendon was equally certain something more dramatic had taken place. He said, in his letter of November 15, that the radical Major Francis White, who had already been thrown off the General Council for suggesting the only power in England was the sword, demanded that the kingdom be put under another government, that is one not headed by Charles. "The soldiers replied 'A king, a king, then 'This king, this king.'" This, the informant said, was not supported by a single officer "which I marvel at".

His next letter, on November 18/20, described how Cromwell had behaved "very gallantly and prudently" at Ware. He "rode among Lilburne's regiment - there without order and wearing Whites in their hats - drew his sword and charged so furiously through it as the regiment (being much astonished therewith) pulled out their Whites and craved mercy."[78]

It was a bad day for Rainborowe with his and the radicals' plans of securing the support of the rank and file for *An Agreement* brutally dashed by Fairfax and Cromwell. But worse for him was to follow. In the immediate aftermath of Corkbush Field, officers and men, angered at the conduct of those they saw as extremists, sent a petition to Fairfax. In it they demanded that Parliament set up a committee to find out who was behind "these seditious Irregularities." In particular it wanted to know what role Rainborowe had played in them. It added for good measure "That Col Rainsborough...may not be suffered to go to sea till this Business be fully examined."[79] The Commons also reacted swiftly. The day after Corkbush, it resolved that "Col. Rainsborough be summoned forthwith to attend the House."[80] His job as vice-admiral, the post he coveted and had faced down Cromwell to get, was now in jeopardy.

Notes for Chapter Six

1. *Commons Journal*, v, pp.317-9; Rushworth, *Historical Collections, vii*, pp. 801-829.
2. *Commons Journal*, v, pp.328-9.
3. Ibid., pp. 339-40.
4. Maurice Ashley, *John Wildman Plotter and Postmaster*, (London, 1947), pp. 9-11.
5. Peacock, *Archaeologia*, vol 46, p. 26.
6. British Library Add.MSS 71532, f. 23.
7. See John Morrill and Philip Baker, 'The Case of the Armie Truly Stated', in Patrick Little (ed.), *Oliver Cromwell: New perspectives*, (Basingstoke, 2009). Other historians, notably S. R. Gardiner and Don Wolfe attribute all of the pamphlet to Wildman.
8. Gentles, *New Model Army*, p. 200.
9. *Clarke Papers*, i, p. 240.
10. Don Wolfe, *Leveller Manifestoes of the Puritan Revolution*, (New York, 1944), p. 223.
11. For the full text see Wolfe, pp. 225-8.
12. Wootton, 'The Leveller Movement' in Burns and Goldie (eds.), *Cambridge History of Political Thought 1450-1700*, p. 413.
13. Elliott Vernon and Philip Baker, 'What was the first Agreement of the People?', *Historical Journal* 53, 1 (2010), pp. 48-9.
14. Geoffrey Robertson, *The Levellers and the Putney Debates*, (London, 2007), p. 43.
15. Ibid. p. 45.
16. Ibid. p. 49.
17. Ibid. p. 45.
18. Ibid. p. 49.
19. Clarke Papers, i, pp. 227-8.
20. Ibid., pp. 230-1.
21. Ibid., p. 246.
22. Ibid., p. 273
23. Ibid., pp. 246-7.
24. Ibid., p. 272.
25. Ibid., p. 304.
26. The Charters of London, (London, 1646), E366(12), p. 12. Quoted in Wotton, 'Leveller Movement' in *Cambridge History of Political Thought*, pp. 248-9.
27. After his appointment to the Navy, his regiment, which he had raised and clearly felt much affection for, was given to Col Richard Deane.
28. Clarke Papers, i, pp. 245-7.
29. Woolrych, *Soldiers and Statesmen*, p. 227. Woolrych writes on the same page that Rainborowe "apparently" hoped to collect his wages both as a colonel and a vice-admiral, although he offers no evidence for this assertion.
30. Baxter, *Reliquiae Baxterianae*, p. 56.
31. Clarke Papers, i, p. 273.
32. Ibid., pp. 272-3.
33. Ibid., p. 287.
34. Ibid., p. 299.

35. He is referred to in Clarke's records as Pettus.
36. Clarke Papers, i, pp. 300-1.
37. Brailsford, *The Levellers*, p. 274.
38. Clarke Papers, i, pp. 301-2.
39. Ibid., pp. 304-6.
40. Ibid., pp. 308-9.
41. Ibid., pp. 309-12.
42. Ibid., pp. 320-23.
43. *Army Book of Declarations*, p. 37.
44. Clarke Papers, i, pp. 324-6.
45. Ibid., p. 328, p. 329, p. 335.
46. Ibid., p. 346.
47. Ibid., pp. 363-7.
48. Dyve, *Letter-Book*, pp. 95-6.
49. Ibid., p. 92.
50. Clarendon MSS, 340, fo.163.
51. Clarke Papers, i, pp. 367-410.
52. Brailsford, *The Levellers*, p. 288.
53. Ibid.
54. Clarke Papers, i, pp. 440-1.
55. Ibid., p. 441; Clarendon State Papers II, Appendix xli.
56. Arthur Sutherland Pigott Woodhouse, *Puritanism and Liberty*, (London, 1938), p. 452.
57. Ibid., p. 453.
58. The dates of these letters do not always tally with the events they purport to describe.
59. Clarendon MSS, ii, p. 40.
60. Ibid.
61. Ibid., p. 41.
62. Austin Woolrych says this was "almost certainly" Lieutenant-Colonel Henry Lilburne, younger brother of the far more radically minded Colonel Robert Lilburne and John Lilburne. See Woolrych, *Britain in Revolution 1625-1660*, (Oxford, 2002), p. 394. Henry declared for the king shortly afterwards.
63. Wilbur Cortez Abbott, *The Writings and Speeches of Oliver Cromwell*, (Harvard Cambridge, 1947), i, p. 551.
64. *Clarke Papers*, i, p. 417. Thomas Harrison (1606-1660) rose to the rank of major-general in the New Model Army. He was a judge at Charles's trial and signed his death warrant. He became increasingly radical in the 1650s, turning against Cromwell's role of Lord Protector. He refused to flee when Charles II became king and was tried, hanged, drawn and quartered.
65. Christopher Hibbert, *Charles I*, (London, 1968), p. 247; Woolrych, *Britain in Revolution*, p. 394; Abbott, *The Writings and Speeches of Oliver Cromwell*, i, pp. 551-2.
66. Colonel Robert Hammond (1621-54) fought in many battles for Parliament, including the siege of Bristol in 1645 with Rainborowe. He at first strongly supported the Army's confrontation with Parliament but by the summer of 1647 had become disillusioned. Fairfax arranged for him to leave military service and become governor of the Isle of Wight. He must have been delighted to have the king turn up on his doorstep. He promised only to treat him with courtesy.

67. *Commons Journal*, v, p. 354.
68. Brailsford, *The Levellers*, pp. 288-9.
69. These were the horse regiments of Fairfax, Fleetwood, Rich and Twistleton and the foot regiments of Fairfax, Pride and Thomas Hammond.
70. William Clarke, 'A full relation of the Proceedings at the Rendezvous of that Brigade of the Army that was held at Corkbush Field in Hartford Parish on Monday last' in Maseres, *Select Tracts*, i, p. 57.
71. Maseres, *Select Tracts*, i, p. 48.
72. Clarke, 'A full relation', Maseres, *Select Tracts*, i, p. 56.
73. Rushworth, *Historical Collection*, vii, p. 876.
74. Maseres, *Select Tracts*, i, p. 49.
75. Clarke, 'A full relation', Maseres, *Select Tracts*, i, p. 57.
76. Ibid. Rushworth, *Historical Collection*, vii, p. 876.
77. Maseres, *Select Tracts*, i, pp. 50-1.
78. *Clarendon State Papers*, ii, App. pp. 41-2.
79. Maseres, *Select Tracts*, i, pp. 46-7.
80. *Commons Journal*, v, p. 359.

Chapter Seven: Revolt at Sea

In the aftermath of the shambles at Corkbush Field, Parliament was furious at Rainborowe's conduct and determined to strip him of his vice-admiralship. He was summoned to attend the Commons, which also set up a committee of no fewer than 33 MPs to inquire into "What Meetings of Persons and Transactions have been in London, for the Dividing of the Army, and Disturbance of the Quiet of this Kingdom." The committee was to meet that very day, November 16, at 2pm to start its inquiry. Two days later it set up a second committee, including several Lords, to look into the role the "London agents" played in "these seditious irregularities" so "exemplary justice" could be meted out.[1] The Commons seemed resolved to get to the bottom of the matter.

But Fairfax, in his long letter to the Lords, not only played down the events at Corkbush but also substantially glossed over Rainborowe's disruptive role. "I thought it my duty to give your Lordship this further account", he told the earl of Manchester, speaker of the Lords, "that Colonel Rainborow, with some others, tendered this enclosed petition, together with the People's Agreement annexed thereunto; and, by what hands I yet know not fully, very many copies of the same Agreement were dispersed amongst the soldiers, thereby to engage them; but, blessed be God! all proved ineffectual."

He ended with an assertion that he knew was untrue, that his army was a happy one. But he also subtly slipped in a warning that the soldiers might just have cause to complain.[2] The issues of arrears and Ireland had not gone away.

The first crunch came on December 10 when the Commons decided by 61 to 58 votes that Rainborowe should not go to sea. It was, surprisingly, the army's senior officers, those with whom he had clashed at Putney and then confronted at Corkbush, who came to his aid. An army council meeting in Windsor on December 22 was turned into a day of "solemn fast" in which the officers, including

Cromwell but not, apparently, Fairfax, "prayed very fervently and pathetically" from 9am to 7pm. Fairfax and his senior ranks, including Cromwell, Ireton, Robert Tichburne and John Hewson and the army chaplain Hugh Peter, then made their decision on Rainborowe.

"Whereas Col. Rainsborough had acted some things which gave offence, that in regard of his present acknowledgement, his former service might not be forgotten; but that the Council would move the General to write to the House, that he would represent to the Parliament as their desire, that he might be made Vice-Admiral; which was assented to by all."[3] What Rainborowe told them is unknown. He never left any documents or letters which explained or defended his behaviour at Corkbush. But it seems likely that before his fellow officers he was contrite. It is unlikely that Ireton, who had good cause at that stage to be angry with him, would have settled for anything less.

Fairfax wrote his letter the same evening. His pitch was simple: the country needed Rainborowe. Perhaps understandably he did not mention that the Army equally needed its own man in charge of the Navy. There was, Farifax claimed, "some want of good guards at sea about the Isle of Wight [where the king was now held]." This endangered the kingdom. Would the Commons therefore re-consider its decision on Rainborowe and send him to do his job at sea. For good measure, Fairfax stressed how this would improve the safety of the kingdom.[4] It did the trick. A second vote was taken two days later which, by 88-66, approved Rainborowe's despatch to sea.[5]

But the Lords remained hostile. Two days after the Commons' positive vote, they not only voted the other way but demanded the MPs' support. After receiving Fairfax's letter describing events at Corkbush, the peers decided "That the Carriage of Colonel Raynsborough at the rendezvous tended much to the disturbance of the quiet and orderly government of the army." They then set their face firmly against him going to sea as commander of the winter guard "conceiving it of most dangerous consequence, that a person who hath had such a character from the general and the army should be employed in a place of so great trust and importance to the kingdom."[6]

The Commons, sitting on Christmas Day, suggested the two sides talk and a conference was duly held on December 28. Meanwhile, Fairfax, hearing there was "some stick with the House of Peers", stepped back into the fray. In a letter to Manchester, Fairfax laid it on with a trowel. While he acknowledged that some had taken exception to Rainborowe's conduct at Corkbush, "he had before (I wrote to the House of Commons) expressed to myself and divers principal officers such a deep sense of the late distempers and miscarriages in those things whereunto he had appeared too inclinable, and such resolutions to decline the like for the future, as gave us large satisfaction concerning him."[7]

Still the Lords said 'No.' Despite the first conference between the MPs and peers revealing that neither Fairfax nor any other officer had made any formal accusation against Rainborowe, the peers held fast. "This house adheres to their former vote upon the whole matter, that Colonel Raynsborough should not command this Winter's Guard" and again repeating their view that he was unfit for this office. Their one concession was to offer more talks with the Commons.[8]

But events came fortuitously to Rainborowe's rescue. There was an attempt to rescue the king by seamen on Parliamentary ships near the Isle of Wight which inevitably provoked fears for his security. The Commons received, on January 1, 1648, letters from commanders of the ships stationed around Cowes on the island and from Colonel Robert Hammond, governor of Carisbrooke Castle where the king was held.

The commanders said that "Captain Burley[9] and some other mutineers" had been captured. The MPs ordered that Rainborowe "be required forthwith to repair to the Isle of Wight with such ships as he shall think necessary for that service." So urgent did the MPs feel about getting Rainborowe to sea that they put the eminent

Edmund Prideaux,[10] an MP and a Parliamentary commissioner, in charge of making sure Rainborowe got his orders. The Commons also ordered ships then stationed off Ireland to sail straightaway for the Isle of Wight.[11] The Lords were not consulted.

Hammond also wrote to Manchester on December 28 saying his fears for the king's security had increased after Charles had turned down the Four Bills, a peace plan based on the Hampton Court Propositions. He told the Lords speaker: "I thought it my duty to take a stricter care than ordinary of the security of the person of the king, and for removing all from about him that are not there by authority of Parliament." Hammond urged that the king should be taken from the island as soon as was convenient or, failing that, he Hammond be relieved of his post, it "being a burden insupportable for me."

He wrote in similar terms to Fairfax. The general told the Commons, in a letter dated December 30, that the young governor felt the king's wellbeing was too great a weight for him to bear. He had accordingly sent three officers, Sir William Constable, his brother-in-law, and Lieutenant-Colonel William Goffe, Whalley's son-in-law, and Lieutenant Colonel Edward Salmon, to assist Hammond.[12] The Lords, still unaware of Rainborowe's despatch, plaintively wrote to the Commons on January 3 asking for a response to their view that Rainborowe should not go to sea. The next day the MPs said they would put aside time for a "speedy consideration" of the Lords' request. By then Rainborowe was with his fleet.

Rainborowe was lucky that the hapless Captain Burley timed his doomed attempt to rescue Charles in the middle of his row with Parliament. He can also consider himself fortunate that Fairfax and other officers of the NMA were prepared to support him. Rainborowe left no explanation or defence of his conduct at Corkbush and whatever pleas he made to Fairfax and his men are lost. It is difficult to understand his behaviour. He himself had stressed at Putney that if the army divided, they were lost. Yet at Corkbush he appears to have made every attempt to split it. Worse, he should not even have been there, or at Putney, as he was no longer an officer in the army. It is too simple to say that Rainborowe was immoderately fired by his radical passions. There were several days between the Putney Debates and the rendezvous, plenty of time for his ardour to cool and common sense to kick in. His time in the field with Fairfax would also have taught him that the general, while endlessly loyal to and supportive of his men, had a line that would not be crossed. Rainborowe's actions on that day seem catastrophically misjudged, acts of wanton folly that defy explanation.

It is perhaps easier to understand Fairfax's forgiving attitude to Rainborowe. Throughout 1645 and 1646, Rainborowe had become an increasingly important solider in the general's army. Not only his inspirational courage but also his assured competence in mounting successful sieges had made him indispensable to Parliament. Fairfax, far less political than many of his senior officers, surely recognised this and more readily forgave him. It was a magnanimous gesture by the general and one that Rainborowe may not have fully deserved.

It is more difficult to understand the forbearance of men like Cromwell, whom Rainborowe scorned, and Ireton. This seems to have embraced not only his presence at Putney but also his rebellious acts at Corkbush. It also was not the first time they had been given assurances by him as to his future conduct. Robert Huntington, a not altogether reliable witness, had broached this in his letter of resignation from the army. After Rainborowe's appointment as vice admiral, Cromwell was asked "How he could trust a man whose Interest was so directly opposite to what he had processed, and one whom he had lately aimed to remove from all places of trust?" He answered, "That he had now received particular assurance from Colonel Rainsborough, as great as could be given by man, that he would be conformable to the judgement and direction of himself and Commissary General Ireton, for the managing of the whole business at sea."[13] Rainborowe had now misled them twice.

The Lords accepted the *fait accompli* of Rainborowe taking over command of the winter guard. But there was still rancour when his named was proposed in March as commander of the summer fleet. They passed the motion but there were two notable opponents, the earls of Manchester and Warwick.[14] Both staunch Presbyterians, they were politically at odds with Rainborowe. But both also knew of his abilities. Manchester was commander of the Eastern Association when Rainborowe's regiment took Crowland in 1644. Warwick, a fellow mariner, had known him for years. Rainborowe's grandfather had been his secretary; Rainborowe's father was a prominent mariner and merchant. Warwick could hardly have doubted Rainborowe's seafaring skills. It looks more likely that they took a harder line than the Commons and the NMA. They had watched his behaviour and thought him unfit for office.

Despite them Rainborowe had got his wish and was now finally at sea. But what type of navy had he taken over? The navy had flourished briefly under Henry VIII, until the disastrous sinking of the *Mary Rose* in 1545. By the time of his death two years later, the navy had about 40 ships, an increase on the five Henry had inherited. But under his daughter Elizabeth, it became increasingly a mix of the Queen's ships augmented by private merchantmen as and when needed. The government paid ship owners bounties for vessels which could be used in war. Many of the ships which saw off the Spanish Armada in 1588 were privateers.

But the last decades of Elizabeth's reign saw an enormous expansion of trade. New routes were opened to Russia and the eastern Mediterranean by, respectively, the Muscovy and Levant companies while merchant adventurers explored the New World and the Caribbean. It all required more and bigger ships. Between 1582-1629, there was a 70% rise in tonnage in England, much from the increased size of ships.[15] This was the era that saw the rise of a new and increasingly rich class of merchants, not just major investors in enterprises but also owners and part owners of the great ships of the day, sometimes also their captains as well. These were the years when Rainborowe's grandfather Thomas, his father William and many of other mariner families made their fortunes.

The government stopped the payment of levies in 1618. But as England was now more dependent on these men to provide ships for war, it encouraged the shipbuilders to equip their ships with guns. So ships like the 500-ton *Sampson*, built and owned by William Rainborowe and his business partners and mastered by Rainborowe himself, was allowed to carry what guns she wished. Ostensibly it was to combat the Barbary pirates off the North African coast they passed on their way to Greece and Turkey, but equally it suited the government to have such ships at the ready.

By the early 1620s, the navy consisted mainly of ships of the merchant marine. When Charles came to the throne in 1625, he had just 28 ships over 200 tons of his own while the merchants had 300 between 200 and 500 tons.[16] Trade was still growing rapidly. Between 1629-41, it grew by 25% and by 1630 "London was regarded as one of the great trading centres of the world."[17] It thrust the tightly knit network of wealthy merchants, united by their strong Puritanism and thirst for profit, into a position of immense power.

By the early years of Charles' reign, they were already beginning to form an opposition to him, both inside and outside Parliament. Inside Parliament, MPs had refused Charles the normal courtesy of voting him tonnage and poundage for life. Outside Parliament, merchants, led by the Levant Company, with which the Rainborowes were closely associated, refused to pay that or any other tax levied by Charles without Parliamentary approval.[18] From their "sudden rise in 1625 or 1626", the powerful merchants were "staunchly allied to the Parliamentary opposition in its struggle against the Crown." By the end of the decade the two sides were "fully merged."[19]

The king's answer was to raise revenue to build and equip his own ships. His means was through Ship Money. Charles had good reasons to build up his navy. Apart from the Barbary pirates, there also threats from the Spanish Dunkirk Squadron, another group raiding English commercial shipping in the Channel. Besides that the French were expanding their navy, as were the Dutch and there was, almost as ever, increased activity by the Spanish off England's coast.

His efforts to collect Ship Money brought growing opposition. This was especially so in 1634-6 when it was imposed without Parliamentary consent after Charles had prorogued Parliament in 1629 and was governing by personal rule. But it also helped strengthen his navy. Rainborowe's father, William played a part in this by serving as an expert on various committees to enhance the navy.

But a more subtle revolution had also taken place. Just as the earl of Manchester had picked men of ability to command his army of the Eastern Association in 1643 rather than the sons of the local squire or aristocrat, so did the navy. But this change came about in the late 1630s. The king had previously relied on his gentlemen captains, but the merchant mariners increasingly choose as captains men of maritime expertise. By 1637, there were few gentleman captains left in the navy. By 1640, merchant mariners dominated it. Inevitably, when civil war came, the navy sided with Parliament. One of the prime instigators of this was William Rainborowe. When the king handed him command of the Sallee expedition to take on the Barbary pirates in 1637, Rainborowe chose as his fellow captains associates from Trinity House who represented the ship owning, shipbuilding community of the Thames. All but one joined Parliament when war broke out in 1642.

Worse for the monarch, it was this same community from the Thames "allied with London merchants with a strong interest in shipping which assumed control of the nation's fleet in 1642."[20] In a few short months they took control not only of the ships but also the administration of the navy. Unawares, the king had invited his enemy into his inner chambers. It was a crucial error.

But if the navy was moving towards Parliament by 1640, it was the king's incompetence which pushed it firmly into its hands in 1642. This was a tale of farce. The earl of Northumberland, a lukewarm supporter of Parliament, was appointed Lord High Admiral of England in 1638. Not wishing to get too involved in the burgeoning dispute between king and Parliament, he appointed a deputy, Sir John Pennington in March 1642. Parliament retaliated by appointing the earl of Warwick to be admiral of the fleet.

Despite his anger, Charles, now based in York, did nothing for three months. Finally he concocted a daft and convoluted plan. With the bulk of the fleet anchored in The Downs off Dover, he decided to send Pennington with letters to all the captains. These both announced the dismissal of Northumberland and the appointment of Pennington as their new admiral. A separate letter would go to Warwick dismissing him.

But Pennington, who was well into his seventies, refused to go. So Charles decided to send two messengers, one a page boy called May to Northumberland and the other Edward Villiers, a courtier, to the fleet with orders for it to sail north to Burlington Bay, Yorkshire. Then, after May had set off, Pennington changed his mind. He would accompany Villiers after all. So new letters were written and the pair went off, this time with the added complication that they would pick up, on route to the fleet, a long retired Royalist naval officer, Sir Henry Palmer.

As a final touch of complexity, May and the Villiers party were expected to time their journeys south so that both arrived at their different destinations at the same time. Failure was, of course, just around the corner. May, unaware of Pennington's change of mind, delivered his letter to Northumberland on July 1. The earl, nothing phased, promptly told Parliament – something the king seems never to have considered. Parliament simply confirmed Warwick in his appointment.

Meanwhile at the Downs, farce took over. Palmer, a lively if crusty old soul, refused to join Villiers in his escapade. One source said it was because Villiers had knocked on his door a bit too early in the morning. Villiers, it was decided, would have to deliver the letters alone while Pennington stayed in hiding, waiting for the moment to announce his presence. Villiers delivered his letters but the problem was that they omitted to name Northumberland's successor.

While Pennington lurked in hiding, Warwick, who was near The Downs but onshore, took the initiative. He called a council of all the ships' captains. All but five declared for Parliament as they were always likely to do. One captain, called Burley,[21] submitted within 24 hours and on July 4, Warwick, when he got official confirmation of his appointment, acted. All four recalcitrant commanders and their ships were surrounded and summoned to surrender. Two, rear admiral Sir John Mennes on *Victory* and Captain Fogge on *Reformation* did so. The two others, Captain Slingsby on *Garland* and Captain Wake on *Expedition* held out briefly. Warwick fired a shot over their bows and sent ships' boats to pick up the captains. They found they had already been arrested by their own men.[22]

This raises the point of whatever was it that persuaded Charles his sailors were loyal to him. In the king's mind there seems to have been no doubt of this. "He had bountifully so much mended their condition and increased their pay, that he thought they would have thrown the earl of Warwick overboard when he should command."[23] The king might have begun the building of a decent fleet but the money went on ships, not men.

There are frequent tales of sailors going without pay, rations and clothing. There are even tales of captains selling ships' equipment to feed their men. In January, 1642, after Charles unsuccessfully tried to arrest the five MPs, 2,000 sailors from Ratcliffe, near Wapping, marched to Guildhall in support of Parliament.[24] The fleet was already as good as lost as Charles' hapless messengers travelled south. He was the first English king to lose his navy. It was a crucial win for Parliament. Without the fleet, it is likely they could have suffered a swift defeat.

But if the fleet was against Charles in 1642, it was never for the NMA of 1647 with its agitators, increasingly radical politics and hardening line towards the king. As the army became more tightly in the grip of the Independents, the navy stayed firmly in the Presbyterian camp. Was it this that gave Cromwell such serious misgivings about Rainborowe assuming command? Did he guess that the radical Rainborowe was about to step into a hornet's nest?

When Rainborowe stepped aboard his ship, the *Happy Endurance*, there were already signs of unrest in Kent which eventually led the county to revolt. There had been a riot in Canterbury on Christmas Day, 1647 after attempts to ban the Anglican religious festival. Further, Kent Royalists, expecting the king to come to the county after John Burley's "rescue", openly declared for the monarch.[25] Dover, hit by a loss of trade and subsequent poverty among residents, was "exceedingly malignant."[26]

But the unrest was not confined to Kent. Other regions were also angry at what they considered to be the unnecessary delay in signing a peace treaty with the king. In February, Colonel John Poyer, the Parliamentary governor of Pembroke Castle in South Wales refused to hand over his command to one of Fairfax's officers, attracting the support of hundreds of fellow officers and men. A month later, he declared for the king, signalling a full scale revolt in the region. In the north the Scots were said to be arming while English Royalists seized Carlisle. Throughout the spring and summer, there were also uprisings in Cornwall, Northamptonshire, North Wales, Lincolnshire and Yorkshire where, in June, Royalists seized Pontefract Castle.

The Commons did little to calm this growing unrest. On January 3, 1648, it passed a vote of no future addresses to the king by the substantial majority of 141-92.[27] This was fewer than three months since it had decisively rejected such a motion from Marten and Rainborowe. The Army backed the MPs on January 9 and the Lords backed them on January 17.

Then, on February 8, it resolved, when drawing up the fleet for the Summer Guard, "That these Ships shall be termed the Parliament's Ships."[28] This simply strengthened the seamen's view that Rainborowe was a political appointee and the minority Independents sought control of the Navy, in defiance of the majority Presbyterians who wanted reconciliation with the king. One observer said many people saw it in just these terms: "that they [the Independents] might establish their Government both by Sea and Land, Rainsborough, the Bell-weather of the Republicans, is set over the Fleet."[29] Later the sailors, in their Declaration of the Officers and Company of Seamen aboard his Majesty's ships, made a great point of this move. "The style of commissions at sea were lately altered, leaving out the King's name, and mentioning only the Parliament and Army, which we understood to be a disherison of his Majesty and his children."[30]

Worse the orders Rainborowe had been given were bound to create further tension. In effect, they raised the new vice admiral to the role of "political commissar."[31] The orders from the Committee of the Admiralty, now firmly in Independent hands, were that "he was to inform himself of the diligence and demeanour of all the captains and commanders in the said fleet, and if there be sufficient cause to suspect any captain or commander he is to put their charge into other hands until further orders from this Committee."[32] It was a blueprint for political cleansing.

Rainborowe seems wisely to have ignored, or at least put aside, this provocative command and tried to get on with his job. Having satisfied himself that the guard on the Isle of Wight and the king were secure, his main concern was with Irish privateers. In a letter to Speaker Lenthall, Rainborowe urged the Commons to speed up its confirmation of the summer guard as "the Irish rebels grow very numerous, and lie in almost every road on the parts of Ireland to the great hazard of the trade in England."

The guard was announced on February 7 but not confirmed. So Rainborowe wrote again, on February 18, that "the Irish men of war do not lessen but increase." They were causing havoc in the English Channel. In one incident, an Irish ship with 22 guns attacked four English ships off Plymouth. In the fight, many men were killed and the master of one of the ships had his legs blown off. Rainborowe said he had been told there were 11 Irish ships between the Isle of Wight and Torbay which had now divided into three squadrons, each able to overpower the Navy's single frigates. His letter ended with reminder that the MPs had promised to move "the parson to some other living." This was a reference to Samuel Kem, William Batten's chaplain and now minister at Deal. It was a request the Commons ignored with disastrous consequences.

Rainborowe's remedy for the Irish challenge was to have two squadrons patrolling the Channel, one at the western end around Land's End, the other around Dover.[33] With pamphlets and newspapers also full of the menace of the Irish ships, described either as pirates or Royalists, the Commons at last responded by confirming the summer guard on March 17. Rainborowe was shifted to command the *Reformation*, at 742 tons, 40 guns and 250 crew, one of the biggest ships in the Navy. He was now in command of 22 ships off The Downs. There were a further 13 ships for the Irish summer guard under vice admiral John Crowther and four under Sir George Ayscue, patrolling around Milford and Land's End which suggested the MPs had at last acknowledged the danger of the Irish men of war.[34] Apparently secure in office, Rainborowe next set about re-organising the fleet.

But in April unrest in the country and resentment in the Navy grew. The Royalist press, sensing a change of mood in the country and seizing an opportunity to attack, revelled in the "disastrous" appointment of Rainborowe. The fear, "almost amounting to a phobia",[35] was not about Rainborowe's skills as a naval commander but against his politics. He was, it claimed, sent to turn the Navy into a replica of the NMA. The sailors had long since rejected that path. The previous year, they had turned down approaches from agitators from the Army to join their cause.[36] They were not about to change their minds. To them, Rainborowe's appointment was a direct provocation.

By the end of the month events began to move fast. Two incidents, certainly connected, deeply alarmed Rainborowe. He reported to Lenthall that the Duke of York, the king's middle son and later James II, "did certainly land at Flushing" the previous

Sunday [April 23]. "He went over in a small pink of that place which lay fourteen days in the river, purposely for him." The Duke, it seemed, had escaped from the Army's custody, apparently disguised as a girl, and reached the continent.

Rainborowe also had late news of James's brother, the Prince of Wales. He had left France although his destination was unknown. Rainborowe called for the captains and lieutenants of three ships, the *Antelope*, the *Swallow* and the *John* to join their vessels. The letter was written on April 28 "past eleven at night" and labelled "Haste, Haste, Haste, post haste with speed."[37] York's escape was confirmed within days when the king made him admiral of the fleet. York immediately demanded that Rainborowe obey his commands and called on the support of the seamen. "If Rainsborough will not submit he [York] intends to make Van Trump his vice admiral...I am told that Rainsborough has written to the Parlt that the mariners are so mutinous, he dare not venture to sea with them... I doubt it is all too good to be true."[38]

As Cromwell set out to crush Poyer's revolt in South Wales, Kent's disquiet intensified. By early May, "a revolt of the whole countryside"[39] seemed probable. While the bulk of the rebels came from central and east Kent, there were pockets of revolt in Romney Marsh on the south coast, in and around Canterbury, in Maidstone and the villages of the Weald. The rebels seemed to have three main aims: capture of the county magazines, seizure of the castle and securing the Fleet off Medway and the Downs.[40]

The grand jury of Kent, representing the Royalist faction, had drawn up its petition by May 11. This called basically for a personal treaty to settle the differences between king and Parliament. This was the petition that the Committee of Kent passed on to Parliament and which the Derby House Committee[41] urged them to suppress, along with the rioters.

The infection had also spread to the seamen. One Royalist observer wrote in what was a letter of intelligence to the royalist Earl of Lanerick: "Tis reported that Capt Swanley and Penne are to come with their ships into Milford to the assistance of Poyer, but it is certain that all the Navy is discontented and wavering."[42] Another Royalist wrote, more specifically as early as May 4, that the seamen "begin to be mutinous against Rainsborow who came to the houses to acquaint them therewith."[43] On May 15, the Commons received Rainborowe's list of his ships and how they were deployed.

But by then the Derby House Committee had begun to get edgy. On May 13, it wrote to the Committee of Kent that assemblies were due to be held in Rochester and Clarke's Heath. "Such meetings may prove dangerous" it warned and ordered the Kent men to do what they could to preserve order.[44] Two days later, it warned the Kent Committee that it expected disturbances in the county and told Fairfax he might appoint one or two troops of horse to be on standby around Greenwich and Dartford. It asked Fairfax to act "as speedily as he may".[45]

On the same day, Rainborowe told MPs of the activities of ships at Dieppe, two men of war ready to take arms and horses to Scotland. MPs also had word that day from the Committee of Kent in Canterbury of more disturbances. In turn they ordered Sir Michael Livesey, Sheriff of Kent, zealous Puritan and strong if maverick supporter of Parliament, "to employ his Care and Endeavours to suppress insurrections and tumults there; and for preserving the peace of the County."[46]

Amidst this quickening unrest, the Prince of Wales apparently landed at Sandwich. At least a man claiming to be Prince Charles landed or arrived in Sandwich on May 19. The following day, Rainborowe wrote a hurried and slightly panicky letter to Lenthall. A fleet of ships had come in "from the westward, and in one of them the Prince of Wales." Dressed in "very mean apparel", he travelled onto to Sandwich "and is now at the Bell." His presence had unsurprisingly caused a stir with many people coming to "kiss his hand." He added, betraying some of the pressure he must have been under, "I dare not take time to write more" lastly adding that he had sent magistrates to hold the man there until Parliament decided what it wished to do.[47]

The "Prince" was a man called Cornelius Evans, a Frenchman from Marseille. Under questioning by the mayor of Rochester, Philip Ward, he told a bizarre story which firmly placed the blame for the episode on Rainborowe. He had been lodging in London and had travelled to Kent to find a passage home. After three days without luck in Dover, Evans moved onto Deal.

There he met a gentleman and a gentlewoman walking in a garden near Deal Castle. Evans said the man led him to believe he was Rainborowe accompanied by his wife. Evans walked on to the Crown Inn in the town. He was immediately joined by three seamen who called for beer and pressed him to drink the King's health, which they all did. One of the seamen, apparently a coxswain, told Evans that he thought he recognised him as the Prince of Wales. The coxswain added, according to Evans, "that Colonel Rainsborrow had sent him to this examinant, wishing him this Examinant to say, that he was the Prince."

Even more, Evans claimed the sailor said: "that if he this examinant would so say, and take upon him to personate the Prince, that the Prince would well reward this examinant for the same, and would come over in a short time." Whether lured by the prospect of money or fired by the beer, Evans readily agreed.

After the seamen left the inn, Evans thought better of the idea and hastily moved along the coast to Sandwich. Here his tale gets increasingly farfetched. On his way, he said he saw seamen, some armed with pistols and swords, rowing quickly in a long boat towards the shore. Evans dived into the Bell Tavern in the town and before long these seamen and townspeople came to the inn where they immediately acclaimed him as the Prince.

Evans resumed his pretence of being the Prince and much of the town seem to believe him. He was "well accommodated" in the Bell and the next morning, he was visited by a Captain Foster, the mayor and town clerk of Sandwich. An unknown woman gave him "One

Hundred Pieces of Gold, and Three Bunches of Asparagus" and after deciding he would like to stay with Foster, he was "carried there accordingly."

At Foster's, two seamen came to him separately and each told Evans that Rainborowe remembered him and "desired him to remember the Message which Colonel Rainsborrough had sent to him whilst he was at Deale; and desired this Examinant to be resolute in affirming that he was the Prince; and that Colonel Rainsborrow bid them tell him this Examinant, that it would not be long ere the Prince came over; and that he would well reward this Examinant for the same."

Evans colourful tale petered out with him going out to sea in the long boat with a few of the seamen for some "sport upon the water with a dog" during which the sailors tried to persuade him to "get a Blue Ribbon, and to wear the same cross his breast."[48] Days before Evans made his statement, the Derby House committee had rightly decided he was a fake and had ordered that he "should be sent up thither." Rainborowe was told that the mayor of Sandwich would deliver Evans to him and "if so you are to put him aboard one of you ships and send him safely up to Parliament." If the mayor failed to deliver Evans, Rainborowe was told to send musketeers and seize him.

But the letter to the vice admiral contained a more serious matter. The Committee, in the letter dated May 23, told Rainborowe: "We are also now informed that Sandwich is garrisoned for the king, but we desire you, if you can with safety to the sea affairs, to remove that garrison if it be in your power, and so preserve that place in the obedience and service of the Parliament."[49] At the same time as the Kent rebels secured the garrison at Sandwich, Peter Pett, the naval commissioner at Chatham dockyard, told Derby House that Parliament's control of the dockyard was "near collapse."[50]

In something akin to panic, Derby House issued a raft of orders. It warned Rainborowe, on May 23, that both ships and equipment at the vital Chatham dockyard were "in danger" because of "the insurrection now in Kent and especially about Rochester." He was ordered to remove two ships, the *Fellowship* and the *Hector*, from the dockyard. On the same day, it asked the Committee of the Admiralty to double the guards on the *Sovereign* and the *Prince*, to appoint "two able and faithful commanders" to the ships who would actually stay aboard the vessels and, finally, all sailors attached to the ships who were then ashore were ordered to join their vessels.[51] Trinity House was simultaneously ordered to do everything to keep the seamen loyal.[52] Other naval commissioners were ordered to protect stores being stolen from Deptford.[53]

But the orders came too late. Peter Pett,[54] Parliament's commissioner at Chatham, had "no power to resist them, being forsaken almost by the whole Navy."[55] The rebels seized Upnor Castle, two miles north east of Rochester, which controlled the Medway; the officers and Navy officials at Chatham declared for the king and the *Sovereign* and *Prince* were seized. Captain Henry Jervoise of the *Fellowship* ignored the order to set sail and his ship was also seized.[56]

A dispiriting letter sent by Rainborowe on May 24 to the Committee of the Admiralty summed up the desperate situation. "The present distemper of this country is such, as has put as sad a face on things as ever England saw; and it has begot a distemper in the Fleet which I am confident (though somewhat allayed at present) will be of as dangerous consequence as any one thing besides, if this gathering be not by some means or other speedily repressed. This, which is the greatest motive to the disturbance of the seamen, is that these parts are wholly for the king."

Forlornly and half-heartedly, he went on to outline his plans for deploying his ships. A few would go to Dublin, two others, the *Convertine* and the *Providence* would go north "if the men will be commanded to it", and others would go to the West Country with ammunition to fight the rebels there. His fears over the *Providence* were real. Many of the men who had met the "Prince" in the Bell at Sandwich were from that ship. He ended his letter rather dramatically

"I am, and shall be unto death, Your Lordship's most humble and faithful servant."[57]

Even as Rainborowe wrote his downcast letter, his enemies were gathering at Sandwich. When the rebels took the town they were immediately visited by Samuel Kem, formerly chaplain to the deposed Captain Batten. Now minister at nearby Deal, he was perfectly placed to stir up trouble on his master's behalf. Kem offered to spread the revolt to the fleet by sending letters to the men of every ship in the Downs.

Matthew Carter, a quartermaster in the king's forces who wrote on the events of 1648 in Kent and Essex, recalled Kem's arrival in Sandwich: the evening that the rebels took the town "came a gentleman who had formerly been a divine, and a captain at sea, and was now a major in the service of Parliament." The self-aggrandising man told the Kent men he was now "very penitent" of having supported Parliament and now promised "the best and utmost of his service to the furthering of the Petition and the engagement of the county."

The rebels were persuaded and agreed to employ him. "Letters were drawn up for him that night to every ship one, and in every letter a copy of the Petition, making this absolute result, that some happy success might follow." The men concluded that if Kem's plan did not work, they had lost nothing.

The next day, May 25, the rebels dismissed the mayor of Sandwich, stripped him and other trained captains of their commissions, seized the town's magazine, loaded a wagon with gunpowder, match and ball and got ready to march on Dover.[58]

Rainborowe went ashore on Friday, May 26 following Derby House's orders to recapture Sandwich Castle. As Rainborowe set about his work, Kem took his chance. Probably in alliance with Henry Palmer, the retired naval officer well known in Kent, and others, he went aboard the *Reformation*, the vice admiral's flagship, with letters and copies of the petition. He was greeted with "great cheerfulness."[59] It immeasurably helped his cause that the *Reformation* and other ships in The Downs were manned by Kentish men regularly in touch with men ashore.[60] He was pushing against an open door. The officers and men of the *Reformation* needed little prompting to side with the rebels. Kem told the Kent commissioners that the mariners, "one and all, declared for the king." Those who disagreed, both officers and men, were "seized and confined in the holds."[61]

When Rainborowe heard the "shouts and huzzas" of men aboard the ships in the Downs, "flourishing his sword over his head in defiance", he rushed back to his ship aboard a small pinnace. There the mariners "forced the boat off, telling him 'He had nothing to do with them, nor should he.' He demanded to know the reason of this sudden and amazing alteration? They immediately answered 'They were upon different designs than those they knew he would lead them upon, or join with them in, having declared themselves for the King and the Gentlemen of Kent."

The mutineers acknowledged that Rainborowe had been a "kind and good natured commander to them" and they would not harm him nor his possessions. But their good will stretched only so far. When Rainborowe, "serious and resolute", demanded a pinnace to take him to London, they refused. A coxswain told him: "Sir, we cannot spare you the least vessel in the Downs; they are engaged for better service: there is a Dutch fly-boat on shore, and for sixpence, you may have a passage in her to London."

Rainborowe, no doubt both perplexed and furious at the turn of events, took the advice, went ashore, collected his wife, children and sisters who were staying at Deal Castle "and made the greatest haste to London."[62]

A similar if less dramatic account was given in a letter from Sandwich. When Rainborowe had completed his work at the town, he set out in a small pinnace to return to his ship but his men refused to allow him to board. The men said "they would obey him no longer but would have the king brought to London." They told him that if he tried to board "it would be at his own peril, but if he pleased he might depart in the vessel he was in, and after many threats and other uncivil passages towards him, he came for London."[63]

Rainborowe landed the next day (May 27) at Landguard Fort on a spit of land east of Harwich. He immediately wrote a doleful letter to Lenthall. "My last was said, this most sad. As I told you my fear, it has now come to pass that my ship, the *Swallow*, the *Satisfaction*, the *Hind*, the *Roebuck*, the *Pelican* are all declared for the king; have imprisoned the officers and all others that stood for you."

Sandwich had been taken and Dover Castle and three others in the Downs were under siege. "Had I not been (according to necessity) employed about securing them, my ship had not been so lost," he wrote. Just two hours before the mutiny, Rainborowe said all the captains, save Robert Nixon of the *Roebuck* who was absent, had sworn allegiance to Parliament and "they knew not aboard any of them the least cause to suspect their men." Rainborowe identified his lieutenant, Lisle as the "chief actor" aboard the *Reformation*. Only four of his men had opposed them.

Now Rainborowe got down to business. He said warnings must be sent to the naval commands at Hull, Newcastle and other northern and western garrisons "to take heed least they be betrayed." He told Lenthall he had sent the *Convertine* and *Providence*, "the two ships I mistrusted", northwards. When he had arrived in Harwich, presumably aboard the Dutch ship, he had found the *Tiger* and *Providence*. From there he moved to Languard Fort.

John Mildmay, captain of the *Providence*, said he had then received a letter from Rainborowe to join him there, clearly testing his loyalty. "I went and after conference I told him I was resolved to stand and preserve the Providence for the use and service of the Parliament with my life and fortune and stand for him as Commander-in-Chief." Rainborowe then boarded the ship, and was "unanimously entertained by the officers and company in loyalty and obedience to the Parliament." Amid the celebrations, the flag was run up and more pledges of loyalty made to Parliament.[64] Later that day, Rainborowe sent the *Nicodemus* to Deptford with the request it be held there.[65] As professional as ever, Rainborowe did his best to limit the damage.

But much of the fleet in the Downs was lost. The motive for the mutiny seems clearly to have been political. There were issues of arrears of pay but the seamen were paid not only more but also more regularly than the soldiers. But their own subsequent statements put politics to the fore. In *A Declaration of the Navy*, drawn up on May 28, they said they had "secured the ships for the service of the king and parliament, and have refused to be under the command of Col. Rainsborough, by reason we conceive him to be a man not well affected to the king, parliament, and the kingdom."

They revealed in their first Declaration that they had "unanimously joined with the Kentish gentlemen in their just petition to the parliament." It was signed, by among others, four of the *Reformation's* company, Lieutenant Thomas Lisle, Andrew Mitchell the boatswain, James Allen, a gunner and Thomas Best, a carpenter.[66] All four signed a similar letter to the commander-in-chief of Dover Castle, Captain Alexander Brafields, which was holding out against the rebels. Pointedly it said they had "engaged their lives and fortunes" for king, parliament and the kingdom.[67]

There was also a religious dimension to their revolt. Besides his politics, the rebels did not like Rainborowe's attitude to their faith. In their second statement, the *Revolted Seamen's Declaration* published on July 8, the men of Kent said the Navy had been put "into such hands as were not only enemies to the king and kingdom, but even to the monarchy itself." The king's name had been removed from the ships of the fleet, "we had no settled form of divine worship, no communions, little or no preaching on board but by illiterate and mechanic persons."

There were plans to put "land-soldiers" aboard all ships "to master and overawe the seamen, things so contrary to the ancient customs and orders of the sea." They had to act in all conscience to save their rights, religion, Parliament, the king and the "liberty of the subject." So "God had put it into our minds, and encouraged our hearts, and strengthened our hands; to remove Colonel Rainsborough from the command of the fleet; a man of most destructive principles both in religion and policy, and a known enemy to the peace and ancient government of the kingdom."[68]

There was also Rainborowe's sometimes fearsome personality to take into account. In their Declaration of May 28, the seamen note that "the insufferable pride, ignorance, and insolency of Colonel Rainsborough, the late vice-admiral, alienated the hearts of the seamen."[69] Certainly the situation in which Rainborowe found himself, head of a navy which opposed his politics and radicalism, required a high level of tact, "a quality in which the vice-admiral was notoriously deficient."[70] But countering this is that the seamen also spoke kindly of him and let him go without harm.

But Royalists provocateurs, like Samuel Kem, also played a significant role. Batten was certainly among those who had, at the very least, sent out feelers to the Scots. Kem was quite probably acting in Kent under his guidance. But their intrigues would not have succeeded if the men were not willing. If Parliament thought it had secured the fleet by appointing its own men as captains, it miscalculated. As Capp wrote: "The conspiracy was carried on mainly by warrant officers in the fleet, who served on a more permanent basis than the captains and lieutenants, and often held great sway with the men."[71]

One of the men who assumed a self-appointed role as leader of the revolt on the *Reformation* was the ship's boatswain's mate, a man named Lendall who immediately styled himself as 'admiral.'

Batten's own *Declaration*, published on August 21, was unsurprisingly full of anger and bitterness. He also damned Rainborowe although he could not bring himself to use his name. But there was not even a hint, let alone an acknowledgement, of his own shady behaviour. He could not, he disingenuously claimed, understand why he had been replaced "by a committee at the headquarters at Putney, with the advice of the Adjutators."[72] However he was correct in concluding he was "not of the temper of the Army."

Batten said he never imagined Rainborowe would ever be appointed vice-admiral of a navy. This must have been a political assessment as Rainborowe, as Batten knew, had been brought up to the sea.

His anger spills over as he related how he had been forced to leave Deal Castle while his wife was sick. "How this wrought upon my brother seamen, I hope all my life I shall thankfully remember. They best knew what service I had done, and now beheld mine and their own reward; whereof they expressed so just resentment, when all these injuries offered to me were repaid to my successor." Rainborowe's treatment by the seamen was justified "it being most reasonable that that man should hold no command, who openly professed himself to be a leveller."[73]

But Batten deluded himself if he thought the seamen's main motive in obstructing and humiliating Rainborowe was to avenge the treatment of their former vice admiral. The seamen had expressed a level of affection for Rainborowe. Peacock summed it up neatly if with slight exaggeration. "No mutiny was ever more successful, or carried out with more regard to the feelings or even comfort of the deposed admiral. We may therefore certainly conclude that the sailors had a formed a high opinion of his character."[74] They wanted him away because of his politics and attitude to religion. It was purely business. As Rainborowe himself said, these were men who were for the king.

Warwick, appointed by Parliament as the new lord high admiral on May 29, arrived at the Down the next day in the *Nicodemus*. He called a meeting of the captains of the revolted ships but Kem, men from Kent and some mutineers from the *Reformation* also attended. Their strategy was to try and persuade Warwick to support a personal treaty with the king and the disbandment of the NMA. This must have been an awkward moment for the earl as he had spent much of 1647, as a Parliamentary Commissioner, encouraging Fairfax and his army to do just that.

This time Warwick stood by the NMA and refused the seamen's demands. In retaliation, the seamen threatened to put him ashore like

Rainborowe. He was eventually allowed to sail away with his self intact but his dignity in tatters. He was saved by his old adversary Fairfax who routed the rebels' army at Maidstone on June 1. The earl returned to the Downs and summoned Lendall. The self styled admiral ignored him. The six original revolted ships had now been joined by the *Convertine*, the *Greyhound* and the *Warwick*.[75]

Almost in desperation, Warwick and, unbelievably, Batten rushed to Portsmouth to try and secure the loyalty of the ships there. This he won on June 4 and, to add to his success, the *Greyhound* and the *Warwick* quietly slipped away from the Downs. The only real choice left to the mutineers was to join the Prince of Wales in the Netherlands. "Fired by Kem and the Kentish gentlemen still aboard, they...sailed for Holland on June 10." Batten joined them a few days later.[76]

Fairfax did not so much as defeat the rebel army in Maidstone on June 1 as crush it. The raw, largely untrained Kent men were no match for the NMA's battle-hardened ranks. About 10,000 of the rebels had held a rendezvous at Barnham Heath, between Rochester and Maidstone on May 29 as Fairfax began his march into the county. The rebels acclaimed the earl of Norwich, a man with no experience of war, as their general. Their army was based mainly around Rochester and Maidstone in the north of the county.

Fairfax, at the head of 7,000 men, marched determinedly towards Rochester but then sent just a small force to attack the town while he turned his main body south towards Maidstone. At 7pm on June 1 in torrential rain, the bitter battle began. Some 2,000 men were defending the town against Fairfax's larger force. Despite disputing every street, house and turning, the rebels were forced back and eventually routed. When men at Rochester heard of the defeat, with at least 300 dead, many began to flee.[77]

Norwich, followed by a minority of his bedraggled army, reached the banks of the Thames where they crossed at Dartford. Some were lucky enough to get in a boat, other swam, many drowned. When Norwich surveyed his forces in Essex, there were 1,500 left. Some

Royalists continued the fight in Kent where they were joined by men from Surrey and Sussex.[78] But Fairfax's focus was now on Essex and the King's forces now gathering in that county.

Norwich, once he crossed the Thames, was joined by hundreds of volunteers, including London apprentices, former Royalist officers ready for one last throw at victory and formidable soldiers like Sir Charles Lucas and Sir George Lisle. When they reached Chelmsford, in the south east of the county, more recruits "poured in."[79]

This growing army was shadowed by Colonel Whalley as it moved out of Chelmsford on June 12, heading north. Norwich was clearly heading for his home region of East Anglia where he no doubt hoped for fresh supplies and more recruits. But he was persuaded by the extrovert and overbearing Lucas to make a detour to Colchester, in the north east of Essex. This was Lucas's home town and where he promised Norwich hundreds more recruits.

But Fairfax was now in full pursuit. He had crossed the Thames on June 11 and by June 12 was just two miles west of Colchester. The next day, the bulk of his army arrived and Norwich and his men were trapped. Fairfax wasted no time and sent his troops in on June 13.

But they were met by both heavy cannon and fierce street fighting led by Lucas, Lisle and Lord Capel, one of the main Royalist leaders in the second civil war. Fairfax made three attempts to storm the town but was driven back with heavy losses.[80] The next day, the siege of Colchester began. It was the nadir of the civil wars.

It is not clear when Rainborowe re-joined Fairfax and the Army. One report suggests he joined Fairfax at the head of half a regiment of foot to fight the Kent rebels and was with him all the way to Colchester.[81] Rainborowe was certainly one of the general's senior officers during the siege but the first mention of him is for June 26.

He was at Languard Fort on May 27 when he wrote his distressed letter to Lenthall and still acting as if he were vice admiral. After Warwick took over, it seems more likely that he returned to London with his wife, sisters and family and from there joined Fairfax. What he would have seen in his short stay in the capital was likely to have both surprised and disturbed him. The City, staunch supporter and paymaster of Parliament, was by the summer of 1648 a "hotbed of Royalism."[82] The City was refusing to pay its taxes, a contributory factor in the soldiers' pay arrears, and in April, up to 4,000 apprentices had marched down Fleet Street demanding a treaty with the king. Fairfax had had to deploy Rich's cavalry regiment to disperse them.[83] When Kent rebelled, hundreds of young London men joined up to the Royalist cause. Fairfax withdrew his men to Southwark which, like the other suburbs, was still loyal to Parliament.

After the defeat at Maidstone on June 1, hundreds of Royalists gathered at Blackheath. When the Derby House committee said it could not withstand an invasion of the City, Parliament made some desperate concessions. This included the release of imprisoned City officials. That and some sharp military moves by Skippon, whose troops controlled London, stemmed the flow of Londoners flocking to the Royalists' aid in Colchester.[84]

Once Fairfax had decided on a siege and needed expert help in building up the siege lines around the town, it became inevitable that Rainborowe would be needed. It was a swift rehabilitation after the humiliation of the naval revolt. Rainborowe was lucky to have a general who so readily indulged him once again.

Fairfax and his men moved quickly. Within three weeks they had built "probably the most sophisticated set of siege lines in either civil war."[85] With the River Colne acting as a barricade north of the town, Fairfax built walls, earthworks and forts from the river in the north west, all around the south to the Colne in the east by East Bridge. Altogether there were ten forts surrounding the town with the siege lines about 1000 metres from Colchester's walls. Rainborowe was put in charge of the troops in the north with the large fort named after him standing directly north of both the town and the Colne. To the east was Fort Bloyes and to the north west Fort Fothersgall.

By June 26, the army had also bridged the Colne upstream of Mile End between the forts of Rainborowe and Colonel Ewer "so the town was entirely shut in on the side [the west] and the royalists had no place to get out but East Bridge."[86] It is not clear which troops Rainborowe initially commanded. However he took over the regiment known as the Tower Guard on July 6. These men had originally been guardians of the Tower of London. Parliament had ordered their number to increase by 400 to 1,000 in April because of the unrest in the City. Under Colonel Simon Needham, another New Englander, they had then been sent to help Fairfax in Kent and then onto Colchester. Needham was killed in the first assault on the town on June 13. His replacement, Lieutenant-Colonel William Shambrook was shot on July 5 and died the next day. Rainborowe then took over the regiment now numbering around 400. Firth reported that Rainborowe was "very active during the rest of the siege."[87]

Both Needham and Shambrook were allegedly killed by poisoned bullets. Parliament was told on June 28 that three prisoners taken, a Kentish man and two London apprentices "had chewed bullets rowled in sand in their pockets, contrary to the Law of Arms; and without doubt, Col. Needham was shot with such, for we have had shots more dangerous than his cured." Again it heard on July 6: "Lieut. Colonel Shambrooke was shot in the body, the bullet since taken out, and we find it poison'd, boiled in coprice; our soldiers hope to be revenged of them the next engagement for this poison'd bullet." Norwich, the Royalist commander in Colchester, denied using poisoned bullets but admitted using "rough cast slugs, they were the best they could send on the sudden."[88]

It was a taste of things to come. While both sides regularly fired artillery at their enemy and the soldiers clashed "almost every day"[89], the siege was also taking on a far darker side. Starvation was an acknowledged part of a siege strategy. But at Colchester both sides also used fire as deliberate tactic. In an age when most buildings were of wood, it was a "wilful infliction of a harm that all town dwellers feared."[90] As the siege ground on, there were reports of not just of poisoned bullets but of rape, torture, maids having their finger tips burned off, boys burned with matches, men and women used as target practice.[91] Amid it all was the constant propaganda battle waged by Parliament. Kites and arrows were sent into the town with messages relating the rout of the king's forces by Cromwell and Lambert at Preston,[92] or making tempting offers of quarter for men who deserted.

But it was hunger and the lack of ammunition which played the decisive roles. By August, the people trapped in Colchester were eating whatever they could find, Carter reported. "Now began horseflesh to be as precious to us as the choicest meats before, the soldiers in general, and all officers and gentlemen, from the lords to the lowest degree or quality eating nothing else unless cats and dogs."

He added that horseflesh had become "so delicious a food amongst the soldiers" that stables were robbed every day "and our horses knocked on the head and sold in the shambles by the pound." Dogs fared no better. There was none left in a short time, he said, "for it was customary for each soldier to reserve half his ammunition loaf, and in a morning walk the streets, and if he discovered a dog, to drop him a piece of bread and so decoy him on till within his reach, and then with the but-end of his musket knock his brains out, and march away with him to his quarters. I have known six shillings given for the side of a dog and yet but a small one neither." [93] In the last month of the siege at least 800 horses were killed for food.

By the end of July, Parliament had cut off all fresh water supplies to the beleaguered town, forcing the inhabitants to drink muddy or contaminated water. This, with the lack of salt to preserve meat, led to diseases, like dysentery and flux. By the third week of August, the town had also run out of malt to make beer or bread.[94]

Amid these horrors, the siege carried on as normal. On July 25, Rainborowe led a party of troops out of his fort, across the River Colne to attack Middle Mill, to the north of the town walls. Rainborowe's men "fell upon them [the Royalist guard] furiously and obliging them to retreat into the town, afterwards set fire to the mill." According to Carter, the sortie ended in disaster for the Parliamentarians. "A party in the town (chiefly gentlemen) marched down upon them, and attacked with such resolution and spirit, that they were obliged to take to their legs and run away, first throwing down their arms."

They retreated in such disarray, that many went to the wrong part of the river to get across and were drowned. Rainborowe lost 12 men in the attack with six more taken prisoner. Carter said it was to have been the start of a major bid to storm the town but "on meeting with this repulse, laid aside their design."[95]

It was the civilians trapped in the town who fared the worst. Starving, without clean water, prey to disease, subject to frequent bombardment from artillery, constantly in fear of fire, they craved an end to their nightmare. Fairfax had been told, in a letter from Capell, Norwich and Lucas on August 21 that the civilians were "ready to starve to death for want of food." . The mayor of the town asked Fairfax if they could leave. The general, rightly but harshly sensing the siege would end sooner if they stayed, refused. But Norwich, faced with nightly demonstrations by townspeople outside his quarters demanding he surrender, had no real answer.

His solution smacked of cynicism. He turned 500 women and children out of the town to the mercy of the Army. They, "with much confidence", marched towards Rainborowe's quarters. "He commands a cannon to be shot off, but so as not to hurt them; they come on notwithstanding; he orders the siring some musquets with powder; that daunts them not; he sends out some soldiers, bids them strip some; this makes them run; but four were stripped." The terrified mass ran back to the town gates but were refused entry. For hours they were trapped in no man's land while Fairfax and Norwich argued.[96] "They can neither have gone backwards nor forwards nor remain where they were but die suddenly."[97]

During the stand off one of Parliament's horses was shot. It led to dozens running out of the town to try and get it. Some were killed before soldiers drove them off. The next day they were back trying to get pieces of the now stinking meat.[98] Meanwhile, the women had eventually been allowed back into the town.

Fairfax had first offered terms for surrender on June 20. There would be honourable conditions for surrender for all except those who had broken their oath not to wage war against Parliament again. The exceptions included Sir Charles Lucas. The terms were scornfully rejected by Norwich, leading Fairfax to withdraw his offer of quarter to officers. By August 17, Norwich was close to desperation. His stores were nearly empty, the ammunition almost gone. There was not bread for more than three days and if the town were stormed, there was only enough in the magazine for two hours' resistance.[99]

Norwich and his council of war decided to sue for peace. On August 17, they sent a local physician, Dr Glyston, to Fairfax. The general's reply was uncompromising. As they had rejected his earlier summons, Fairfax told them "best conditions we must expect from him must be to submit to mercy." Only the ranks and junior officers would be allowed to go home.[100] He followed up his terms with a hail of arrows on August 22, carrying the messages that all except senior officers, lords and gentlemen would be allowed to go. These must "submit to mercy."

On August 24, the crushing blow of the defeat of Hamilton at Preston, ending all hope of relief, reached the town, courtesy of more of Fairfax's arrows and kites. To tighten the screw, the general also stepped up his preparations for what looked like a plan to storm the town.

The next day, rumours that Lucas, Lisle and other seniors officers were planning a break out spread around the town. The men and the civilians would be left to their own devices. It was a poor return for nearly 75 days' brave defiance amid soul destroying hardship. It instantly ended the unity and loyalty that kept the resistance alive.[101] Two days later the articles of surrender were signed.

"We had scarce left uneaten one cat or dog in the town, some horses we had yet alive but not many...as for bread, there was not corn left for one day's provision, and there were many mouths to feed, and we had made all kind of corn the town could afford, as malt, barley, oats, wheat, rye, peat, and all we could recover into bread, for eight weeks together to lengthen our store, still contented to undergo any hardship that might probably tend to the advancement of the general good; but our hopes were now quite dissolved into absolute fear of unavoidable ruin."[102]

Rainborowe was among the commissioners appointed by Fairfax to handle the peace negotiations. More significantly, he was also on the council of wear which dealt with the last remaining issue of this bitter siege: what to do with the Royalist officers who, in the first civil war, had taken an oath not to take arms against Parliament again. This proved to be every bit as bitter as the siege itself.

Many Royalists believed that Fairfax's hardball tactics in the run up to surrender were the result of him being the "tool of his council of war", in particular of Ireton and Rainborowe. These two, former opponents at the Putney Debates less than a year ago, were now "united in a relentless demand for retribution." If fair quarter officially meant that those who surrendered would not only escape with their lives but also get fair treatment, for these two it stood for something a lot harsher. They would keep their skins but not much else. By the same measure, mercy meant surrender but "without certain assurance of quarter."[103] In fact Fairfax shared these tough views. The leaders of the town's defiance could expect the worst.

After negotiations that took ten days, Rainborowe and the other commissioners signed the terms of surrender at 10pm on August 27. By 10am the next morning, all arms and artillery had to be given up and all men and junior officers to assemble at the East Gate to receive fair quarter. An hour later the senior officers, lords and gentlemen were to be in the King's Head to surrender to the mercy of Fairfax.

In the afternoon the regiments of Rainborowe and one other colonel entered the town. They "saw a sad sight of so many fair houses burnt, and so many inhabitants sick and weak, with living upon horses and dogs, and eating the very draught and grains for preservation of their lives."[104] At 2pm Fairfax himself entered the town. After inspecting the defences which had defied him for 75 days, the general retired to his new headquarters in the town hall and called a meeting of his council of war.

Later that afternoon Colonel Isaac Ewer was sent to the King's Head to bring them Lucas, Lisle, Sir Bernard Gascoigne and Colonel Farre to the council. Carter, writing with insight, said they at first thought Ewer had come to visit but soon realised "he brought a sentence of death in his heart." Lucas must have guessed something similar for Carter said he "took his solemn leave of the Lords and the rest of his fellow prisoners." With Farre already escaped, Ewer then led his three captives back to the town hall.[105] An hour later, a messenger from Lucas arrived at the King's Head, asking that "a chaplain might immediately be sent to him: this struck a dead sorrow in the hearts of all."[106]

The council of war wasted little time. When Lucas and Lisle arrived, they were told: "That after so long and obstinate a defence, it was highly necessary, for the example of others, that some form [of] military justice should be executed; and therefore, that Council had determined, that they, Sir Charles Lucas, and Sir George Lisle, should be immediately shot to death."

The pair, along with Gascoigne who was also sentenced to death, were then taken to a dungeon in the county jail in the town's castle. With Rainborowe and Colonel Whalley accompanying him, Ireton then told the three to prepare for death.[107]

Lucas pointedly asked by whom he had been condemned, whether it was Fairfax or the council of war. Ireton, the lawyer, replied that it was "by the Parliament upon your own actions." To drive his point home, Ireton then lectured the three that those who had waged against parliament for a second time were "traitors and rebels and they (Parliament) do employ us as soldiers by authority from them to suppress and destroy."

Lucas claimed he fought within the law under a commission from the king. It did not wash with Ireton who told him: "There was no assurance of quarter given to any of you, and the general did expressly declare that he would be free to it."[108]

After being refused time to settle their affairs and prepare their souls, the three prayed with the chaplain. "Then they were hurried out of the castle, and conducted to a green spot of ground on the north-side of the said castle, a few paces from the wall." There they were confronted by three rows of musketeers. Also again present to witness the executions were Ireton, Rainborowe and Whalley.

The first to be shot was Lucas. He fell to his knees to again pray than rose and "with a cheerful countenance, opened his doublet, and showed them his breast, and then placing his hands by his side, called out to his executioners, 'See, I am ready for you, and now do your worst.'" A moment later he was dead.

Lisle, according to Carter, met his death with equal courage. After exchanging banter with the musketeers about whether they were too far away to hit him, Lisle "kneeled down for prayers for some minutes, and after uttering many invocations in the name of Jesus Christ, rose up, and said, 'I am now ready; traitors do your worst.' Which words were hardly out of his mouth, before they fired at him, and some of the shot going through his body, he dropped down dead."[109] Gascoigne was reprieved because as an Italian, Fairfax feared his death might lead to reprisals against English people in Italy.

Fairfax's instant justice produced instant martyrs. Almost overnight the deaths of Lucas and Lisle became the stuff of myths. A pamphlet, entitled *'An elegie on that most barbarous, unparalleled, unsoldierly murder, committed at Colchester, upon the persons of the two most incomparable, Sir Charles Lucas and Sir George Lisle'* was just one of many produced by Royalists in the months after their deaths. Marchamont Needham[110] wrote in *Mercurius Pragmaticus*, a strongly Royalist newspaper, in the edition for the week September 5-12, 1648 that Lucas and Lisle had been shot "in cold blood."

Needham reported that Fairfax had discovered his "bloody inclination" and with a "council of war consisting of the prime leading saints of his Army had ordered the two to be "shot to death." Noting "what sweet justiciaries this crew of Levellers are", it makes clear that neither Lucas nor Lisle had a chance to defend themselves in a court. Lucas, he claimed, was "tied to a pillar and cruelly butchered by two desperate soldiers." Lisle's manner of heroic death left his enemies "smitten with horror." Both, Needham assured his readers, were now martyrs.

But while these scathing reports in *Mercurius Pragmaticus* must have infuriated Royalists into believing that the two knights had been unlawfully killed, neither mentioned Rainborowe by name. In his summing up that the pair had been murdered in cold blood, Needham names only "Tom Fairfax, Ireton, Whalley and those other monsters of Independency."[111]

The legend took hold, at least in Royalists circles, that the two had been wantonly killed. Their deaths embraced "illegality, bad faith, cruelty, and murder." The conditions in which they were killed, the state of the country, the fact of war and a bitter siege were swept aside. Even the characters of the two men did not matter – Lucas was capable of being a nasty piece of work, guilty, according to Whalley, of putting prisoners to death in the first civil war. Even Clarendon, the faithful Royalist historian, did not like him much.

It all had little to do with "the myth of their martyrdom, which depended on the commitment to the king's cause that they shared with their panegyrists, the wickedness ascribed to the villains, and their unflinching and principled courage."[112] As their cause was stamped out in the wet miserable summer of 1648, first at Preston and then at Colchester, the Royalists needed something to cling to. Lucas and Lisle fitted the bill.

Years later when their tombstone over their bodies in St Giles' Church, Colchester, where they were buried, was engraved, it repeated the same theme: by the command of Fairfax they had been "in cold blood barbarously murdered."

As ever Fairfax said little about it and Rainborowe and Ireton nothing. In a letter to the earl of Manchester, speaker of the Lords, the day after the surrender, the general matter of factly reported the deaths. "For some satisfaction to military justice, and in part to avenge for the innocent blood they have caused to be spilt, and the trouble, damage and mischief they have brought upon this town, this country and the kingdom, I have, with the advice of a Council of War, of the chief officers, both of the country forces and the army, ordered two of the men who were rendered at mercy, to be shot to death before any of them had quarter assured them.

"The persons pitched upon this example, were Sir Charles Lucas and Sir George Lisle; in whose military execution, I hope your lordships will not find cause to think your honour or justice prejudiced." The speaker's reply made no reference to the execution, suggesting he found no cause for complaint. It merely thanked him for his "good service done in [the] regaining of the said town" and asked that Norwich and Capell be sent to Windsor Castle under guard. It was signed "your friend and servant", again suggesting nothing was amiss.[113]

The only other time Fairfax referred to the executions was years later. In his war memorial, he wrote: "Sir Charles Lucas and Sir George Lisle, being mere soldiers of fortune, and falling into our hands by chance of war, were executed; and in this I did nothing but according to my commission, and the trust reposed in me."[114] "Here Fairfax stretched the term 'soldier of fortune' beyond it limits and clearly intended it as an insult." Whatever may be thought of Lucas, he was not at Colchester for the money.

But as the condemnation of Fairfax, Rainborowe and Ireton ballooned, there was a far more worrying explanation being put forward for the death, at least, of Lucas. Fairfax, having been thoroughly bested by Lucas's rampant cavalry at Marston Moor in 1644, simply wanted revenge. Andrew Hopper, biographer of Fairfax, believes there is something in this. "Although Fairfax acted within martial law, these executions were unprecedented and clearly motivated by vengeance."[115] Phil Jones, in *The Siege of Colchester*, quotes an unnamed MP saying the executions were "wholly an act of revenge."[116] It is impossible to say this is the case. What can be said is that even many Royalists thought it was out of character for Fairfax, a commander regarded as a man of honour. Hence the blame heaped on the radical Rainborowe and Ireton.

But there is an alternative explanation. At the end of the siege, Fairfax, Ireton, Rainborowe and Whalley were angry men. Royalists, fired by the refusal of a slippery and deceitful king to sign any peace treaty, had started a second civil war. After four years in which hundreds of thousands had died and been maimed, fighting had started again across the country when most people yearned for peace.

Worse, they had just spent 75 days besieging a town in effect held hostage by the group of these Royalists. Some had surrendered in the first war's battles and skirmishes and promised never to fight Parliament again. Yet here they were involved in what became a thoroughly nasty siege where fire, hunger and even disease became tactical weapons. Lucas, Lisle and Capell were just as fanatical as Rainborowe was held to be. When the Colchester siege was over what was to stop them – as they surely would – continuing the fight another day, in another town. Execution may have seemed the best way to stop this and deter others.

Manchester's warning that the king only had to win once but Parliament had to win every time may have rung in their ears. With London possibly changing its loyalties, risking all that had been gained by the years of fighting, Fairfax and his officers not only wanted a quick end to more fighting but an conclusion that sent an unmistakeable message to potential Royalist rebels: this is what will happen to you. It meant summary justice for the two held to be the worst. Others who took part in Royalist uprisings in 1648, including Capell, the earl of Holland and the Duke of Hamilton were all executed after being tried the following March. It was the *summary* deaths of Lucas and Lisle that created the fury. It cost Rainborowe his life.

After the ending of the siege, Rainborowe returned to London but also seems to have spent some time at the new Army headquarters in St. Albans. The crisis that had gripped the City was largely over. The heroic Skippon had kept the lid on most of the Royalist unrest and the victories at Preston and Colchester had ended the Royalist dreams. But the situation was far from stable.

The radicals were boosted by the release of John Lilburne, one of the Leveller leaders, and John Wildman, Rainborowe's ally at Putney, from prison in August.[117] Henry Marten, Rainborowe's republican ally, was also again active, helping to organise a major petition in London. It contained all 27 of the main points of the Leveller programme and, according to Lilburne, attracted 40,000 signatures. It was presented to Parliament on September 11.[118]

To counter this, Presbyterians, like Denzil Holles, had now resumed their seats in the Commons. Their main aim was to negotiate a peace with the king. The vote of "no Address", passed in January, was repealed in August and talks with the king got underway on September 15 at Newport on the Isle of Wight. But if the Commons, with the Presbyterians once again dominant, were again moving towards a deal with the king, army leaders were moving in the opposite direction. The immense anger at the unnecessary second civil war was homing in on Charles himself, the "man of blood". If Rainborowe had believed, since August 1647, that it was not possible to reach an agreement with a man like Charles, others were now joining him.

There is no record of Rainborowe being involved in any radical activities in the autumn although it seems likely that he would have spoken with his brother, William, to his fellow, like-minded MPs, like Marten, and perhaps even with Wildman. But surprisingly, it was Ireton, the innately conservative lawyer at Putney, who emerged as the Army leader opposed to a deal with the king. Partly from the scars of the second civil war, Ireton had considerably changed his views.[119] He was now convinced the Army should stop any agreement between Charles and Parliament and put the king on trial.[120]

Rainborowe was required for other duties. While the second civil war was largely over, Pontefract Castle in Yorkshire was still holding out for the king. Fairfax, mindful that Rainborowe was his best siegemaster, ordered him north to take the town. But the Royalists were still seething at Rainborowe for his role in the execution of Lucas and Lisle. There had already been one attempt on his life. The Commons heard, on September 30, that Rainborowe and a captain were "set upon by three of the King's Party between London and St. Albans... the Cavaliers seeing their gallantry and resolution, put spurs to their horses and rode for it, and being extraordinary well mounted over rid them."[121]

But by that time Rainborowe, under the shadow of death, was already riding north.

Notes for Chapter Seven

1. Commons Journal, v, p. 359.
2. Lords Journal, ix, pp. 526-528.
3. Rushworth, *Historical Collections*, vii, p. 923-52.
4. John Rowland Powell and E. K. Timings (eds.), *Documents Relating to the Civil War 1642-48*, (London, 1963), pp. 296-7.
5. Commons Journal, v, p. 401-4.
6. Lords Journal, ix, pp. 605-12.
7. Lords Journal, ix, pp. 614-615; Powell and Timings, *Documents*, p. 297.
8. Lords Journal, ix, pp. 616-7. Powell and Timings, *Documents*, pp. 297-8.
9. John Burley was captain of the *Yarmouth Castle* and was involved in an alleged plot on December 27 to free the king. He was charged with treason, tried at Winchester in January, 22 and executed on February 3. There were claims that Parliament had planted "stooges" on the jury to obtain a guilty verdict. Little is known of Burley or what prompted his "plot."
10. Edmund Prideaux, a Cornish lawyer, was appointed solicitor general in November 1648 but resigned shortly afterwards, refusing to take part in the trial and execution of the king. He died in 1659.
11. Commons Journal, v, p. 413.
12. Lords Journal, ix, pp. 619-621.
13. Huntingdon, "Sundry Reasons", *Lords Journal*, x, pp. 406-14.
14. Lords Journal, x, pp. 115-6.
15. Mike Braddick, 'An English Military Revolution?', *Historical Review* 36, no. 4 (1993), p. 970.
16. Andrew Thorn, 'Naval Finance and the origins and development of Ship Money' in Mark Charles Fissel (ed.), *War and Government in Britain 1598-1650*, (Manchester, 1991), p. 135.
17. Braddick, *Military Revolution?*, p. 970.
18. Tonnage and poundage was a tax levied on the maritime community to pay for the country's naval defence. By the time Charles became king the "lion's share...had long been swallowed up by the Royal Household." Thorn, 'Naval Finance', p. 141.
19. Brenner, *Merchants and Revolution*, p. xii and p. 233.
20. Andrews, *Ships, Money and Politics*, p. 80.
21. This could possibly be the same Captain John Burley who in 1648 attempted to rescue Charles from Carisbrook Castle.
22. Powell and Timings, *Documents*, pp. 2-3. Stephen Greenberg, 'Seizing the Fleet in 1642: Parliament, the Navy and the Printing Press', *Mariner's Mirror*, No 77, 3, (1991), pp. 229-230.
23. Clarendon, *History of the Rebellion*, v, p. 215.
24. Greenberg, 'Seizing the Fleet', pp. 228-9.
25. Alan Everitt, *The Community of Kent and the Great Rebellion 1640-60*, (Leicester, 1966), p. 231 and p.232.

26. *Newes from Kent A true and most exact relation of the particular commotions and transactions of the Kentish designe*, (London, 1648), p. 2. Everitt, *Community of Kent*, p. 235.
27. Commons Journal, v, pp. 415-6.
28. Ibid., v, pp. 457-8.
29. George Bate, *Elenchus motuum nuperorum in Anglia, 1685*, p. 86. Quoted in Kennedy, 'Naval Revolt', p. 250.
30. The Declaration of the Officers and Company of Seamen aboard his Majesty's ships, quoted in Powell and Timings, *Documents*, pp. 354-5.
31. Powell and Timings, *Documents*, p. 300.
32. SP 16/515, 134, quoted in Powell and Timings, *Documents*, p. 312.
33. Tanner MSS, lviii, ii, 707. Quoted in Peacock, *Archaeologia*, pp. 29-30.
34. Commons journal, v, pp. 502-5.
35. Robert Ashton, *Counter Revolution The Second Civil War and its Origins, 1646-8*, (London, 1994), pp. 412-3.
36. The agitators had sent a letter, dated June 21, 1647 to the "honest seamen of England" urging them to unite in a common cause. See Wolfe, *Leveller Manifestoes*, pp. 144-6.
37. Tanner MSS, lvii, 23. Quoted in Peacock, *Archaeologia*, pp. 31-2 and Powell and Timings, *Documents*, p. 324. A pink is a small sail boat. The three absent captains were Edward Hall, Edward Popham and Edward Miott.
38. Clarendon MS 30 (2), 2689. Quoted in Jones, *Thomas Rainborowe*, p. 103, Peacock, *Archaeologia*, p. 32.
39. Everitt, *Community of Kent*, p. 241.
40. Ibid., pp. 243-71.
41. The Derby House Committee was in effect the Cabinet which oversaw the conduct of the war and foreign policy. It was previously known as the Committee of Both Kingdoms until early 1648 when the Scots were removed from it and sent home.
42. *Hamilton Papers 1638-50*, Samuel Rawson Gardiner (ed.), (Camden Society, 1880), 120, p. 188. The letter is dated April 25, 1648 but the writer is not named. William Penn was appointed captain of the frigate, *Assurance* for the winter guard of Ireland for 1647-8. There is no mention of a Captain Swanley in the Parliamentary list.
43. Henry Oxinden, *The Oxinden and Peyton Letters 1642-1670*, Dorothy Gardiner (ed.), p. 38. Quoted in Kennedy, 'Naval Revolt', p. 250.
44. CSPD, 21/24, p. 56.
45. Ibid., pp. 58-59.
46. Commons Journal, v, p. 559.
47. Tanner MSS, lvii, 91, quoted in Powell and Timings, *Documents*, pp. 327-8.
48. Lords Journal, x, pp. 288-91. Not all Royalists were taken in by Evans. Matthew Carter, a quartermaster in the king's forces, visited him and quickly concluded he was an impostor. Carter in his booklet, *A true relation of that honourable though unfortunate expedition of Kent, Sussex and Colchester in 1648*, (Colchester, 1789), wrote: "The youth carried on the cheat upwards of a week, having a guard of musketeers attend him." Evans was eventually taken first to the Isle of Thanet, then to Canterbury and finally to Newgate Prison. Pp. 37-9.
49. CSPD 21/24, p. 68. Also quoted in Powell and Timings, *Documents*, p. 329.
50. Bernard Capp, *Cromwell's Navy The Fleet and the English Revolution 1648-1660*, (Oxford, 1989), p. 19.

51. CSPD 21/24, pp. 71-3.
52. CSPD 1648-9, pp. 78-81. Capp, *Cromwell's Navy*, p. 19.
53. CSPD 21/4, p. 75.
54. Peter Pett helped build the *Sovereign* with his father Phineas Pett. It was the ship Charles offered to William Rainborowe. Despite his links with the Crown, Pett was strongly for Parliament and later served the Commonwealth.
55. Historical MSS Commission, part i, Portland MSS, pp. 460-1.
56. Capp, *Cromwell's Navy*, pp. 19-20.
57. Tanner MSS, lviii, i, p.100; quoted in Peacock, *Archaeologica*, p. 35, Powell and Timings, *Documents*, pp. 329-330.
58. Carter, *A true relation*, pp. 34-5.
59. Ibid., p. 43.
60. Everitt, *Community of Kent*, p. 250.
61. Carter, *A true relation*, p. 43.
62. Ibid., pp. 43-45.
63. *A Letter from Sandwich*, Thomason Tracts, E.445, 32, quoted in Powell and Timings, *Documents*, pp. 331-2. The letter is dated May 25 which cannot be correct.
64. Tanner MS, lvii, 117. Powell and Timings, *Documents*, pp. 334-5. Mildmay's letter to Lenthall was written on May 28.
65. Tanner MS, lvii, 115. Powell and Timings, *Documents*, pp. 330-1.
66. *A Declaration of the Navy*, Thomason E. 667, 36, 12. Powell and Timings, *Documents*, pp. 332-3.
67. *Newes from Kent*, pp. 12-13. Brafields refused to join the rebels or surrender the castle. It held out until relieved on June 6, 1648.
68. Thomason E. 669, Folio 12, 69. Powell and Timings, *Documents*, pp. 354-5.
69. Thomason E.667, 36, 12. Powell and Timings, *Documents*, p. 334.
70. Powell and Timings, *Documents*, p. 300.
71. Capp, 'Naval Operations', p. 180.
72. The meeting of the Admiralty Committee which had planned to dismiss him was held in London.
73. Thomason E. 460, 13. Powell and Timings, *Documents*, pp. 364-5. Batten was not much trusted by the sailors with whom he defected. He was shortly put ashore and lived quietly during the Commonwealth years. He became an MP and Surveyor of the Navy after the Restoration and worked with Samuel Pepys who seems to have disliked him. Batten died in 1667.
74. Peacock, *Archaeologia*, p. 37.
75. Capp, 'Naval Operations', p. 182.
76. Ibid., p. 183.
77. Everitt, *Community of Kent*, pp. 262-3.
78. Ibid., pp. 264-5. Resistance in Kent continued until August when the last attempt at an uprising was defeated.
79. Barbara Donagan, *War in England 1642-1649*, (Oxford, 2008), p. 317.
80. Ibid., p. 322.
81. Peacock, *Archaeologia*, p. 37. He gives no source for this information.
82. Ian Gentles, 'The Struggle for London in the Second Civil War', *Historical Journal* 26, no. 2 (June, 1983), p. 290.

83. Ibid., p. 287.
84. Ibid., p. 293.
85. Donagan, *War in England*, p. 323.
86. Phil Jones, *The Siege of Colchester 1648*, (Stroud, 2003), p. 74.
87. Firth, *Regimental History*, pp. 573-4.
88. Rushworth, *Historical Collections*, vii, pp. 1169, 1181 and 1179.
89. Carter, *A true relation*, p. 87.
90. Donagan, *England at War*, p. 330.
91. Jones, *Siege of Colchester*, p. 125.
92. Cromwell's and Lambert's defeat of the Scots army under Hamilton and the northern Royalist forces under Langdale at Preston on August 17 marked the end of major resistance in the north.
93. Carter, *A true relation*, pp. 147-8.
94. Donagan, *England at War*, p. 338.
95. Carter, *A true relation*, pp. 142-3.
96. Rushworth, *Historical Collections*, vii, pp. 1236-7. The incident happened around August 18-20. It was reported to Parliament on August 22.
97. Clarke MSS 114, fo. 60.
98. Rushworth, *Historical Collections*, vii, pp. 1236-7.
99. Carter, *A true relation*, p. 156.
100. Ibid., p. 157.
101. Jones, *Siege of Colchester*, p. 128.
102. Carter, *A true relation*, p. 160.
103. Donagan, *England at War*, p. 357.
104. Whitelock, *Memorials*, ii, pp. 393-4. Rushworth, *Historical Collections*, vii, p. 1242.
105. Carter, *A true relation*, p. 182.
106. Ibid., p. 184.
107. Ibid., p. 185.
108. Clarke Papers, ii, pp. 35-6.
109. Carter, *A true relation*, pp. 187-90. The two versions of the deaths of Lucas and Lisle, in the Clarke Papers and in Carter, are similar in the words Ireton and Lucas exchanged. However Carter's is a more florid account which feels as if it feeding the legend which grew up around Lucas and Lisle.
110. Marchamont Needham (1620-1678) emerged as a leading pamphleteer in *Mercurius Britanicus*, a Parliamentarian newspaper in the 1640s but was jailed for savage attacks on the king. On release, he switched sides and wrote *Mercurius Pragmaticus*, an equally savage Royalist paper. Again he was jailed, in 1649. He emerged from prison as a leading supporter of classical republicanism in the 1650s. At the Restoration he worked as a doctor but still found time to write occasional polemics on leading politicians of the time.
111. Marchamont Needham, *Mercurius Pragmaticus* E.462, issue 23, September 5012, 1648, pp. F3-4 and p. G.
112. Donagan, *England at War*, p. 367.
113. Lords Journal, x, pp. 476-81.

114. Short Memorial of Thomas Fairfax in Masere, *Select Tracts*, i, p. 450. Bodleian, MS Fairfax 36, 4r-v. Andrew Hopper, *'Black Tom' Sir Thomas Fairfax and the English Revolution*, (Manchester, 2007), p. 87.
115. Hopper, *'Black Tom'*, p. 87.
116. Jones, *Siege of Colchester*, p. 142.
117. They had been jailed in January, 1648, Lilburne in the Tower, Wildman in the Fleet after holding an inflammatory meeting in Wapping, Rainborowe's home patch. They were charged with "treasonable and seditious practices."
118. Pauline Gregg, *Free-Born John The Biography of John Lilburne*, (London, 1961), p. 249.
119. Ireton's biographer, Robert Ramsey puts the change in his views to three causes: the rejection by the king of his Heads of Proposals, the defection to the Royalists of his protégé Edward Wogan; and the death of his friend Francis Thornhagh at Preston. Robert Ramsey, *Henry Ireton*, (London, 1949), p. 50.
120. Ireton actually met up with Wildman, Lilburne and other supporters of the Independent party at that radical haunt, the Nag's Head Tavern in the Strand. At the meeting Wildman called for the execution of the king and the purging of Parliament. A second meeting was held there on November 15 by which time Ireton had drawn up, on behalf of the soldiers, the *'Remonstrance of the Army'* which called for Charles to be tried as an enemy of his people. Ramsey, *Henry Ireton*, p. 112.
121. Rushworth, *Historical Collections*, vii, pp. 1248-1280

Chapter Eight: Aftermath

As soon as the House of Commons heard of the death of Rainborowe, it ordered Cromwell "forthwith to make a strict and exact scrutiny of the manner of the horrid murder."[1] The lieutenant general was the most senior officer in the north. When Rainborowe was attacked and killed in Doncaster on October 29, 1648, Cromwell was just 41 miles to the north in Boroughbridge. Ironically Cromwell was the man who gained most from this death, ridding him of a fierce rival in the crucial endgame over the fate of King Charles, now being played out in London. The long expressed view of Rainborowe that the king should put on trial was now in the ascendancy among senior officers in the Army. But Cromwell was still apparently dithering over what to do and consequently was losing ground. He still held enormous stock as a brilliant cavalry commander and the driving force of the successful New Model Army. In that he was unassailable. But his dogged pursuit of a treaty with the king had seriously alienated him from the more radical officers and men in his army, like Thomas Rainborowe. Now his uncertainty was again costing his dearly.

The second and unnecessary civil war, fought with increasing bitterness and decreasing gallantry, had made up the minds for many in the Army and among the radicals. But even by the early autumn, Cromwell was undecided about what to do with Charles. His enforced absence from London during the summer and autumn of 1648 had also left a vacuum which his opponents readily filled. But it was not just long standing enemies who stepped in. His son-in-law, Henry Ireton, a conservative lawyer and staunch Cromwell ally at the Putney Debates, not only joined, but soon led, the call for the king to be tried. Others, like John Wildman, author of the quasi-republican document *An Agreement of the People* and, with Rainborowe, a leading radical speaker at Putney, were already calling for the king's execution.

But while it may have suited Cromwell to be rid of his turbulent foe, there is no evidence at all that he had any hand in Rainborowe's death. Instead he seemed genuinely both saddened and angered that a former friend and a fellow officer had been killed. When Parliament ordered him to pursue and capture the men responsible, he did exactly that. Wilbur Abbott wrote that Rainborowe's death "was construed by Parliament and by Cromwell as the deliberate murder of a man who had been one of the first to advocate the trial of the king. Greatly distressed at the loss of such a valued officer, Cromwell did what he could upon his arrival to discover the murderers and to prevent further raids."[2]

Cromwell arrived at Pontefract within a couple of days of Rainborowe's death and set up his headquarters first at Byron House in the town and then at nearby Knottingley. He was not impressed by what he found. In a letter to Speaker Lenthall, Cromwell wrote: "the siege of Pontefract...had lost all semblance of a military operation."[3] His first act was to order up more supplies and to tighten the cordon around the castle. He clearly expected a long operation. But events in London were moving at an alarming speed. They demanded his presence.

Rainborowe's death helped fire an intense period of radical activity. It "inflamed radical opinion in London" and rapidly transformed him into a martyr for the Leveller cause.[4] Like Cromwell, many radicals believed his death "was the deliberate murder of one of the king's most outspoken antagonists."[5] Sir Henry Cholmley was openly blamed for his "ill management of the siege", in particular for letting out and then letting back the men who killed Rainborowe "and not a pistol fired at them."[6] Later others pointed the blame at Army grandees, notably Fairfax and Cromwell.

But at first there was, among the radicals, a deep grief that they had lost one of their leading lights. At this time of heightened radical action, the regimental petitions which arrived at Army headquarters contained not just the now usual demands for arrears, redress of grievances and an end to peace talks with the king. There was now a new demand for vengeance against Rainborowe's killers. The regiments of Fleetwood, Whalley and Barkstead, both officers and men, sent in a petition to Fairfax which spoke of the "most desperate and inhumane murdering of Col. Rainsborough" and demanded the incident be investigated.[7]

A couplet in a long eulogy to the dead man, printed in *The Moderate*, a tract supporting the Levellers, ran:

Now Cholmley laugh, and let malignants grin,
You know from hence your reckoning will begin
Up them stout souls, born for the peoples good,
Mount him to's grave, and next revenge his blood.
For though imtombed with honour Rainsborow lies
Yet still his dust for satisfaction cries.[8]

In the immediate aftermath of Rainborowe's death, it was, surprisingly, Ireton who took up the radicals' baton. Almost certainly converted by the viciousness of the siege of Colchester, the once conservative lawyer wanted a quick end to the whole business. More importantly, he wanted the Army to be the arbiter. Probably without savouring the irony, the humourless Ireton had stepped into Rainborowe's shoes.

As Rainborowe's body made its way south, Ireton drew up the first draft of the *Army Remonstrance*. Its central points were that peace talks with the king should end and he be put on trial; that Parliament be purged; and that a new body be elected on a much wider franchise. It was presented to the Army Council on November 7 but rejected by Fairfax and the moderate officers.

Rainborowe's body reached north London on Tuesday, November 14. An announcement of the funeral was made in *The Moderate*. It was clearly meant to be a vehicle for a grand demonstration of radical solidarity. The body of the "never to be forgotten English champion" would be met by his brother William and other relatives at Tatnam (Tottenham) High Crosse." All the well-affected in London and parts adjacent are desired to accompany them." The cortege would leave no later than 10am.⁹ The mourners gathered in their thousands. The women were in 50-60 coaches. Men on horseback numbered about 3,000. It was among the biggest funerals that London had yet seen. The procession wound through Islington, past St. Paul's Cathedral, along Cheapside and across the river into his birthplace of Wapping. There the service was conducted by Thomas Brooks, his navy chaplain, who preached on "How God's saints who have been treacherously murdered here below will be glorified in heaven."

Brooks told his congregation: "The more I think of the gallantry and worth of this champion the further off I am from discovering his worth. I think he was one of whom this sinful nation was not worthy; he was one of whom this declining Parliament was not worthy; he was one whom these divided, formal, carnal Gospellers are not worthy. He served his generation faithfully. Though he died by the hands of treachery, I am fully satisfied, with many more he is now triumphing in glory and it will be but a day before he shall see his enemies at the bar."[10]

The sermon lasted two hours before Rainborowe was buried next to his father in the graveyard of St. John's. There was one other highly significant aspect of this day of both mourning and celebration. Many of the thousands who attended wore Rainborowe's own colours of sea green and black. From then on, they were adopted as the colours of the Leveller cause.

The death and funeral were also the trigger for an outpouring of verse for the dead man. While the Leveller tracts eulogised a great man, the Royalists ones mocked him viciously. *The Moderate* printed *In Memoriam Thomae Rainsborow Pro Populo, Principe, Parliamento, Chiliarche Fortissimi.*

The proposed epitaph read:

He that made Kings, Lords, Commons, Judges shake,
Cities, and Committees quake;

> *He that fought nought but his dear Countreys good,*
> *And seal'd their right with his last blood,*
> *Rainsborow the just, the valiant, and the true,*
> *Here bids Levellers adue.*[11]

The *Mercurius Militaris*, another Leveller tract, wrote the spirit of "brave Rainsborough...

> *Lives 'above your rage, and in our thoughts we find,*
> *The fair republic built in his brave mind;*
> *In this dark night of error with a clear*
> *Unspotted light his view did appear.*

It concluded:

> *Yea, had his life been to his virtues spunne*
> *Out to a length, he had outliv'd the Sunne.*[12]

Not all were so acclamatory. Perhaps inevitably some saw his death as deserved revenge for the execution of Lucas and Lisle. A song which appeared shortly after his killing, *Colonel Rainsborough's Ghost* did just that. Part of it read:

> *For when the town they did surrend*
> *I plotted all against them then;*
> *I quickly brought unto an end*
> *The lives of two brave gentlemen.*

> *Sir Charles Lucas and Sir George Lisle,*
> *Two worthy men whom I did hate,*
> *The glory of the British Isle,*
> *Whom I did make unfortunate.*

With resolution stout they died,
And called me traitor to my face.
I did no whit abate my pride,
I saw them fall in little space.

The death of them revenged hath been
On me by those that loved them well.
Sweet Jesus Christ forgive my sin,
For by my means these worthies died.[13]

But it was the snobbish Royalist tracts which overflowed with contempt for the dead man. Marchamont Nedham, "the acid-tongued editor of *Mercurius Pragmaticus* wrote: 'The carkasse of Rainsborough was attended through London by a regiment of horse, and all the rag-tags of the faction that were able to hire horses, and entered at Wapping among his fellow swabbers and skippers.'"[14] The *Mercurius Elenticus* was equally sneering, claiming the funeral was attended on by "a great number of the well affected of all professions, Will the Weaver, Tom the Tapster, Kit the cobbler, Dick the Doore Sweeper, and many more apron-youths of the City who trudg'd very devoutly both before and behind this glorious saint, with about 100 of the she-votresses crowded up in coaches, and some 500 more of the better sort of brethren mounted on hackney beasts."[15]

The *Mercurius Melancholicus* topped them all with a vicious assault on Rainborowe's memory. It imagined him being transported to hell where he was "placed up to the chin in a bath of liquid lead, there to disturb all hell with his laments, cursing the hour that he procured the slaughter of these thrice noble heroes Sir Charles Lucas and Sir George Lisle." In verse, it accused Rainborowe of treachery, ambition, lust, pride, an insatiable desire for blood, sedition, killing Lucas and Lisle and, "worst of all" contention.

It warned readers that his "furious ghost" may appear

And fright poor England, shaking yet
Into a second ague fit.

The doggerel concluded, after again wishing him endless torture in hell,

While unto Charles, his crown is given
And he when dead convey'd to heaven
Looking down thence shall laugh to see
Rainsborough howl in misery.[16]

The Royalist attacks on Rainborowe continued well into the New Year and after the king's execution. *The Famous Tragedy of King Charles I* appeared about halfway through the year.[17] In this feast of doggerel, waywardly styled on Shakespeare and perhaps Marlowe, Rainborowe is depicted from the start as lusting for the death of Lucas and Lisle. He is, according to the author, known only by his initials E. D., determined that they pair should "die without mercy" as soon as the siege was over. Urged on by Ireton, Rainborowe is shown as persuading a reluctant Fairfax to put them to death.

Rainborowe's own death is inevitably drawn as revenge for the executions. Stranded at night in a lonely wood, wracked by guilt and haunted by the ghosts of Lucas and Lisle, Rainborowe is surprised by Michael Blackbourne and his men, his actual killers. Accused by his attackers of many crimes including treason, murder and rape, Rainborowe finds that guilt hangs too heavily on him to fight back. He falls, declaring 'Let all those who have sought their Sovereign ruin, look upon me and my deserved Destiny.'

The next scene shows Cromwell and Mrs Lambert "in their night robes" discussing their night of passion when Ireton brings news that the king has been executed.[18] For some reason *The Famous Tragedy* does not appear in the *Oxford Companion to English Literature*.

But if Royalist attempts to discredit Rainborowe increasingly verged on the ridiculous, his memory stayed strong in many parts of the country. A petition to Fairfax from the people of Rutland and Northamptonshire complained of the "miseries of a Civil War" and announced it had set up its own defence force. After Parliament had ignored petitions from Hull, York, Leicester and London, the people of Rutland and Northamptonshire now feared being massacred "as our beloved Rainsborough was."[19]

But despite its grandeur and intimidating display of radical solidarity, Rainborowe's funeral had no affect on the Presbyterian dominated House of Commons. On the very day of the burial, November 15, it voted for Charles to return to London to continue the talks for a peace treaty and the resumption of his throne. But the sheer size of the turnout and its obvious display of affection, even reverence, for the dead man may have had some affect on the MPs at a personal level.

What spurred them was a letter from Fairfax about a man whom he clearly both liked and admired. He was fulsome in his praise of his former comrade: "If the gallantry and faithfulness of that gentleman in his service to this kingdom were not fully known to every one I should speak more particularly."He noted with approval that the Commons, on hearing of Rainborowe's death, had indicated it would give financial help to his widow, Margaret, and their two children. This was something "myself, the Army and all honest men have cause to thank you."

But there was a problem. Rainborowe's "many losses and considerable expenses in your service were not fully laid before you." He asked that Parliament now consider Margaret Rainborowe's petition for recompense.[20] The response was favourable although nothing concrete was done for several weeks, until in fact after Parliament was purged.

The MPs considered both Fairfax's letter and Margaret Rainborowe's petition on December 19 and decided to set up a committee. This, under the guidance of a Mr Scott, met the same day and reported back to the Commons a week later. On hearing Scott's report, the MPs immediately ordered that £500 debt which

Rainborowe had incurred during the Irish Expedition six years before, "be left to the Committee of Adventurers for the Sea Expedition, for satisfaction thereof."

They also awarded £2,000 to Mrs Rainborowe, making it clear this was in addition to an earlier £1,000 awarded to her husband in late 1647. The money was awarded for the "losses and sufferings of Colonel Rainborowe" and again in addition to the arrears due to him for his Army service under Fairfax.[21] In a further act of generosity, the Commons ordered, six weeks later on February 13, 1649, that the money to be paid to Mrs Rainborowe was "without Deduction of Free Quarter."[22]

The Commons returned again to the matter of Rainborowe's money four months later. It planned to give William Rainborowe and Stephen Winthrop, Thomas's New England brother-in-law, a sum of £3,000 to be held in trust for Margaret and her children. Originally the money was to come from what seemed to be church lands. But a month later, on July 20, the MPs said the sum was to be "charged upon Sir Francis Doddington's Estate, or the Estate of such other Delinquent as the Committee shall bring in."[23]

But the matter dragged on. Parliament had numerous bereaved widows to deal with and it was not until June 22, 1650 that it got around to the first and second reading of a bill to settle lands on Margaret and her son William. But on the same day, the MPS ordered that "the Sum of One hundred Pounds, at *Michaelmas* next, and Two hundred Pounds *per Annum*, from thenceforth, by quarterly Payments, until an Act shall be passed, in Parliament, for settling Lands upon the said Margaret Rainborow" for the maintenance of her and her children.[24] The matter seems to have been left there.

It was a generous settlement, if a long time coming, and one that attempted to provide a pension while the land was settled on Mrs Rainborowe. But it begs the question of why Rainborowe's widow was so in immediate need of money. Despite his absence, the family's merchant shipping business seems to have continued and Rainborowe also had property in Southwark. By the standards of the day, they were comfortably off at the very least. The only explanation can be that, like his ally Henry Marten, Rainborowe spent much of his own money on Parliament's cause.

On the more pressing matter of what should be done with Rainborowe's regiment, the MPs were unsurprisingly more decisive. The Tower Regiment was withdrawn from Pontefract in the aftermath of Rainborowe's killing and probably returned to Army headquarters at St Albans. It was one of the several regiments which presented a petition to Fairfax opposing any deal with the king. The opening of their petition mourned their loss of the man they affectionately referred to as "The General": "Though the sad sense of the unhappy loss of our highly esteemed Colonel, may cause us to bear low in our reputation, and sink us into a slowness to such high actings as the vigour of his noble spirit might have enabled us to."[25]

On November 25, the Commons voted "that the Tower Regiment, late under the Command of Colonel Rainborough, be forthwith disbanded."[26] In a move which gives a clear indication of the disdain in which they held the MPs, Fairfax and his council simply ignored the order and changed the regiment's name.[27] But it also gives an insight into the fear in which the Commons held the regiment of the Army's top ranking radical and its potential for revolt. No other regiment was picked on in this fashion.

When the Army presented its *Remonstrance* to the Commons on November 20, one of the officers involved was a Lieutenant-Colonel George Cooke. He later took over Rainborowe's old regiment which as late as January was still being referred to in the press as the "regiment of the late Colonel Rainsborough." Cooke was yet another New Englander who returned to take part in the Civil War. He was a captain in the colony's artillery company in the 1630s and would have known Israel Stoughton. He served under Needham in New England and again under him at Colchester where Needham was killed. Cooke had stayed on with the regiment when Rainborowe took over.[28]

The formidable crowd which accompanied Rainborowe's cortege, if it had little effect on MPs, did probably help stiffen some

Army sinews. As the MPs cleared the way for the return of the king, Ireton, Hugh Peter and Colonel Harrison – the officer who had damned Charles as a "man of blood" – met the Levellers in the Nag's Head. They agreed on the main points of the *Remonstrance* and, a day later, the Army Council approved it.

It was presented to Parliament four days later but decisively rejected by 125 votes to 58. In brutal retaliation, the Army moved towards its headquarters nearer to London in readiness for its second occupation of the capital, this time to purge the Commons of its opponents. This was exactly what Rainborowe had told the king's secretary, Berkeley, in July, 1647, that the Army would do if the MPs stood in its way.

At the new headquarters in Windsor, Fairfax was getting agitated. With the fighting largely over, he was being pushed, not entirely unwillingly, into the background. But he wanted his deputy, with his sharper political antennae, back as soon as possible. He sent Cromwell a note on November 28 urging him to return to headquarters as speedily as he could. Despite this, Cromwell still delayed. After handing over control of the siege to Lambert, he finally set out for London on December 1. Still apparently paralysed by uncertainty, he took his time.

But this lack of decision finally told against him. He arrived in the capital on the evening of December 6. By this time, the Army had once again entered London[29] and earlier that very day, Colonel Pride had begun his notorious purge, barring any MPs sympathetic to the king from the Commons. Cromwell had, for the moment, lost control of events. But with him or without him, events were now on an inevitable course. Within seven weeks, the king was tried, found guilty and executed.

In Pontefract, the Royalists held out until March 22, 1649. Cromwell had left orders with Lambert to enforce the siege with all vigour. This he did although the late arrival of cannon and the plentiful provisions within the castle delayed the end. Lambert also acted against the disgraced Cholmley by disbanding his regiment of horse in early January, along with that of Colonel Edward Rhodes. These were the two men who had earlier ignored a plea for help from Cromwell while he was pursuing the Scots. But the castle held out with unexpected determination and it was not until March that talks on surrender began.

From the start, Lambert was prepared to offer mercy to the garrison save for six named men. The main quarry were John Morrice, the leader of the Royalist faction which had taken the castle back in June 1648, and Cornet Michael Blackbourne and Lieutenant Alan Austwick, son of the mayor of Pontefract, Thomas Austwick. Blackbourne and Austwick were both suspected of the actual killing of Rainborowe. The other three, Major Ashby, Sergeant Floyd and Ensign Smith, were the men who had betrayed the castle to Morrice.

Lambert seemed not to have suspected any of the three Paulden brothers or others, like Marmaduke Greenfield or Charles Dallison, who were named in some reports as members of the party which tracked Rainborowe down in Doncaster. William Paulden had, in any case, died of fever in the castle in February, 1649. The youngest Paulden brother, Timothy, escaped but died two years later while fighting for the Royalist cause at Wigan in 1651. But Thomas Paulden, who wrote the self serving account of Rainborowe's death, was still in the castle on the day of surrender.

Amid the chaos of the last few days of the siege, Morrice and Blackbourne successfully charged through the Parliamentary lines and escaped. Smith was killed in the attempt. The three others all escaped after the surrender on March 22. They had hid in a sally-port of the castle. "Thence they made their escape the next night after the castle was surrendered, and all lived till after the King's return."[30] Morrice and Blackbourne fared less well. They were arrested at Lancaster ten days after escaping, the former "disguised as a beggar."[31]

They were tried at York Assizes on August 16. Morrice interrupted the proceedings so often that he was first put in leg and hand irons and then removed from the court. He and Blackbourne were both found guilty and sentenced to death. Two days before their execution was due they made a dramatic bid to escape. Morrice had successfully lowered himself by rope over the castle wall at York but Blackbourne fell and broke his leg in his attempt. Chivalrously, Morrice refused to leave his comrade and both were re-captured. They were executed on August 23. Before he died, Morrice spoke warmly of his great mentor, Thomas Wentworth, earl of Strafford, himself executed by Parliament. He was buried in the eponymous village Wentworth near the grave of his former employer.[32]

Thomas Paulden escaped from Pontefract and "went again beyond the sea, and, upon King Charles the second's Restoration, returned into England." However he also claimed to have been a secret agent for Charles, returning on several occasions to England. "I was once betray'd, and brought before Cromwell; but I denied my name, and nothing could be proved against me." Nonetheless, Cromwell had him committed to the Gatehouse in Westminster "from whence I made my escape...by throwing salt and pepper into the keeper's eyes." Paulden ended his recollections by hoping that "this attempt at Doncaster may not be altogether forgotten by posterity."[33]

By the time of Paulden's death in 1710, eight years after he completed his memoirs, Rainborowe's death was fading into history. But back in 1649, it was still fresh and raw for many radicals. The opening months of that year saw growing unrest both in the Army and among radicals in London – the two things the Army grandees utterly feared. The second *An Agreement of the People*, calling for "a secure and present peace, upon grounds of common right, freedom and safety", which had been approved by Army officers in late 1648, was presented to the Rump Parliament on January 15.

But after the execution of Charles on January 30, the Army grandees adopted a far tougher line against radicals, with Cromwell in the vanguard. In February they attempted to curb the influence of radical outsiders on common soldiers. Next they tried to stop the soldiers petitioning Parliament without the consent of their officers.

In an Army now used to extensive rights of protest, there was inevitably a backlash. Eight soldiers petitioned the Council of Officers on March 1 to assert such rights. The response was out of all proportion. After one recanted and two vanished, the remaining five were court-martialled, violently punished and cashiered. When Captain-Lieutenant William Bray backed them, he was thrown off the Council and later, when he criticised Fairfax, imprisoned at Windsor Castle. In Cromwell's eyes, Bray was a recidivist. As a junior lieutenant, he had connived at the revolt of Robert Lilburne's regiment at Corkbush and argued with Ireton about the role of kings at Putney. He was throughout strongly supported by his men.[34]

The mounting unrest was a suitable opportunity for two of the leading Levellers to castigate the grandees of the Army. Richard Overton published his attack on the officers, *The Hunting of Foxes*, in direct reply to the cashiering of the soldiers, on March 21.[35] In it, Overton accused the grandees of betraying the soldiers and the kingdom by not introducing Leveller solutions to the country's ills.

But John Lilburne cast caution to the wind when, three days later, he published *The Second Part of England's New-Chaines Discovered*. Amidst his withering attack on the grandees, Lilburne also accused them of being responsible for Rainborowe's death. These officers "had shot a soldier to death" at Corkbush – a reference to the execution of Private Richard Arnold after the failed revolt - for backing *An Agreement of the People*, and criticised Rainborowe for his support of the pamphlet.

Rainborowe had then, claimed Lilburne, been removed from the Army "by a plausible but only titular command at sea" in which he had no power to stop the naval revolt or "preserve himself from being expulsed at the seamen's pleasure." With Rainborowe still sticking to his principles, the grandees had then "put him upon that dangerous and unhappy service before Pomfret (notwithstanding a commander had been appointed thereunto by the committee of York) whither he went with much reluctancy and discontent, as wondering at the cause of his being design'd thither, and expressing as much to his friends, his sad soul presaging the misfortune, which after befell him."

Lilburne pressed on regardless, next accusing the Army of trying to stop William Rainborowe "in searching after, and prosecuting the causes of that so bloody and inhumane a butchery." It was this, Lilburne said that was "the greatest cause of grief and suspect to his [Rainborowe's] friends."[36]

Not much of this was accurate. It was Rainborowe himself who had coveted the navy post; Cromwell had actually tried to stop him. Rainborowe would also have known full well why he was being sent to Pontefract, although he surely regretted being removed from London as the politics were hotting up. Nor had Lilburne jumped to Rainborowe's aid when the latter asked for his support for *An Agreement* in 1647. The sorrow sounds a little fake. But Lilburne was pursuing a vendetta against the Army grandees, in particular his former friend Cromwell. He, like Overton, fervently believed the grandees had betrayed the men. The truth did not really come into it. Some of the Levellers had opposed the execution of the king, including Lilburne, and now saw Cromwell's ascent to power not only as illegitimate but also a betrayal of the rights of the common soldier. Hence the vehemence of Overton's and Lilburne's prose.

But the two articles did the trick of incensing the elite. The Council of State was already "alarmed by the discontent among soldiers"[37] caused by Overton's article. The House of Commons was beside itself. On March 27, three days after the appearance of Lilburne's diatribe, and the day it received word of the surrender of Pontefract Castle, it was informed of this "scandalous and seditious book".

The MPs heard that the pamphlet "does contain much false, scandalous, and reproachful matter; and is highly seditious, and destructive to the present Government." It was likely to cause a mutiny in the Army, a new war in the Commonwealth and damage the present attempts to relieve Ireland.

They voted that "the Authors, contrivers, and framers of the said Paper are guilty of High Treason, and shall be proceeded against as traitors." The Council of State was ordered to find out who wrote and published the two pamphlets. Fairfax was ordered to find out if any of his soldiers were involved and the declaration of high treason against the perpetrators was to be posted throughout the kingdom.[38] But they did not have far to look. Overton, Lilburne, William Walwyn, a leading Leveller who probably had little input in either article but had fallen out with Cromwell, and Richard Prince, the publisher, were arrested the next day and packed off to the Tower.

Support for the Levellers had been beginning to fade, with the death not just of Rainborowe but also of the king. Cromwell in particular took on a far more resolute stance against the radicals with whom he had once flirted. There were allegations that he had openly bullied Henry Marten, the stout republican MP and Rainborowe ally, into curbing his outspokenness.

Marten, a regicide, had helped organise the Levellers' petition in London the previous autumn. But the *Mercurius Pragmaticus* reported a disturbing incident where Cromwell had, on March 4, 1649, drawn his dagger in the Commons, laid it next to him and "expressed great anger against Harry [Marten] and his levelling crew."[39] A generous grant from Parliament for Marten, who had squandered much his vast inherited fortune on wine and women, may also have helped tighten his tongue.

The officers were also cajoled. Most had approved the second *An Agreement of the People*, in late 1648. But by April only one of note, Major John Cobbett, still openly backed it.[40] Bray's burst of radical independence had been quickly punished. Another officer who courted suspicion was Lieutenant Colonel John Jubbs who, in May, called for support for reforms originally proposed by Rainborowe.

None of this was welcome to Cromwell. Dissent, let alone revolt, was enough to put the grandees on edge. It was not so much the petitions that the Army was receiving from the regions, like the one from Rutland and Northamptonshire. What really unnerved them was potential unrest in the Army and in London. The arrests by Parliament made this far more likely.

Despite being jailed, Lilburne stepped up his campaign against the Army. "Throughout the month of April, he and Overton strove with all their might to inspire the rank and file to overthrow their officers, take charge of the army and implement the Leveller agenda for England."[41] Early that month, several hundred women, some sporting the sea green colours of Rainborowe and now the Levellers, brought a petition to Parliament, signed by 10,000 women, demanding the adoption of the second *An Agreement* and also drawing attention to the fact that people in London were starving to death. After being told by one MP to go home and wash the dishes, the women returned the next day and the day after, at one point threatening Cromwell with his life. They were back again in May berating the MPs for their patronising attitude to them.[42] The *Mercurius Militaris* celebrated their demonstrations with some lively verse:

> *Thus the bonny Besses*
> *In the seagreen dresses*
> *Are come to the hall today*
> *To crack a louse*
> *With it the house th'elves*
> *In the merry month of May.*
>
> *But Nol and his asses*
> *Do fear the brave lasses*
> *And therefore begin to flee*
> *So speed them well*
> *In their journey to hell*
> *And high then up go we.*[43]

But theirs was one of several protests in April which culminated in the first Army revolt at the end of the month in Bishopsgate in the

City. After eight weeks of mounting unrest, Fairfax and Cromwell were set on moving regiments out of London, away from the influence of radicals. But a small troop of men from Whalley's regiment refused to go, took hold of the regiment's colours and locked themselves in the Bull Inn, a Leveller meeting place. There they demanded their pay arrears and for Lilburne and his three colleagues to be freed. Their defiance continued until the next day when Fairfax and Cromwell appeared on the scene as 15 of the mutineers were arrested. All were court-martialled the next day and six sentenced to death. Five were reprieved but one was executed.

This was Robert Lockyer, a 23-year-old Baptist from Bishopsgate. Lockyer had signed up at 17, served in Cromwell's Ironsides and fought at the Battle of Naseby. But he was also a radical who had supported Rainborowe and *An Agreement of the People* at Corkbush. Amid the growing tumult, Fairfax was determined to make an example of at least one man from the mutiny. Many thought it was Lockyer's politics that marked him out as that man. Certainly Lilburne reacted with his predictable fury, accusing Fairfax of murder and demanding Lockyer's pardon. It made no difference.

On the morning of April 27, Lockyer was led into the yard of St. Paul's Cathedral and shot by six musketeers. In his last speech, he said it was a pity to die over a claim for pay arrears rather than for the nobler cause of freedom. After refusing a blindfold, Lockyer chided the musketeers that he stood "for nothing but what is for your good."[44] His funeral was another vast show of solidarity by the radicals. Up to 5,000 attended, more than at Rainborowe's, again many wearing sea green ribbons, now the accepted Leveller colours. No doubt much to Cromwell's consternation, some of the mourners were serving soldiers.

But the execution of Lockyer did little to quell the now deep unrest. Four days after his death, the cavalry regiment of Colonel Adrian Scroop refused to go to Ireland until the General Council was reconvened, complete with agitators, to redress their grievances. Others speedily joined the protest, among them men from the regiments of Ireton, Harrison, Skippon and Horton. Trouble was also brewing in Oxfordshire. Here the instigator was William Thompson, a rabble rouser and man of violence. After beating up the occupants of a house which refused him and his followers quarter in Essex, he moved onto Oxfordshire where he managed to raise some 300 men, many the disaffected soldiers from the regiment of Colonel John Reynolds. In his rallying cry on May 6, Thompson invited the disaffected men to join him.

Reynolds caught up with Thompson's band at Banbury and routed them, although Thompson escaped with a few men to Chipping Norton. But the revolt was still spreading. Agitators were by now at work in most cavalry regiments and the tireless Lilburne was still doing his best to encourage an uprising. Even when Fairfax and Cromwell mustered five regiments in London on May 9 to move westwards to take on the rebels, some of the men turned up wearing sea green colours. These were peremptorily ripped from their hats.[45]

Major Francis White, a radical with much sympathy for the Levellers demands, made valiant but ultimately fruitless attempts to negotiate a peace between the two sides. The men's anger was deep and genuine. They felt that the grandees had betrayed them by failing to honour the Engagement, made at Newmarket on June 5, 1647, to discuss their grievances at meetings of the General Council. "You keep not your covenant with us" they men bitterly said of the grandees.

By May 14, Fairfax decided the time for talking was over. That day, he and Cromwell advanced on the Oxfordshire town of Burford, where the 900 mutineers were now gathered. Cromwell with some 2,000 horsemen and dragoons arrived in the town in the dead of night. They achieved complete surprise and there was little fighting. About 600 of the mutineers fled, 340 were captured and locked up in the local church. Only two men died – one from each side.

The Council of the Army decided it had the right to execute all 340 of the prisoners but chose in the end to pick out four of the ringleaders for the extreme punishment. Cornet James Thompson, younger brother of William, Corporal John Church and Corporal Perkins were lined up against the churchyard wall on May 17 and shot. The fourth man singled out, Cornet Henry Denne, an ordained priest who had worked with White on a peace deal, was pardoned as he stood in the churchyard. Fairfax had taken note of his extravagant contrition and ordered him to preach to the other prisoners of the wickedness of their late deeds. He did so with gusto, "howling and weeping like a crocodile."[46] William Thompson was killed a few days later in a clash with Parliamentary forces. Burford marked the end of the Leveller influence on the Army.

The demise of the radicals meant the memory of Rainborowe began to fade. It was perhaps inevitable. Fate had dealt him two lethal blows. First, he died relatively young, when still in his late thirties and before his potential had been reached. He could have expected to live for perhaps another 20 to 30 years, certainly throughout the Commonwealth years in which he may well have played a major role.

It is idle to speculate on what Rainborowe would or might have achieved had he lived. Hugh Ross Williamson, in his 1949 essay on Rainborowe, felt that he would have pushed hard for the adoption of the first *An Agreement of the People* which he championed at Putney. "It would have been carried or, at last, have precipitated a third Civil War with Cromwell and Rainsborough as the opposing leaders." Had this happened, "it is inconceivable that Cromwell would have had so easy a victory over the Levellers at Burford in 1649 had Rainsborough been leading them."[47] It is true his death left a leadership gap among Army radicals that was never even vaguely filled. But whether, after his sobering experience at Corkbush, he would have led the mutiny in 1649 is an unknown.

But it is likely that his death and the grim manner of it galvanised the Army grandees, like Ireton, into adopting a far harsher attitude to Charles. Ireton's biographer, Robert Ramsey wrote that while Ireton, post-Colchester, was clear the king needed to be punished, he "was not yet fully convinced that he must actually die." There was no doubt, Ramsey argued, that Rainborowe's killing "intensified the bitterness of the extremists against the king and probably had not been without its influence on both Cromwell and Ireton."[48]

What is more certain is that, after the king's execution, Cromwell would not have had such a smooth ascent to power had Rainborowe been alive. They were both great soldiers, fighting on the same side although few would argue that Rainsborough's clinical efficiency outstripped Cromwell's genius. But off the battlefield, the two were intense political rivals. Whatever Cromwell might have muttered about their "friendship", there was little love lost between them, certainly on Rainborowe's part. Their beliefs and temperaments were also incompatible which sharpened the antagonism.

What split them was the king. The calculating, painstaking and innately conservative Cromwell favoured a peace settlement with the Charles and a return to monarchy. He pursued this with dogged recklessness. The impetuous and radical Rainborowe saw, long before most, that no deal could reasonably be made with a man as slippery as Charles. The alternative, as he saw it, was to make the people sovereign and give every man a say in who ran the country. This was a startling vision.

But it was Rainborowe's view that gained ground. As Charles' tiresome policy of playing his opponents off against one another with no intention of signing a peace treaty became obvious, a growing number of soldiers firmly opposed a deal with him. For them, Rainborowe was the man who had got it right. By the end of the Putney Debates, with Cromwell and Ireton still clinging to the idea of a deal, the Army was close to splitting along these lines with one side led by the grandees and the other by Rainborowe.

To exacerbate Cromwell's discomfort, Rainborowe emerged from the Debates with his reputation among the soldiers solidly enhanced. His spirited advocacy of their rights and his eloquence in promoting their aspirations endeared him to the common soldier. On the other hand Cromwell appeared as the defender of the king they had risked their lives to defeat. It was the radicals' failure of

Corkbush that diffused the situation. The escape of the king, perhaps fortuitously for Cromwell, quickly united the Army against its common enemy. The second Civil War was little more than an unwanted distraction from what many saw as the main problem: the future course of the kingdom.

But the horrors of Colchester, as Charles continued his compulsive game playing throughout 1648, hardened the attitude of many to the king. The Army, the compelling power in England, edged towards Rainborowe's long stated view that he must be punished for his crimes against the people. It seems reasonable to suppose that had he lived, he would have been a powerful and leading figure in the move to try the king. He certainly would have had the strong support of much of the Army rank and file. But by the time Cromwell reluctantly supported the trial of the king, Rainborowe was dead. The man who had called it right and forced him to change his mind had been removed from the scene. After Charles' execution, this left Cromwell with a clear run.

The second lethal blow that Rainborowe suffered was that the moving words he spoke at Putney of soldiers' rights and people's liberties were lost for nearly 250 years. These words were recorded by Sir William Clarke, secretary of the Army in 1647, in his own shorthand and later transcribed by him. His son, Sir George Clarke eventually bequeathed his father's papers to Worcester College, Oxford University in 1736. There they lay largely unnoticed and untouched for many years. A Mr Coxe had catalogued some of them by 1852 but historians showed little interest.

When more of what became known of the Clarke Papers were found later that century, the librarian of Worcester College, H. A. Pottinger drew them to the attention of the historian Charles Harding Firth. To his delight, Firth discovered the new finds included the transcripts of the Putney Debates as well as a treasure trove of details about the crucial meetings of the Army Council in the frenetic year of 1647. Firth published these documents in 1891, 244 years after the words were spoken.

Before that the radicals of the 1640s got scant attention from historians. The Thomason Tracts, which contain most of the Leveller (and Royalist) pamphlets were available from 1760s. But they were not used by campaigners for Parliamentary reform in the late 18th and early 19th centuries. Nor did the Chartists like being compared with them.[49]

Samuel Rawson Gardiner was publishing his landmark work on the Civil War in the 1880s[50] as Firth was researching at Worcester College. Gardiner's work consequently did include the Putney Debates. But he glossed over the role played by radicals in the war. He does mention Rainborowe and his supposed Republicanism,[51] but Wildman, author of the groundbreaking first *An Agreement of the People*, and Sexby, the common soldiers' champion at Putney, get scant mention.

But even when Firth's books came out, other historians at first took little notice. Rainborowe's vision of a country where the people were sovereign and each man had a vote had still not come about. Queen Victoria was grantedly less powerful than Charles I. But just a generation before, the Victorians had seen off the working class Chartist movement which included in its six demands a call for one man, one vote. Universal manhood suffrage was not finally introduced until 1918 while women had to wait a further ten years before all of them were also granted the vote.

The re-assessment of the radicals and the role they played in the 1640s was, perhaps ironically, certainly inadvertently, begun by the work of Firth and Gardiner. But it was spurred on by men like Henry Noel Brailsford, a prolific left wing historian and journalist in the first half of the 20th century.[52] Earlier writers had ignored the radicals of the 17th century as being men who did not write in Latin, did not quote recognised authorities and were not, in their terms, educated men. But Brailsford was one of the first generations to experience universal suffrage and the coming to power of socialist and communist parties. He saw the radicals in a different light, as forerunners, not men with irrelevant ideas.[53]

A current historian, Philip Baker dates the change in attitudes to radicals from the 1940s. This, interestingly, was through the work of North Americans historians who, writing against a background of fascism and communism, saw traces of the origins of Western liberal democracy in the conflicts of mid-17th century England.[54] However in Britain, Baker says, it was the Marxists who made the running into research on the radicals. He identifies Christopher Hill's *The World Turned Upside Down* (1972) as a crucial work in which the historian argued that the radicals provided a vision of a new country. "That vision was of a popular, demotic phenomenon that fundamentally challenged the axioms of the day 'and looked towards a total revolution.'"[55]

But the pendulum then swung the other way. Historians in the 1980s and 1990s, called "revisionists", like Mark Kishlansky, subsequently argued that too much attention was given to the radicals and that they were not that important. But other historians pushed the belief that the aim of the radicals was a fundamental shift in power. It was not about superficial change but about major upheavals that would have involved the abolition of bishops, a written constitution and guaranteed basic rights.[56]

This seems a more accurate assessment. It also gives radicalism a more central role in the politics of the 1640s and, more markedly, those of 1647. It moves in that decade from being a movement which was noisy but on the fringe to one that, albeit briefly, occupied centre stage. This was in 1647 when, at the Putney Debates, supporters of *An Agreement of the People* demanded a written constitution and guaranteed rights. Furthermore, for the first time in England, someone called for one man, one vote. He was not looking for a superficial change. He wanted nothing less than an upheaval of the then political structure.

So where does this leave Rainborowe and his reputation? Like fate, historians have not been particularly kind to him. One of the most vitriolic verdicts on him came from John Rowland Powell. The naval historian, writing in his 1962 book *The Navy in the Civil War*, first accused him of "fanatical republicanism."[57] Warming to his theme, he concluded: "He possessed unconsciously the maddening self-righteousness of the convinced reformer which may explain the complaint, made later on by the seamen 'of his insufferable pride, ignorance and insolency.' His fanaticism provoked the dislike of most people and the affection of none. To put in bluntly, he was an impossible person."[58]

Much of this is nonsense which may derive from Powell's own lack of knowledge of the man. Rainborowe himself made clear, when challenged at Putney, that he was not against kings in themselves. Relying to a speech by Ireton about whether there should be a king or not, Rainborowe had replied: "I do very much care whether there be a king or no king, Lords or no Lords, property or no property; and I think if we do not take care we shall all have none of these very shortly."[59] What he was against was a treacherous king like Charles. It is not the same thing.

In the bitter aftermath of the naval revolt, Powell is correct in what the sailors said of Rainborowe. But it is also correct that Matthew Carter in his account of the revolt in Kent and the subsequent siege of Colchester, said that the seamen acknowledged that as Rainborowe had been a "a kind and good-natured commander to them, in return for which, no injury should be done to him."[60] It was not as clear cut as Powell makes out.

Finally Rainborowe was more than well liked. His men were devoted to him, Fairfax stuck his neck out on his account more than once when he did not have to and some 3000 people attended his funeral. Powell's remarks are in defiance of the reality.

The assessment of Robert Ashton, in his book *Counter Revolution The Second Civil War and its Origins 1646-8*, published in 1994, was also harsh. Ashton described the account by John Rushworth of Lord Norwich, commander of the Royalist forces in Colchester, sending out 500 women from the town. These had headed towards Rainborowe's quarters. In response Rainborowe had first fired a cannon over their heads, then some musket fire, and then ordered soldiers to strip them. The women were then left for hours exposed in no man's land before Norwich let them back into the besieged town.

This was one of many horrors at Colchester. Ashton wrote: "With these agonizing circumstances in mind, it is perhaps difficult to feel much regret about Rainsborough's earlier humiliation at the hands of the mutinous sailors the previous May, or even his later assassination by Morrice's soldiers at Doncaster in October; or to express relief at the reprieve which saved Norwich from execution early in the following year."[61]

No side had any right to feel proud of what happened at Colchester and Ashton is correct in drawing attention to the sufferings of the "hapless inhabitants of that town, and especially the women and children, bullied, starved and molested in a conflict in which their own concern was at most marginal."[62] But still his verdict Rainborowe might have deserved to die because of it seems unduly severe.

Austin Woolrych's is a much fairer but still flawed assessment. Woolrych rebuked Rainborowe, claiming that his "active support of the Leveller interest lasted less than two months."[63] There are three points here. First Rainborowe was known as a radical long before the Putney Debates. Richard Baxter, the sanctimonious scholar, had spoken of the "distaste" leading Worcester citizens for him when Fairfax appointed him governor of that city in 1646.[64] Secondly Rainborowe had been fully occupied as a leading colonel in the Army since 1644, whose main job was defeating the enemy not pursuing political agendas. Lastly, what evidence is there that that Rainborowe had any interest in promoting the Levellers? His views were not the same. They derived partly from his religious beliefs, as those of most radicals did, and, more crucially, from his talks with New Englanders in his regiment. It was they who bolstered or perhaps planted the ideas of sovereignty and people's rights which he set forth at Putney, not John Lilburne or Richard Overton.

But Woolrych's final assessment of Rainborowe is both accurate and fair. "He gives the impression of an impetuous man, generous in his sympathy with the underdog, undoubtedly brave, instinctively radical, but apt to keep his fiery temper on too short a fuse."[65]

It compares with the far fuller commendation that Brailsford gave him. The left wing historian, who did much to enhance the standing of the 17th century radicals, wrote that Rainborowe's death "inflicted a heavy loss on the Leveller movement." He added: "As famous for his ingenuity as a tactician as for his fabulous courage, he had the warmth of feeling and the ability to express it which are among the indispensable gifts of a popular leader. What he said at Putney echoes in English ears to this day. He ranks among the few talented soldiers of these wars, who cared passionately for a principle and nothing at all for their careers."[66]

But he backtracks when it comes to political leadership. After suggesting that an earlier biographer, Williamson had exaggerated Rainborowe's importance, Brailsford asked whether Rainborowe's failure to contain the naval mutiny threw doubt on his ability as a leader of men while the affair of the fake Prince of Wales may have indicated he was easily deceived.

He concluded: "A man who is an able leader and popular leader in military matters may fail in the more complicated field of politics. Rainsborough, as I read his character, was too impulsive, too hot-headed and perhaps too simple-minded to make a successful politician."[67]

Thomas Rainsborough was the son of a wealthy and highly regarded mariner and national naval hero. He shared the strong puritan beliefs of his family and their tightly knit seafaring community of Wapping. He grew to be a powerfully built and supremely self-confident man who appeared set to follow his father into the shipping trade, specialising in currants bought from the Greek islands and sold, very profitably, as luxury items in London.

The Civil War and its bitter politics changed what might have been a quiet, anonymous and prosperous life into one of action, drama and controversy. After displaying notable courage in clashes at Hull and Crowland, he became a colonel in Parliament's New Model Army, forged solely to defeat the Royalists. It was clear even by then that Rainborowe was a natural leader. His tall stature, his courage, his readiness to do battle with the enemy seem to have readily won the support and, later, the devotion, of his men and the admiration of his superiors.

In Parliament's cause he showed quite astonishing courage. He helped win the day at the crucial battle of Langport and quite probably turned the battle at Bristol. There his selfless fighting considerably impressed Cromwell. In addition he successfully besieged a string of Royalist strongholds, ranging from castles and country houses to cities. He never once failed to break the resistance. By the time the first Civil War ended in 1646, Rainborowe had emerged as a great soldier, a brilliant siegemaster and probably second only to Cromwell in terms of military prowess. At the least, he was indispensable to the NMA's commander, General Fairfax in his all conquering campaign in the West Country and the Midlands. More likely, Fairfax could not have succeeded without him.

In the battle over the peace, Rainborowe's radicalism surfaced. Almost certainly it was nurtured at camp fire talks with the many men from New England who had joined his regiment. They talked of how most men in their community had a say in the government of both the church and the settlement. It clearly struck a chord with Rainborowe. His Puritanism would have shown him that in England many men could discuss and decide on church affairs. From there it was a short step to include civil affairs as well. Many radicals took similar step.

But none was as long as the leap that Rainborowe made. If John Wildman, in the first, groundbreaking *An Agreement of the People* laid out the theory of how England could be governed after the war, it was Rainborowe who began to add the details. Wildman argued for a country where the people were sovereign with inalienable rights and the power of the people they elected to represent them was second only to their power. There was no mention of a king.

Rainborowe argued at Putney that all men should have a say in who governed the country, regardless of wealth or status. Men of property had no claim to greater rights than men without property. And no man should be subject to the rule of a tryant – that was why the people had to be sovereign. It was a strongly revolutionary blueprint for a complete restructuring of English society. It was no surprise it horrified not only the Royalists but also men of his own side, like Cromwell and Ireton.

The choice of words that he spoke at Putney merely increased the impact of what he was saying. They were and remain one of the most simple and elegant pleas for a society based on fairness: "For really I think that the poorest he that is in England hath a life to live as the greatest he; and therefore truly, Sir, I think it's clear, that every man that is to live under a Government ought first by his own consent to put himself under that government."

It eloquently expressed exactly why many of the men volunteered for and fought in the NMA. Faced with a man who seemingly wished to dispense even with the small franchise Parliament of the 17th century, they wanted change, not a return to the old status quo.

For nothing else, forgetting his immense skills as a soldier, his gift a natural leader, Thomas Rainborowe deserves to be remembered for his vision at Putney of a society based fairness not privilege. It says something of how far ahead of his time he was that his vision, politically at least, did not become reality for more nearly 300 years.

But England does not warm to its radicals or visionaries. The statute in the grounds of Westminster Palace, the home of British democracy, is of Cromwell, the man who opposed one man, one vote, not of Rainborowe, the man who actually proposed it. John Wildman whose words in *An Agreement of the People:* "These things we declare to be our native rights" later helped inspire the American and

French revolutionaries. Thomas Payne also spurred these men to action. Both are little known or recognised in this their own country.

In the small east Devon town of Colyton, there is a plaque which proudly boasts of how many of its young men joined the Duke of Monmouth in his attempt to wrest the crown from his uncle James II in 1685. At the subsequent Battle of Sedgemoor in July, Monmouth's untrained army was routed by Royalist forces under the Earl of Faversham and Colonel John Churchill. But many of the rebels against the Catholic king again wore sea green ribbons or even tunics in the battle. In Colyton itself, there is also a large cut out of a typical soldier who fought in the battle. Beneath his brown sleeveless coat, his shirt is sea green.

Few would know the history of those colours but it is one of the very few reminders of the life of Thomas Rainborowe. In the churchyard of St. John's, Wapping where Rainborowe is buried next to his father – the church has long been de-consecrated – a plaque in his memory was put up in 2013. It briefly recalls his life and how he had made:

"King, Lords, Commons, Judges shake
Cities and Committees quake."

But it does not say why. There is no mention that he wanted to see all men vote for the government of their choice. That might have made it a more compelling tribute.

In the small and attractive riverside church of St. Mary's, where at least part of the Putney Debates were held, there is a small museum which details the main points of the Debates, who was there, who said what, what was the context of the Debates with commentary from eminent historians, like Quentin Skinner, and politicians, like the late Tony Benn. But it is Rainborowe who gets pride of place.

On a blue grey pelmet looking down onto the aisle of the church are written, in gold, capital letters his great words: "For really I think that the poorest he that is in England hath a life to live as the greatest he."

Thomas Rainborowe deserves to be remembered for those 21 words - but also for a lot more as well.

Notes for Chapter Eight

1. Commons Journal, vi, p. 69.
2. Abbott, *Writings and Speeches of Oliver Cromwell*, iv, p. 673.
3. Ibid., p. 672.
4. Ian Gentles, 'Political Funerals during the English Revolution', in Stephen Porter (ed.), *London and the Civil War*, (London, 1996), p. 217.
5. Gentles, *New Model Army*, p. 271.
6. Rushworth, *Historical Collections*, vii, p. 1319.
7. *The Moderate*, November 7-14, 1648, E472 (4), pp. 5-8.
8. *Ibid., p. 8.*
9. *The Moderate*, October 31-November 7, 1648, p. 5. E472 (15).
10. Thomas Brooks, *The Glorious Day of the Saints Appearance*, E474 (7). Quoted in Williamson, *Four Stuart Portraits*, pp. 141-2.
11. *The Moderate*, November 7-14, 1648, E472 (4), pp. 5-6.
12. *Mercurius Militaris*, November 14-21, 1648, p. 4. E473 (15).
13. Thomas Wright, *Political Ballads*, (1841), quoted in Williamson, *Four Stuart Portraits*, pp. 136-7.
14. Gentles, 'Political Funerals', p.218. *Mercurius Pragmaticus*, November 14-21, 1648, E473(7).
15. *Mercurius Elenticus*, November 15-22, 1648, E473 (9), pp. 503-4.
16. *Mercurius Melancholicus*, November 14-21, 1648, E472 (26), p. 4.
17. The first edition of the play gives no exact date for its publication but references to Blackbourne as Rainborowe's killer suggest it was after the end of the siege of Pontefract in March, and probably a little later.
18. *The Famous Tragedy of King Charles I*, (London, 1649).
19. *A Petition presented at a Common-Hall in London on Saturday last concerning the kings majesty*, p. 4, quoted in Sarah Barber, *Regicide and Republicanism*, (Edinburgh, 1998), p. 84.
20. Tanner MS 57, fo. 411.
21. Commons Journal, vi, pp. 99-104.
22. Ibid., p. 139.
23. Ibid., p. 265.
24. Ibid., pp.428-30.
25. *The Moderate*, November 14-21, 1648, E472 (4), quoted Firth and Davies, *The Regimental History of Cromwell's Army.*, p. 577.
26. Commons Journal, vi, p. 87.
27. Firth and Davies, *Cromwell's Army*, p. 577.
28. Ibid., pp. 577-9.
29. The Army entered London on December 2, the same s day Charles indicated he would reject the peace proposals from Parliament.
30. Paulden, *An Account*, p. 22. The king referred to is Charles II.
31. Edmund Ludlow, *The Memoirs of Edmund Ludlow*, (Oxford, 1894), i, p. 199.
32. Nathan Drake, *Nathan Drake's Account of the Siege of Pontefract Castle*, Publications of the Surtees Society, (London, 1861), xxxvii, pp. 114-115. Drake's account covers mainly

the first two sieges of Pontefract. The coverage of the third siege is made up of writings from various authors including Thomas Paulden.
33. Paulden, *An Account*, pp. 23-25.
34. Gentles, *New Model Army*, p. 320. Gentles believes Bray's men took part in the Burford Mutiny in May.
35. Richard Overton, *The Hunting of the Foxes*, (London, 1649). The full text is in Wolfe, *Leveller Manifestoes*, pp. 355-383.
36. John Lilburne, *The Second Part of England's New-Chaines Discovered*, (London, 1649), quoted in William Haller and Godfrey Davies, *The Leveller Tracts 1647-1653*, (New York, 1944), pp. 178-181.
37. Haller and Davies, *Leveller Tracts*, p. 171.
38. Commons Journal, vi, p. 175.
39. *Mercurius Pragmaticus*, February 27-March 4, 1649, E546/4, quoted in Gentles, *New Model Army*, p. 530N. Gentles suggests this report from the royalist newspaper should be taken "with more than a grain of salt."
40. Gentles, *New Model Army*, p. 320.
41. Ibid., p. 322.
42. Ibid., p. 324.
43. *Mercurius Militaris*, May 8, 1649, E554/13, p. 32. Nol was a dismissive nickname for Cromwell.
44. *The Army's Martyr*, (London, 1649), p. 5, quoted in Lindsey German and John Rees, *A People's History of London*, (London, 2012), p. 63.
45. Gentles, *New Model Army*, p. 335.
46. *The Levellers (Falsly So Called) Vindicated*, (August 20, 1649), E571/11, pp. 7-8, quoted in Gentles, *New Model Army*, p. 345. The pamphlet condemned Denne as a spy planted by the grandees in the mutineer's camp. One of the authors of the tract was Robert Everard, an agitator and prominent speaker at Putney. He was in Scroop's regiment by 1649 and still committed to the Leveller cause.
47. Williamson, *Four Stuart Portraits*, p. 125 and p. 125N.
48. Ramsey, *Henry Ireton*, p. 140.
49. Blair Worden, 'The Levellers in history and memory c.1660-1960', in Michael Mendle (ed.), *The Putney Debates of 1647*, (Cambridge, 2001), pp. 260-272.
50. Gardiner, *Great Civil War*, (London, 1886), vols. i-iv.
51. Ibid., vol iii, pp. 200-1.
52. Henry Noel Brailsford, usually known as H. N. Brailsford (1873-1958) wrote 40 books, including one novel, on a wide range of political topics. His one book on the 17th century, *The Levellers and the English Revolution* was published in 1961, three years after his death. It was edited by the Marxist historian Christopher Hill.
53. See Wootton, 'The Leveller Movement' in Burns and Goldie (eds.), *The Cambridge History of Political Thought 1450-1700*, (Cambridge, 1991).
54. Philip Baker, 'Radicalism in Civil War and Interregnum England', *History Compass* 8/2 (2010), p.152. He cites A.S.P. Woodhouse's *Puritanism and Liberty* (1938) as an example of his view.
55. Ibid., p. 153. The last phrase is a quote from the inside cover blurb of Hill's book.
56. Ibid., p 156.
57. Powell, *Navy in the Civil War*, p. 133.

58. Ibid., p. 134.
59. Clarke Papers, i, p. 304.
60. Cater, *A True Relation*, p. 44.
61. Ashton, *Counter Revolution*, p. 474.
62. Ibid., p. 475.
63. Woolrych, *Soldiers and Statesmen*, p. 227.
64. Baxter, *Reliquiae Baxterianae*, p. 56.
65. Woolrych, *Soldiers and Statesmen*, p. 227.
66. Brailsford, *The Levellers*, p. 360.
67. Ibid., p. 377N.

Bibliography

Primary Sources

Add. MSS 71532, fol 23. British Library.

Addl. MS11, 602, fol 38. British Library.

Army Book of Declarations, (London, 1647).

The Army's Martyr, (London, 1649).

Bate, George. *Elenchus motuum nuperorum in Anglia*, (1685).

Baxter, Richard. *Reliquiae Baxterianae*, ed. Matthew Sylvester, (London, 1696).

Brooks, Thomas. *The Glorious Day of the Saints Appearance*, (London, 1649).

Calendar of State Papers, Domestic, The National Archives.

The Charters of London (London, 1646).

Clarke, Sir William. *The Clarke Papers*, ed. Charles Harding Firth, (London, 1891).

Clarendion MSS. The Bodleian Library, Oxford.

Clarendon State Papers.

Commons Journal.

Dyve, Sir Lewis. *The Tower of London Letter-book*, ed. H. G. Tibbutt, (Bedfordshire Historical Society, 1958).

The Famous Tragedy of King Charles I, (London, 1649).

The Levellers (Falsly So Called) Vindicated, (London, 1649).

Lilburne, John. *The Juglers Discovered*, (London, 1647).

Lilburne, John. *The Second Part of England's New-Chaines Discovered*, (London, 1649).

Londons Liberty in Chains, (London, 1646).

Lords Journal.,

Mercurius Elenticus.

Mercurius Militaris.

Mercurius Melancholicus.

Mercurius Pragmaticus.

Overton, Richard. *The Hunting of the Foxes*, (London, 1649).

Oxinden, Henry. *The Oxinden and Peyton Letters 1642-1670*, Dorothy Gardiner (ed.), London, 1937).

Paulden, Thomas. *An Account of the Taking and Surrendering of Pontefract Castle*, (Oxford, 1747).

Portland MSS, 13th report of the Historic Manuscript Collection, The National Archives.

Rushworth, John. *Historical Collections*, (London, 1721-2).

The Moderate, (London, 1648).

Sexby, Edward. *The Case of the Armie Truly Stated* (London, 1647).

Sprigge, Joshua. *Anglia Rediviva*, (London, 1647).

Tanner MSS, The Bodleian Library, Oxford.

The Tangye Collection of Cromwelliana, The Fairfax Correspondence. Museum of London.

Thomason Tracts. The British Library.

Vicars, John. *The Burning Bush not Consumed*, (London, 1646).

Wildman, John. *An Agreement of the People* (London, 1647).

Wildman, John. *Putney Projects* (London, 1647).

Worcester Archives.

Secondary Sources

Abbott, Wilbur Cortez. *The Writings and Speeches of Oliver Cromwell*, (Harvard Cambridge, 1947).

Ackroyd, Peter. *Thames Sacred River*, (London, 2007).

Acts and Ordinances of the Interregnum 1642-60, eds. Firth, Charles Harding and Rait, R.S., (3 volumes, London, 1911).

Adamson, John. *The Noble Revolt*, (London, 2007).

Andrews, Charles M. *The Colonial Period of American History*, (Yale, 1964).

Andrews, Kenneth R. *Trade, plunder and settlement Maritime enterprise and the genesis of the British Empire 1480-1630*, (Cambridge, 1984).

Andrews, Kenneth R. *Ships, Money and Politics: Seafaring and naval enterprise in the reign of Charles I*, (Cambridge, 1991).

Ashley, Maurice. *John Wildman Plotter and Postmaster*, (London, 1947).

Ashton, Robert. *Counter Revolution The Second Civil War and its Origins, 1646-8*, (London, 1994).

Atkin, Malcolm. *The Civil War in Worcestershire*, (Stroud, 1995).

Baker, Philip. 'Radicalism in Civil War and Interregnum England', *History Compass*,(2010).

Barber, Sarah. *Regicide and Republicanism* (Edinburgh, 1998).

Barber, Sarah. *A Revolutionary Rogue Henry Marten and the English Republic* (Stroud, 2000).

Barratt, John. *The Battle of Langport 1645*, (Bristol, 1995).

Binns, Jack. *Yorkshire in the Civil Wars*, (Pickering, 2004).

Bottigheimer, Karl. *English Money and Irish Land*, (Oxford, 1971).

Braddick, Mike. 'An English Military Revolution?', *Historical Review*, (1993).

Brailsford, Henry Noel.*The Levellers and the English Revolution*, (London, 1961).

Bremer, Francis J. *First Founders*, (Durham, New Hampshire, 2012).

Brenner, Robert. *Merchants and Revolution: Commercial Change, Political Conflict, and London's Overseas Traders 1550-1653*, (Cambridge, 1993).

Brogan, Hugh. *The Penguin History of the United States of America*, (London, 1985).

Burne, Alfred Higgins and Young, Peter. *The Great Civil War: A Military History of the First Civil War 1642-1646*, (London, 1959).

Capp, Bernard. *Cromwell's Navy The Fleet and the English Revolution 1648-1660*, (Oxford, 1989).

Capp, Bernard. 'Naval Operations' in John Philips Kenyon and Jane Ohlmeyer, *The Civil Wars A Military History of England, Scotland, and Ireland 1638-1660*, (Oxford, 1998).

Carlyle, Thomas. *The Letters and Speeches of Oliver Cromwell*, ed. S. C. Lomas, (London, 1904).

Carter, Matthew. *A true relation of that honourable though unfortunate expedition of Kent, Sussex and Colchester in 1648*, (Colchester, 1789).

Chaplin, W. R. 'William Rainsborough (1587-1642) and his associates of the Trinity House,' *The Mariner's Mirror* (London, 1945).

Earl of Clarendon (formerly Edward Hyde), *The History of the Great Rebellion and Civil Wars in England*, ed. W. Dunn MacRay, (Oxford, 1888).

Coleman, Donald. C. *The Economy of England 1450-1750*, (Oxford, 1977).

Coward, Barry. *The Stuart Age: England 1603-1714*, (Harlow, 1994).

Coward, B., *Oliver Cromwell Profiles in Power* (London, 1991).

Crawford, Patricia. *Denzil Holles 1598-1680 A Study of his Political Career*, (London, 1979).

Cust, Richard. *Charles I A Political Life*, (Edinburgh, 2007).

Darby, Madge. *Waeppa's People: A History of Wapping*, (London, 1988).

Donagan, Barbara. *War in England 1642-1649*, (Oxford, 2008).

Drake, Nathan. *Nathan Drake's Account of the Siege of Pontefract Castle*, (London, 1861).

Everitt, Alan. *The Community of Kent and the Great Rebellion 1640-60*, (Leicester, 1966).

Firth, Charles Harding and Davies, Godfrey. *The Regimental History of Cromwell's Army*, (Oxford, 1940).

Gardiner, Samuel Rawson. *The History of the Great Civil War* (London, 1886).

Gentles, Ian. 'The Struggle for London in the Second Civil War', *Historical Journal*, (June, 1983).

Gentles, Ian. *The New Model Army*, (Oxford, 1992).

Gentles, Ian. 'Political Funerals during the English Revolution', in Stephen Porter (ed.), *London and the Civil War*, (London, 1996).

German, Lindsey and Rees, John. *A People's History of London*, (London, 2012).

Gimelfarb-Brack, Marie., 'Maximilian Petty', *Biographical Dictionary of British Radicals in the Seventeenth Century*,(London, 1984).

Glover, Samuel Dennis. 'The Putney Debates: Popular versus Elitist Republicanism', *Past and Present*, (Oxford, 1999).

Greenberg, Stephen. 'Seizing the Fleet in 1642: Parliament, the Navy and the Printing Press', *Mariner's Mirror*, (1991).

Gregg, Pauline. *Free-Born John The Biography of John Lilburne*, (London, 1961).

Haller, William and Davies, Godfrey. *The Leveller Tracts 1647-1653*, (New York, 1944).

Hamilton Papers 1638-50, Samuel Rawson Gardiner, (ed.), (London, 1880).

Hardman Moore, Susan *Pilgrims: New World of Settlers and the Call of Home*, (London, 2007).

Hibbert, Christopher. *Charles I*, (London, 1968).

Hill, Christopher. *World Turned Upside Down*, (London, 1972).

Holmes, Clive. *The Eastern Association in the Civil War*, (Cambridge, 1974).

Hopper, Andrew. *'Black Tom' Sir Thomas Fairfax and the English Revolution*, (Manchester, 2007).

Jones, Phil. *The Siege of Colchester 1648*, (Stroud, 2003).

Jones, Whitney R. D. *Thomas Rainborowe, Civil War Seaman, Siegemaster and Radical*, (Woodbridge, 2005).

Kennedy, D. E. 'The English Naval Revolt of 1648', *English Historical Review*, (1962).

Kingston, Alfred. *East Anglia and the Great Civil War*, (London, 1897).

Kishlansky, Mark. 'The Army and the Levellers', *Historical Journal* 22 (1979.

Kishlansky, Mark. *The Rise of the New Model Army* (Cambridge, 1979).

Knafla, Louis. 'John Wildman', *Biographical Dictionary of British Radicals in the Seventeenth Century*, (London, 1984).

Little, Patrick. 'Lady Bankes Defends Corfe Castle', *History Today*, (2015).

Ludlow, Edmund. *The Memoirs of Edmund Ludlow*, (Oxford, 1894).

MacCormack, J. R. 'The Irish Adventurers and the English Civil War', *Irish Historical Studies*, (1956).

Maseres, Francis. *Select Tracts Relating to the Civil Wars*, (London, 1815).

Morrill, John and Baker, Philip. 'The Case of the Armie Truly Stated', in Patrick Little (ed.), *Oliver Cromwell: New perspectives*, (Basingstoke, 2009).

Peacock, Edward. 'Life of Thomas Rainborowe,' *Archaeologia*, XLVI, (London, 1881).

Peter, Hugh. *A True Relation of the Passages of Gods Providence in a Voyage for Ireland*, (London, 1642).

Powell, John Rowland and Timings, E. K. (eds.), *Documents Relating to the Civil War 1642-48*, (London, 1963).

Purkiss, Diana. *The English Civil War A People's History*, (London, 2006).

Ramsey, Robert. *Henry Ireton*, (London, 1949).

Roberts, Keith. *Cromwell's War Machine: The New Model Army 1645-1660*, (Barnsley, 2009).

Robertson, Geoffrey. *The Levellers and the Putney Debates*, (London, 2007).

Sabine, G.H. (ed.), *The Works of Gerrard Winstanley*, (Cornell, 1941).

Sharpe, James A. *Early Modern England: A Social History 1550-1760*, (London, 1987).

Slack, Paul. *The Impact of Plague in Tudor and Stuart England* (Oxford, 1985).

Stearns, Raymond. *The Strenuous Puritan Hugh Peter*, (Urbana, 1954).

Stow, John. *A Survey of London*, (London. 1598).

Tawney, Richard Henry. *Religion and the Rise of Capitalism*, (London, 1926).

Thompson, George Malcolm. *Sir Francis Drake*, (London, 1972).

Thorn, Andrew. 'Naval Finance and the origins and development of Ship Money' in Mark Charles Fissel (ed.), *War and Government in Britain 1598-1650*, (Manchester, 1991).

Underdown, David. *Pride's Purge*, (Oxford, 1971).

Vernon, Elliott and Baker, Philip. 'What was the first Agreement of the People?', *Historical Journal* (2010).

Wanklyn, Malcolm and Jones, Frank. *A Military History of the English Civil War 1642-1646*, (Edinburgh, 2005).

Waters, Henry Fitz-Gilbert, Waters, Henry F and Greenwood, Isaac. *The Rainborowe Family* (New York, 1886).

Whitelock, Sir Bulstrode. *Memorials of the English Affairs*, (Oxford, 1705).

Williamson, Hugo Ross. *Four Stuart Portraits*, (London, 1949).

Winship, Michael P. *Godly Republicanism*, (Cambridge, Massachusetts, 2012).

Winthrop, John. *The Journal of John Winthrop 1630-1649*, Richard S. Dunn and Laetitia Yeandle (eds.), (Harvard, 1996).

Winthrop, John. *History of New England*.

Withington, Phil. *The Politics of Commonwealth* (Cambridge, 2005).

Wolfe, Don. *Leveller Manifestoes of the Puritan Revolution*, (New York, 1944).

Wood, Alfred. *A History of the Levant Company*, (London, 1935).

Woodhouse, Arthur Sutherland Pigott. *Puritanism and Liberty*, (London, 1938).

Woolrych, Austin. *Soldiers and Statesmen*, (Oxford, 1987).

Woolrych, Austin. *Britain in Revolution 1625-1660*, (Oxford, 2002).

Wootton, David. 'The Leveller Movement' in J.H. Burns and Mark Goldie (eds.), *The Cambridge History of Political Thought 1450-1700*, (Cambridge, 1991).

Worden, Blair. 'The Levellers in history and memory c.1660-1960', in Michael Mendle (ed.), *The Putney Debates of 1647*, (Cambridge, 2001).

Wright, Thomas. *Political Ballads*, (1841).

Zaller, Robert. 'Edward Sexby', *Biographical Dictionary of British Radicals in the Seventeenth Century*, (London, 1984).

Made in the USA
Charleston, SC
11 July 2015